MANAGEMENT INFORMATION SYSTEMS
CONCEPT AND APPLICATIONS IN COOPERATIVES

MANAGEMENT INFORMATION SYSTEMS

CONCEPT AND APPLICATIONS IN COOPERATIVES

By

Dr. M.Karthikeyan

Assistant Professor

Department of Cooperatives

Institute of Cooperatives & Development Studies

Ambo University

P.B. No. 511

Ambo University

ETHIOPIA

DPH

DISCOVERY PUBLISHING HOUSE PVT. LTD.

NEW DELHI-110 002

First Published - 2010
Reprinted - 2014

ISBN: 978-81-8356-615-5

Management Information System
Concepts and Applications in Cooperatives

Published by:
DISCOVERY PUBLISHING HOUSE PVT. LTD.
4383/4B, Ansari Road, Darya Ganj
New Delhi-110 002 (India)
Phone: +91-11-23279245, 43596064-65
Fax: +91-11-23253475
E-mail: discoverypublishinghouse@gmail.com
sales@discoverypublishinggroup.com
web: www.discoverypublishinggroup.com

Printed at:
Infinity Imaging Systems
Delhi

Preface

I am very much glad to present a book on *Management Information Systems (Concept and Applications in Cooperatives)*, which is a pioneering effort in the field of MIS applications in cooperatives. This work is based on my experience as teacher, trainer and researcher in the field of cooperatives for more than 13 years. This book is very unique in the field of both information systems and cooperatives. No attempt has been made in this line of applications of MIS in cooperatives.

This book will be very much useful to the practising managers in companies and cooperatives, the trainers who are working in various training establishments and the students of management at M.B.A. and similar post-graduate level.

I have drawn the inputs from various materials; papers, journals, books and I have consulted several of my friends, colleagues and field experts. I am ever grateful and thankful to them for their immense support and healthy criticism.

I hope that the readers of this book will get knowledge on MIS as also the applications of MIS in cooperatives. Any useful comments, suggestions to improve the present version are welcome and solicited from the readers.

I thank Mr. Parul Wasan of Discovery Publishing House, New Delhi for publishing book neatly under his renowned label for the knowledge community.

M. KARTHIKEYAN

Contents

Contents

PART–I

MIS–A CONCEPTUAL FRAMEWORK

PART I

MIS: A CONCEPTUAL FRAMEWORK

1
Information Systems

The Evolution of Information Systems

Between 1965 and 1975 the organizations concentrated on automating those functions where they could make large efficiency gains. Typical targets were those that processed many routine transactions, such as pay-rolls, inventory and financial transactions. Department managers often delegated responsibility for information management to their information systems department. These became very skilled at running large, routine and usually centralized systems. The IS function also became influential, and line managers were rarely involved in discussions of IS strategy and development. The technologies had little effect on smaller organizations. The objective of most applications was to process routine transactions more efficiently.

In the following decade automated systems spread widely. Technical developments made smaller systems possible and more attractive to managers in other parts of the organization such as planning, manufacturing and distribution. More departments discovered the possibilities of computer-based information systems and their managers became familiar with issues of budgeting for hardware, requesting support, defining requirements and setting priorities – alongside established IS departments. Suppliers developed systems that were suitable for smaller organizations.

Since the mid-1980s the information systems environment has continued to change significantly. Technical developments have brought information systems to the foreground of corporate policy. Systems that for decades have supported the business functions of finance, manufacture and distribution continue to develop and employ more modern technology. In addition, computer-based systems have extended to serve many other business functions. Software suppliers have expanded product lines to support functions as diverse as production forecasting, supplier rating and project management. Information technology often supports managers and professional staff directly. Non-technical staff or small business owners now depend heavily on computer-based information.

Examples of such new developments are:

- the emergence of fast, relatively cheap and portable computer power;
- the ability to link these into networks (local and in a wider environment);
- the use of the internet to link computer systems with those in other organizations;
- using information technologies for communication – such as email and video-conferencing;
- creating integrated database that staff can use in different applications throughout the organization, for example in customer relationship management (CRM).

The rise of the internet since the mid-1990s has further stimulated these developments. It challenges many traditional organizations to innovate their processes and change their operations. But it also enables completely new "dot.com" firms to enter the market place with totally new ways of doing business, and to challenge established players. Figure 1.1 depicts a clear picture on the widening role of information systems for many organizations. The early stages featured single, unconnected systems for separate business functions. In stages 3 and 4 managers are linking systems together and using them to make radical changes to previously separate processes. In stage 5 they are using common information systems based on the internet to move information between organizations and often having direct electronic links with their customers.

Stage 1 One business function supported by an Information system

Stage 2 More business functions supported by Information systems

Stage 3 Information systems linked and integrated By joint database

Stage 4 Competitive use of information system Process innovation By innovating business processes

Stage 5 Joint information systems Amongst organizations, Process innovation amongst orgns. e.g., by using the internet

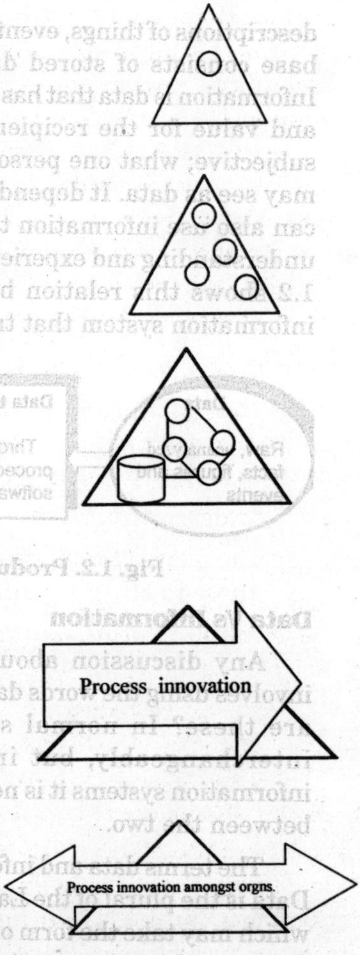

Fig. 1.1. The widening effects of information systems in organizations

THE ROLE OF INFORMATION IN ORGANIZATIONS

Data, Information and Systems

Organizations store and process large amounts of data, which may or may not convert into information. Data refer to recorded descriptions of things, events, activities and transactions. A database consists of stored data items organized for retrieval. Information is data that has been processed so that it has meaning and value for the recipient. This means that information is subjective; what one person perceives as information another may see as data. It depends on their interests and role. People can also use information to create **knowledge** – the expertise, understanding and experience that comes from learning. Figure 1.2 shows this relation between data, information and the information system that transforms the one to the other.

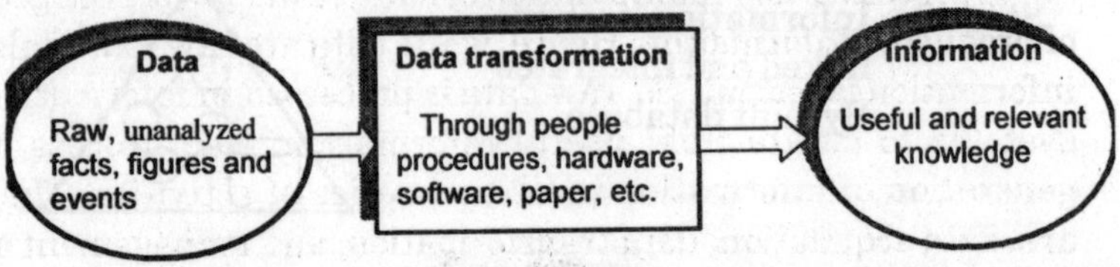

Fig. 1.2. Producing information from data

Data Vs Information

Any discussion about information systems inevitably involves using the words data and information. But what exactly are these? In normal speech the words are often used interchangeably, but in talking about computer-based information systems it is necessary to make a careful distinction between the two.

The terms data and information do not mean the same thing. Data is the plural of the Latin datum, literally a "given", or fact, which may take the form of a number, a statement, or a picture. Data are the raw materials in the production of information. Information, on the other hand, is data that have meaning within a context. Information can be raw data or data manipulated through tabulation, addition, subtraction, division, or any other operation that leads to greater understanding of a situation.

Data is the raw material of organizational life; it consist of disconnected numbers, words, symbols and syllables relating to the events and processes of the business. Data on its own can serve little useful purpose; in fact, a serious problem for the manager is the need to make sense of the deluge of data that threatens to overwhelm him or her in the normal course of the job. The ability to select those items of information which are truly necessary from the flood of irrelevance is a key management skill. The extent of the information explosion can be seen from the fact that 75 per cent of all information available on the earth today has been created in the last 20 years! And it has been estimated that the total amount doubles 10 years or less!

Generating Information

A process is any manipulation of data, usually with the goal of producing information. Hence, while data are raw materials, information is output. So, raw data is processed in information systems to create final useful information. The process of generation of information involves a series of activities. They are: data acquisition, data transformation, and management of information. *Data acquisition* means capturing data. What ever may be the sources of data, it may be initially recorded and later verified for accuracy and authenticity. This activity is named as data capture. Data may be captured by punching with keyboard or scanning with scanning devices, facts from documents on which they were recorded. The data captured for business information systems are organized in data files. Each file contains records relating to various data elements (fields) expressed with the help of different symbols (characters). These files are linked to databases based on the hierarchy of data in business information systems. *Data transformation* may be done by performing any of the operations, such as rearranging data in some specified order (sorting of data), classifying the data on the basis of the selected variables / factors, calculating the data by series of calculations, summarizing, which is a process of aggregating various data elements, reducing the bulk of data to a more meaningful form. *Management of information* can be performed either by communicating the transformed information or by storing it for future reference. The appropriate channel of communication, the report format and storage medium should be selected and used. Such activities of communicating and/or storing information may be termed as managing information.

Historically people recorded data on paper, transformed it into information and presented it on paper. Now they are more likely to use some form of computer-based information system to record, transform, store and present information. An information system is a set of people, procedures and resources that collects and transforms data into information and disseminates this information. Figure 1.3 presents the elements of a computer-based information system.

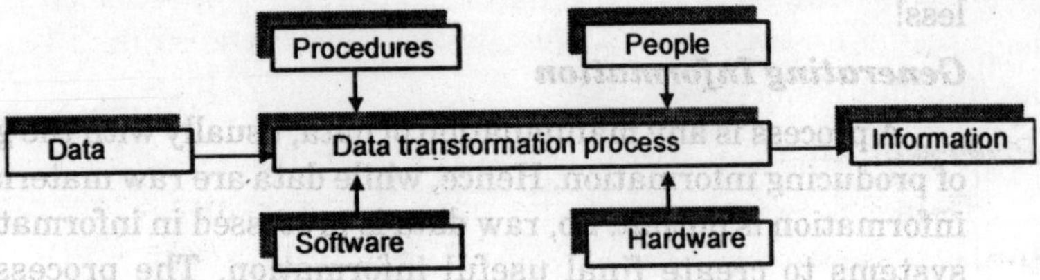

Fig. 1.3. The elements of a computer-based information system

The Nature of Data Processing

Information comes from data that has been processed to make it useful in management decision-making. The task of date processing is one which has been performed by people since the earliest days, whether we consider the stone tables of prehistoric man or the quill pens of Dickensian England. Now, increasingly, this task is being undertaken by computes, but the steps are essentially the same whether the process is undertaken manually or electronically.

Stages in Data Processing

Origination

At some point, new data comes into existence. This could be when a customer rings in to a sales department and places an order for a product; at this time new data relating to the customer and his or her needs is identified, where none existed before. From this point on, these data items are processed, partly electronically by formal computer and communication systems and partly by other less formal means such as word of mouth and manipulation in manual records.

Input and Transaction Recording

After origination, the next step in producing information is collecting and introducing data, known as input, into the information system. These data result from transactions undertaken in the course of business. These transactions can be recorded on paper and later entered into a computer system, or they may be directly recorded through terminals of Transaction Processing Systems (TPSs). At this stage input devices such as the keyboard, infrared devices that sense bar codes, and voice recognition systems are used to enter data in an information system.

Processing

Data can be manipulated in an infinite number of ways, but, in practice, most data processing tasks can be described in surprisingly simple terms. Data items can be sorted into appropriate sequences; one item can be compared with another and decisions made on the basis of the comparison; numerical data can be maintained by calculation; and, finally, data can be summarized, i.e. condensed into a form showing less detail. The computers' greatest contribution to information systems efficient processing of data, which is essential to a robust information system. The computers' speed and accuracy let organizations process millions of pieces of data in several seconds; in the past, such quantities of data could not have been processed quickly enough to be meaningful.

Storage and retrieval

A prime need of any business is the storage and retrieval of data. Large organizations can require the filing of staggering amounts of data. We now take for granted that such a mass of records will be stored and retrieved using automatic systems. A major contribution of electronic computer systems in management has been the cost-effective storage and efficient retrieval of data, which electronic storage systems provide. The computer's internal memory stores data and programmes while processing them. For longer storage periods, the computer transmits data to external storage devices such as magnetic and optical discs and tapes, in a form that lets the computer retrieve and process them.

Output

When data has been processed, or retrieved from a storage system, then it will be communicated to data user in some way. This could be achieved by word of mouth, or in the form of a written report or diagram. Computer systems employ a number of methods for outputting data, including display on a VDU screen and printing reports and documents. However, computers can communicate output through speakers in the form of music or speech and can also transmit it to another computer or electronic device in computer-coded form, for later interpretation.

The main (but no means the only) criterion for deciding about information is its usefulness in decision. This point has a number of considerations: firstly, if information is to be useful, then clearly its value depends to a large extent on the recipient and how it is to be used. Information is only useful to somebody and a prime criterion of its value relates to decision. Of course, the decision in question may not be immediate; information can be useful when it informs decisions to be made at some time in the future. In fact, learning is about storing information which may be useful at some time in the future.

All this implies that information which is useful to one person may be quite useless to somebody else, thus we may say that one manager's information may be another manager's data. Consider the staff in a sales office checking sales orders to allocate trade discounts: in this situation, details such as the customer's name and type of business may be items of information used to make a decision about the discount allowable. Now consider the sales manager in the same office as he or she decides whether to allocate more salespeople for the amount of business to be achieved that month: in this instance, the total order value achieved so far may be the key piece of information and the details of individual customer names are irrelevant to the decision.

If we were to tell you that, today being Monday, tomorrow is Tuesday, then this piece of information will not be very valuable to you! The information has no surprise value, it tells you nothing you do not already know. Information is of more or less value to the extent to which it reduces our uncertainty about our word. If you were considering placing a bet on the favourite in the 3.30, then the would be uncertainty as to the outcome. If there were not, then you would find it hard to place a bet, because everybody would have knowledge of the result. But there is always uncertainty about the outcome of future events (in management as well as in horse racing). The information you receive about the race and about the horses may act to reduce this uncertainty, and is more or less valuable accordingly. For example, knowing that a horse is favourite tells you something about the possible outcome. Of course, just because the horse is favourite does not mean that it will win; but to a certain degree, your uncertainty about the outcome has been reduced. Knowing the odds, then, on the horses in a race reduces to some extent our uncertainty about the outcome (even if not very much) and hence this information has a certain value.

Essential tools for the input, processing, storage and output of most companies' information systems, computers also introduce another component to information systems: the need to translate instructions from natural - or human - languages into computer languages. Computers understand, give computers directions on how to interpret and manipulate data, and in what form (visual, aural or otherwise) to provide information to the organization. Thousands of programming languages are in use today.

Computer Equipment for Information Systems

The following are the basic components of the computer system within an information system:

- Input devices introduce data into the information system (IS);
- The computer processes data through the IS;
- Storage devices store data and information.
- Output devices display information;

In addition to communication that takes place between computer components, communication occurs between computers over great distances (call telecommunications).

Communications technology lets users not only access multiple input, output and storage devices with a single computer but access data and resources of more than one computer as well. This way, a computer's power may be augmented with the power of an entire computer network.

Desirable Characteristics of Information

In order that it should be valuable to the recipient, information must be of sufficient quality to make it useful in decision. But what is information quality? In practice, there are several rule-of-thumb criteria which help to create better information:

Relevant information

The need for information to be relevant to the purposes of the recipient in decision-making cannot be overstressed. Irrelevant information constitutes a substantial problem, because it distracts attention from important issues and wastes managers' time. It should be remembered that information which is relevant to one person may well be quite irrelevant to another who has different responsibilities. A further point is that information which is relevant now may become less so over time.

Accurate information

Information should be accurate enough for the purposes in mine. Clearly, wrong and misleading information can only have harmful consequences, and perhaps is worse than no information at all. However, at the same time, unnecessary numbers of decimal positions which add spurious accuracy will serve no purpose. The level of accuracy, therefore, should be chosen to suit the circumstances: sterling values to the nearest penny are necessary for personal payslip details; values to the nearest pound may be suitable for supervisors' reports; values accurate to the nearest thousand are usually chosen for the company's published accounts. This point is reinforced in the next paragraph.

Concise information

The problem of an 'information explosion' for management has already been mentioned. An essential quality of useful information is that it should represent the minimum necessary to convey what is required for the decision in hand. Anything extra beyond what is essential serves only to add to the manager's information overload, and also acts to increase processing costs unnecessarily.

Timely information

Information which arrives after a decision has been made is clearly of little use, however, accurate and relevant it may have been. Hence the value of most information reduces sharply over time. Computers have often been introduced to lend their very fast processing speed specifically in order to improve the timeliness of information flows.

Well-presented information

The manner in which information is presented to information has a dramatic effect on its usefulness in decision-making. If key information is hidden in huge volumes of printouts, or if tables of numerical statistics are issued to show trends which might have been better displayed on a graph, then the decision-maker will not have been given the necessary assistance in his or her understanding of the information. Apart from these general points, there is some evidence to show that individuals have certain preferences for information types; for example, some people respond better to information presented visually in the form of pictures or graphs while others are happier if the same information is supplied in a verbal or textual form.

Complete information

In order to make a decision, the manager need all the information relevant to that task; if key parts of the information set are missing then this will obviously detract from its value.

Upto date information

Information must reflect the current known facts relating to a decision; if it show details relating to the past when more recent information would be of greater use, then, in a sense, it is not longer accurate.

Cost-effective information

Providing information always costs money (although often the true costs of creating it may be hidden); any decision, however important, can only have a certain value. Information which costs more to provide than the value that can result from a better decision, is not cost-effective. Often it is just as difficult to ascertain the true benefits from use of information as it is to evaluate the cost of producing it (this point will be taken up in the next chapter.) Nevertheless, the creation and processing of information is a large item of expense for most organizations, and it is necessary to be careful that the benefits derived are not outweighed by the costs of production.

The computer, when employed with care, can assist in the achievement of these desirable characteristics. The successful design and implementation of information systems is rooted in an understanding of how these characteristics can be achieved.

Clearly, the creation and provision of information which has one or more of the above qualities may result in conflict with the other characteristics. For example, to produce information which is complete in all respects may well take too long, so that the information is no longer timely; or to take the extra care required to make sure it is well presented may result in the information no longer being cost-effective. In practice, producing information requires us to select a suitable compromise between the desirable characteristics, which represents the best we can do in a given situation.

Information Value and Costs

Assessing the value of information is not always easy, and there are different views as to how this should be done. Nevertheless, an attempt must be made to consider this point because providing information certainly entails outlay. If you consider the cost of a large computer system and the specialist staff required to run it, then the costs may be very high indeed. How are we to judge whether the costs is worth while without knowing the value of the information provided?

Returning to our racing example, if we could entirely reduce your uncertainty about the outcome of the horse race, then the information would surely have a specific (and possibly very high!) value. The point is that you could calculate quite specifically how much it would be worth paying to have that information. In general, we try to apply the same principles to estimating the value of information in management, i.e. by attempting to assess the value arising from decisions which could be taken more accurately on the basis of the information provided.

In a management setting, information can clearly be seen to have value if it results in somebody taking action which increases profitability. If that extra profit can be measured, then we have a direct assessment of the value of the information which achieved it. For example, if we provide information about optimum stockholding levels and the information can be acted upon so that a direct reduction in stockholding costs of £10000 per year ensues, then we can claim that the information is worth that much, i.e. it would pay us to spend up to that value to obtain the information.

Unfortunately, the issues are rarely so clear-cut in the management world. The value of information is usually dependent on the recipient's needs and abilities to act in a given situation, and so there is usually no absolute or constant value of any piece of information. This is particularly true for management information systems where information may relate to decisions which in themselves are hard to quantify, or to situations which might arise in the distant future. In practice, then, the costs of information systems are usually justified using qualitative as well as quantitative arguments about the benefits which are to accrue.

Management use of Information

Of course, individuals differ in the ways in which they respond to information and this inevitably affects the way in which decisions are taken. It has been shown, for example, that people have different cognitive styles, i.e. some people prefer information which is structured and follows a clear path from beginning to end (analytic or systematic style) while others prefer a more intuitive approach and like to see where the information as a whole is going (intuitive or heuristic style).

An oft-quoted example of this style difference is shown in the case of two people who are planning for a car journey. One prefers to drive to the approximate location to see if he can fine it-the intuitive/heuristic approach-while the other person prefers to trace a map route from beginning to end-the systematic/ analytic approach. Either approach may be more or less effective and successful depending on the circumstances; but the individual's response to information will, of course, be different. Differences such as this call for information systems, which are tailored to the cognitive styles of the people who are to use them. However, this degree of sophistication in business systems design is rather rare.

System

Simply put, a system is an array of components that work together to achieve a common goal, or multiple goals, by accepting input, processing it, and producing output in an organized manner. Needless to say, not every system has a single goal. Often, a system consists of several subsystems – components of a larger system – with subgoals, all contributing to meeting the main goal. Sub-systems can receive input from, and transfer output to, other systems or subsystems. Systems are closed or open, depending upon the nature of information that flows within an organization. A closed system stands alone, with no connection to another system: nothing flows from another system; nothing flows out to another system. An open system interfaces and interacts with other systems.

Information and Systems

With an understanding of the words information and system, the definition of an information system is almost intuitive: "an information system (IS) is all components that work together to process data and produce information. Almost all business information systems consist of many subsystems with subgoals, all contributing to the organisation's main goal."

An information system is an orderly way of providing information that an organization needs to operate in a successful way and, for a business organization, in a profitable way. Various methods and procedures are combined in numerous means and in various subsystems to make up what may be called an IS. In many companies there may be no formally designated system, but an IS must exist or the company would not continue to operate.

The way in which similar functions are performed tend to vary from one organisation to another. In some companies many systems functions are performed manually or orally, whereas in other companies the same functions require extensive use of data processing and communications equipment. The basic functions of an IS rarely change, but methods and procedures do change. Thus 'systems work' focuses on indentifying and applying the most effective combination of methods and procedures for a particular organization. Over the years a number of creative people within the business environment have recognized the basic principles required in good business systems. At the same time they have developed the skills and techniques to enable them to design better systems than those in existence.

The IS and its components

In an organization, an information system consists of data, hardware, software, telecommunications, people, and procedures as summarized in Exhibit 1.1. Generally defined, the term information system does not have to include electronic equipment. However, "information system", a system with a computer at its centre to which peripheral equipment is connected. That is how we use the term here. In a computer-based information system, computers collect, store, and process data into information, according to instructions people provide via computer programmes.

Exhibit 1.1
Components of an information system

Data	Input that the system takes to produce information.
Hardware	A computer and its peripheral equipment: input, output and storage devices. It also includes data communication equipment.
Software	Sets of instructions that tell the computer how to take data in, how to process it, how to display information, and how to store data and information.
Telecommunication	Hardware and software that facilitate fast transmission and reception of text, pictures, sound, and animation in the form of electronic data.

People	Information systems professionals and users who analyse organizational information needs, design and construct information system, write computer programmes, operate the hardware, and maintain software.
Procedures	Rules for achieving optimal and secure operations in data processing. Procedures include priorities in dispensing software applications and security measures.

Several trends have made the use of information systems very important in business. They are: computers' power has grown tremendously while their prices have dropped; computer programme's variety and ingenuity have increased; quick and reliable communication lines and access to the internet and world wide web have become widely available and affordable; the fast growth of the internet has opened opportunities and encouraged competition in global markets; and an increasing ratio of the workforce is computer literate.

Information Systems and Management

Most organizations, even down to the very smallest, utilize computers in some way or another. The uses to which the computers are put vary enormously, ranging from word processing and elementary accounting systems through to on-line enquiry, sophisticated decision support systems and mathematical modeling for corporate planning. It is probably true that many of today's businesses simply could not function effectively without automated information processing systems of some form or another. The costs and delays arising from manual processing methods would be truly daunting without automated data processing; consider, for example, the raw data processing involved when next you write a cheque or buy a plane ticket. Increasingly, information systems are seen as a strategic resource within the organization; that is, they have an important impact on key operations which determine the livelihood of the organization.

But it would be wrong to overemphasize the role of computers alone. In practice, most management information systems are an amalgam of human and computer-based activities, where man and machine have different but complementary roles to play in achieving the successful working of the system. The question as to which aspects are best done by machine and which are best done by people is a fascinating one, and, of course, the answer is changing constantly with rapid advances in technology. Table 1.1 compares some of the different capabilities of human and computer as information processors.

Table 1.1. Human and computer compared

	Human	*Computer*
Overhead costs	expensive	cheap
Running costs	expensive	cheap
Performance over time (stamina)	deteriorates	constant
Reliability/ consistency	poor	excellent
Computation ability	poor	excellent
Handling the unexpected	good	poor
Commonsense abilities	excellent	poor
Language abilities	good	poor

The Advantages of Computerized Information Systems

There are several distinct advantages, which can accrue from the successful use of computer systems. We use the word can carefully here; it is not certain that any benefits will accrue just because a computer is installed: far from it. In practice it is necessary to plan computer systems withy great care and to implement them skilfully in order to realize the full benefits. This book is intended to provide guidance for realizing those benefits and for avoiding some of the pitfalls which may arise.

There are significant advantages to be achieved from the successful implementation of computer-based systems; but these can take several different forms, and it is worth while being quite clear as to which benefit(s) are being sought. Generally, the concrete advantages fall into four categories:

1. information cost-effectiveness;

2. enhanced business growth potential;
3. the automation of decisions;
4. enhancement of decision quality.

Information cost-effectiveness

Computers have greatly reduced the need for clerical date processing; at the same time new work roles have arisen, and new information workers have appeared to fill them. In general, computers can process raw data very much more cheaply and accurately than human beings, and this has meant a dramatic reduction in the costs of elementary data processing. Many organizations have justified the introduction of computer systems on the basis that specific cost savings will accrue as result of a direct saving in clerical effort. Most mature organizations will by now have already shed or relocated clerical effort where this can be directly replaced by automated systems and so further cost reductions here are not so easy to achieve. In practice, the direct replacement of human data processing by computers is rarely straightforward and clerical cost reductions must be balanced against a whole host of new costs associated with the new systems.

Enhanced business growth potential

Many organizations find that they are hampered in their search for growth by their administrative paperwork systems, or by the lack of consistent information. The introduction of computer-based systems can overcome these hurdles and allow growth in sales to occur. The costs of manual data processing tend to rise linearly with the volumes of data; i.e. ignoring any learning effects, it costs twice as much to cope with 200 documents as it does to cope with 100. This is usually because the dominant cost element is people. However, this will not be the case with a computer system; once initial installation costs have been overcome it may cost little to expand the system to cope with extra volumes of data.

It can be seen that with small data volumes the computer system initially costs more than an equivalent manual system, because of the capital outlay on equipment and set-up costs. However, as data volumes rise, so the manual system costs rise with them while the computer costs remain roughly constant. This is because more data needs more people, but the computer can take on more work until its capacity is reached. At a certain point, the computer will have reached its limit and will need enhancing or replacing, resulting in a step-change in costs. Thus there is an area of the graph where the computer costs are constant while manual costs are rising. A carefully designed system will exploit the capacity of the computer to soak up increased volumes with little cost increase. (This is of course a simplification of reality, and in reality the people function will be a stepped cost also and there will be a host of other factors to consider.)

The automation of decisions

The work of and organization can be seen as being made up of countless elementary individual decisions. Most of these decisions are usually quite straightforward, but the decisions must be taken none the less, and good solutions arrived at or the organization cannot function. Examples of these elementary decisions are legion, but include the allocation of sales discounts to customers depending on pervious sales records, or the calculation of PAYE income tax depending on earnings and tax code. A computer system can handle such decisions accurately and tirelessly, according to a fixed set of rules called an algorithm. A great advantage of the computer is that it can make decisions no matte how complex the decision factors are, always providing that these factors can be defined. This enables consistency and accuracy to be achieved in the organization's work and enables management and staff to concentrate on aspects requiring human judgment and skills.

Enhanced decision-making

Much of the development work in information systems for management is aimed at improving the quality of human decision. This is a different matter altogether from the automation of decisions discussed in the previous section. The intention now is to provide information to enable the manager to make a decision, which, based on more accurate information or assisted by a computer model of the factors involved, will permit him or her to achieve better outcomes than if the decision was made unaided.

Recent developments in decision support systems (DSS) and executive information systems (EIS) have had far-reaching effects on strategic decision-making by senior managers. Decisions, which have crucial long-term effects on the organization can be supported by computer-generated information and decision models so that the long-term effects of different options can be reviewed. Further enhancements to decision quality are possible as a result of developments in the comparatively new field of computer-base artificial intelligence and expert systems. In addition to these cited advantages, information systems are increasingly being considered as strategic; in overall terms they can crucially affect an organization's survival.

The Benefits of Human-Computer Synergy

After having understood the advantages of computer-based systems, we should know about the benefits of human-computer synergy also. It is important that computers can only carry out instructions that humans give them. Computers can process data accurately at far greater speeds than people can, yet they

Exhibit 1.2

Qualities of human and computers that contribute to synergy

Human	Computers
Think	Calculate and perform programmed logical operations extremely rapidly
Have common sense	Store and retrieve data and information extremely rapidly
Can make decisions	Perform complex logical and arithmetical functions accurately
Instruct the computer	Execute long, tedious operations
Learn new methods and techniques	Perform routine tasks less expensively
Accumulate expertise	Adaptable (programmed & re-programmed)

are limited in many respects – most importantly they lack common sense. However, combining the strengths of these machines with human strengths creates synergy. Synergy (from the Greek word *'synergia'* means "work together") occurs when combined resources produce output that exceeds the sum of the outputs of the same resources employed separately. A computer works quickly and accurately; humans work relatively slowly and make mistakes. A computer cannot make independent decisions, however, or formulate steps for solving problems. Thus, human-computer combination allows the results of human thought to be translated into efficient processing of large amounts of data (Exhibit 1.2). The following exhibit depicts a clear picture on the qualities of human and computers that contribute to synergy.

TYPES OF INFORMATION SYSTEM

Formal and Informal Information Systems

Because we concentrate a great deal on formal information systems: accounting reports computer printouts and so on, we tend to forget that, in fact, managers pay a lot of attention to other, less formal, sources of information. These include managers' own observations of events, and especially the face-to-face and telephone contacts they have with the people around them. In fact, the typical manager spends most of the time gathering information in this way (or being exposed to it) an hence the informal information sources make up a significant part of the manager's world (see Table 1.2).

Of course, the informal information is completely different from the sort of thing, which we usually think of as 'management information'. It consists of word-of-mouth reports about events and people in the organization, usually reported verbally and with little quantitative content. Often the information is inaccurate, it comes form 'the grapevine' and tends to be newsy with snippets of detail about people and events, which are of general personal interest.

The informal information system has obvious drawbacks as regards accuracy, validity and reliability. Nevertheless,

Table 1.2 Formal and informal information systems compared

Formal	*Informal*
How communicated	
word of mouth, gossip,	printed reports
computer terminals	hearsay
How created	
MIS, computer-based systems	personal contacts, 'grapevine'
By whom created	
staff specialists	managers' interpersonal
IS department	networks, including
corporate planning	colleagues, subordinates,
department	superiors, friends and allies
Information types	
quantitative	qualitative
financial	personal
economic	non-economic
Information characteristics	
regular, scheduled	unscheduled, chance contacts
summarized	disaggregated
aggregated, selected	fragments of detail processed

managers seem to prefer their informal systems to the formal systems for some aspects of their information needs. The reasons for this are not hare to find: the informal information usually has a more immediate character to it, i.e. it relates to the here and now; also, it may be easier to digest and to act upon than a complex report or financial summary. In extreme circumstances informal information may be more trusted than the formal information passed down by senior management.

In fact there are circumstances where informal information is of the utmost importance to managers. Consider the sales director who visits his office in the morning and reads the monthly sales analysis for his division; this report-from the formal information system-tells him which customers have placed orders, and for how much. In the evening he plays a round or golf with a friend from one of his most important client companies; his friend tells him of a rumour-the informal information system-that the client company may be about to place its business elsewhere. This is serious and worrying news (if true) which the sales director acts on the next day by contacting the client directly.

Clearly, the informal information system has a tremendous importance in this instance because it advised the sales director of possible future events. The formal information system would have told him of the problem only after the client company had withdrawn its custom. The issue here is that informal information systems serve a key purpose for most managers, and that formal, computer-based systems have a complementary role. They do not necessarily replace all previous information systems.

The role of computers in management has a broad range of possible applications. Since these different applications often have quite different aims and objectives it is essential to discriminate among the various groups of information systems: data processing, transaction processing systems, management information systems, decision support systems, executive information systems, expert systems, geographical information system, office automation systems, intelligent knowledge-based systems and the personal information systems.

Data Processing

The aims of data processing are to process large amounts of data quickly, cheaply and accurately. Automated data processing (ADP) was the first major application of computers in management, and, indeed, automated date processing of one kind or another had been carried out long before computers became generally available in the 1950s. Herman Hellerith developed the punched card in the late nineteenth century so that machines could process the results of the US population census. The improvements, which these punched-card methods produced, were adopted by many of the larger business organizations, which sought to reduce the costs of their elementary data processing tasks. Payroll and elementary accounting systems were among the first and most popular systems to be automated. The electronic digital computer greatly improved the scope and cost-effectiveness of ADP, and the new technology became known as electronic data processing (EDP). Now it is taken for granted that the elementary data processing tasks of a business will be performed wherever possible by computer; indeed for many firms it is an essential part of their competitive business strategy.

Transaction Processing Systems (TPS)

The earliest electronic information systems in business consisted of computers and programmes used to record and report transactions. Called TPS they are the most widely used information systems. The TPS's predominant function is to record data collected at the boundaries of organization, in other words, at the point where the organization transacts business with other parties. The TPSs include cash registers, which record sales; automatic teller machines, which record cash withdrawals, deposits and transfers; and purchase order systems, which record purchases. After data are collected, the information system either automatically processes the data into information or stores it for later processing on demand.

Management Information Systems (MIS)

The MIS grew naturally out of the earlier simple data processing systems. While processing data quickly and economically, it was a small extra step to summarize and select information which would help mangers make decisions. For example, while processing the payroll, there is little extra computer processing involved in producing totals of overtime payments, or an analysis of days worked by each department.

In time, it came to be seen that information produced by the computer system could be produced to standards of speed and accuracy which were just not possible before, and that this information could act as a platform achieving a far more efficient business organization. There came to be a special emphasis on the value of management information and this resulted in systems being designed specifically for their information outputs, rather than purely for the data processing benefits. These systems were planned so as to create all (or almost all) the information needed for the monitoring and controlling of an organization's affairs.

Although there is some dispute over the definition of these terms, MIS usually means a system which contains large amounts of information which has been structured to assist management in decision-making. (The relationship between data and information has already been defined in this chapter). Typically, the information is held on some form of database, consisting mainly of financial data from internal company systems, and is used mainly by middle management in monitoring and controlling the organization's business. Management information systems are essentially historic, being concerned with past actions and outcomes.

In recent years there has been a swing away from large-scale MIS systems. It was found that these large, integrated systems were very expensive to build, cumbersome in operation and did not always achieve all the benefits that were expected. Today, it is probably fair to say that there is still and important role for the MIS, but it is no longer seen as the ultimate and final expression of the organization's information needs. Rather, the MIS takes its place among the other types of computer-based information systems, which an organization may utilize.

Decision Support Systems (DSS)

These systems were created, at least in part, as a response to some of the perceived failings of MIS. The MIS, because it was based mainly on internal financial data, did not directly address the needs of top management, or of strategic decision-making. A DSS usually contains specially designed models which provide the user with the means of assessing the consequences of decision. An example of this is known as a "what if?" facility: given the task of deciding between various forms of investment, for instance, the system user can see the consequences of each option when the system evaluates the effect on profitability using a financial model of the organization's finances.

Executive Information Systems (EIS)

Executive information systems or Executive support systems help high-ranking officers direct an organization. Often programmed to integrate thousands of pieces of data and produce summary reports, these systems evolved in the mid-1970s to help executives focus on long range strategic planning within an organization. These information systems generate strategic information and are used by top level managers. They help in identifying options, evaluation of alternative scenarios and making informed choices regarding the business options.

Expert Systems (ES)

Often managers or other workers may need expertise to make certain decisions, not just formulas. In the past, only human experts in a specific line of work could provide advice to decision makers. Now, information systems can be developed that incorporate human expertise. These systems are called expert systems. These expert systems aim at formalizing expertise and make it available for repetitive type of business decisions. They use artificial intelligence tools to generate knowledge out of the information, existing theories, beliefs, and experiences of managers in various business activities.

Geographical Information Systems (GIS)

In some cases, the information decision makers need is related to a map. In such cases, special information systems called geographical information systems can be employed to tie data to physical locations. A GIS application access a database that contains data about part of a city, a city, a county, a state, a country, or even the entire world. By representing data on a map in different graphical forms, a user is able to promptly understand a situation taking place in that part of the world and act upon it.

Office Automation Systems (OAS)

Information technology (IT) is a broad term which has been coined to refer to the range of electronic facilities used in modern management. These facilities include personal computers, word processing and desk-top publishing (DTP), electronic mail, electronic point of sale (EPOS) and electronic funds transfer

(EFT). Many of these techniques remove the need for paper-based filing systems of communications, and have given rise to the expression 'the paperless office'. However, most offices are still anything but paperless and the strength of the technology lies primarily in the utilization of computer and communications technology together in information processing and transmission.

Intelligent Knowledge-based Systems (IKBS)

The search for a means of creating human-like computer systems has been carried out in research departments of universities since the very earliest days of computers. In recent years this has been supplemented by substantial commercial development, particularly in expert systems. The capacity of computers to reproduce human skills and abilities is known as artificial intelligence (AI). A number of special techniques have been developed over the years which enable computers to go some way towards emulating these skills. The IKBS utilize AI techniques in order to provide specialist expert systems. It is now possible to store the knowledge of human experts in a computer and to enable the knowledge to be tapped by an enquirer who consults the computer. The system reviews the problem, asks questions if necessary and provides a diagnosis and suggestions for a solution.

Personal Information Systems (PIS)

The personal information systems are used by managers to improve their productivity at work. They help managers perform their jobs more efficiently. The personal information systems involve the use of microcomputers along with softwares for word processing, electronic spreadsheets, personal database management systems, graphics and business presentations and desktop organizing. The PISs are less expensive to install and simple to use as compared to other business information systems. They are more flexible and protected because they are single-hand handled systems. Since they are personal, a manager can use it the way he finds it more productive for him.

Information Systems in Business and Sectors

Without exception, every business function in every business sector employs information systems. Information systems are key tools in transaction processing, decision making, problem solving, and operations of all business entities. The foolowing section briefly discusses these information systems uses. Chapter 5, "MIS and Business Functions (Functional Areas)" discusses these information systems in business functions in detail.

Information systems in functional business areas

Different types of information systems serve different purposes of an business organization. Functional areas of business include, but are not limited to, accounting, finance, marketing, production, and human resources; they exist in one form or another.

Accounting

In accounting function, information systems help record business transactions, produce periodic financial statements, and create reports for making business decisions.

Finance

The purpose of financial systems is to facilitate financial planning and financial control. In finance, information systems support prepare budgets, manage cash flows, analyse investments, and make decisions that could reduce interest payments and increase revenues from business financial transactions.

Marketing

Marketing information systems provide information on product, price, physical distribution, promotional activities, and public relations. These information support given by the information systems help the managers to decide the things regarding marketing.

Production

Information systems help production function by providing proper information for production planning and control. The materials information is also provided by the information systems so as to have proper materials system in the business organization.

Human Resources

Human resources management systems encompass the human resource planning, recruitment and selection, training and development, performance appraisal systems. The information systems help to make decisions in all respects of human resources management system.

Information systems in business sectors

Different business sectors use information systems of all types. Also, systems are often adapted for specific needs of the sectors in which they are used. Information systems in different business sectors are discussed hereunder.

Manufacturing

Information systems are used throughout a manufacturing operation, from inventory control to paying supplies. Information systems help allocate resources, such as personnel, raw material, and time, to optimize production and productivity. Manufacturing operations use information systems to process customer orders, prepare production schedules, perform quality assurance, and prepare shipping documents.

Service

Information systems play such a central role in the service sector that they are often the backbone of service organizations. The best example can be the banking sector. Without information systems what banks would do? Bank information systems' input consist the type of account (as well as the dates and quantities of deposits and withdrawals); their output consist of statements on interest paid or owed, balances, etc.

Retail

Because information systems enable a large retail chain to run as a single big store, retail chain gained significant economies of scales using information systems. The major purpose of these information systems is to minimize understocking and overstocking in any of the chain's stores.

Government

In recent years governmental and commercial organizations have installed computer-based information systems to automate the processes and replace the human labour. The business of the government depends heavily on information systems for collecting taxes, paying social security, and purchasing goods and services for various departments.

Enterprise Application Systems

The enterprise application system are in existence, which are information systems that tie together the different functional areas of a business. Such systems allow business to operate more efficiently by avoiding duplication of information and avoiding rework. The most pervasive type of enterprise applications is Enterprise Resource Planning (ERP) systems, which actually help in more areas than only planning.

At the outset, information systems support all types of organizations in gathering data, processing, storing and dissemination of information wit IT infrastructure and resources.

2

Management Information System : A Conceptual Framework

Introduction

Today the need for updated information has become inevitable to arrive at an effective decision in all walks of life. Whether it is industry, commerce, defence, banking, education, economics or politics, information is needed. The managers in the organization spend more time on collecting or gathering, recording, searching, absorbing and communicating information. Information is 'live' as it is required to be updated all the time and is renewable. It is substitutable and transportable and can be made to travel.

The resources of an organization are: money, manpower, machines, materials and methods. Information is considered to be the sixth resource. Figure 2.1 presents the flow of information as resource in a production organization along with other resources.

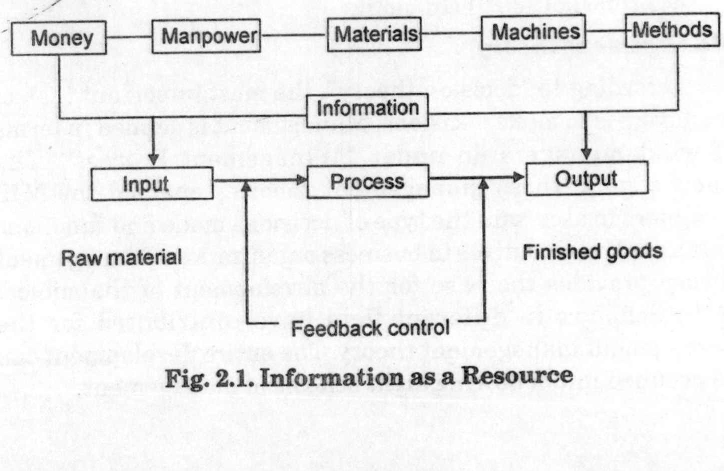

Fig. 2.1. Information as a Resource

Evolution of MIS

The complexity of modern business organizations has been responsible for the use of system approach to management. System approach looks organizations as a sum of interrelated elements that are working together to achieve common goal. For integrating the elements of the organization, management needs information and this led to the evolution of Management Information System, familiarly known as MIS. Information can be defined as the knowledge communicated by others or obtained from investigation, analysis or study. The nature and form of information needed would vary according to the level of decision-making. The level of management activity viz., strategic management, management control and operations management, significantly influences the characteristics of information.

There is confusion that whether MIS is the product of information revolution. It is not true. The subject of MIS is predates to the use of computers. However, it cannot be ignored that the advancement of computer technology activated the use of MIS. Many of the ideas of MIS are the contributions of accounting and management sciences. The four areas, which are having important bearing on the development of MIS is:

1. Management Theory
2. Management Science
3. Managerial Accounting
4. Information Technology.

Management theory

According to "decision theory", the most important task of managers is to make decisions. Management is defined in terms of what managers do under "Management Process". The knowledge of these management theories enabled the MIS designers to ascertain the type of decisions made and functions performed by executives in business organizations. Management theory provides the base for the development of the subject MIS. Scholars in different field have contributed for the development management theory. The entire development can be grouped into following eight schools of management.

1. Scientific management
2. Behavioral Science
3. Social
4. Systems Management
5. Contingency Management
6. Decisional Management
7. Quantitative Measurement
8. Management Process.

These developments facilitated the managers to understand the relationship between the man and the other factors of production and develop decision models, which are so useful for the growth of MIS.

Management science

Operations research and model building are the two important areas in management science, which contribute for the development of MIS. Operations research is concerned with developing systematic approach to problem solving by using mathematical models and statistical procedures. By using the mathematical and statistical procedures the researchers study the behavior of organizations under different conditions under model building. In both the cases the common techniques used by the researchers are:

1. Stimulation
2. Queuing Theory
3. Game Theory
4. Decision Theory
5. Linear Programming
6. Integer Programming
7. Dynamic Programming.

At present researchers have developed ready to use software for using these techniques for managerial decision-making. Management science techniques were incorporated in the MIS design to make quantitative and analytical information available to users of MIS.

Managerial Accounting

There are two areas in managerial accounting. One is financial accounting, where financial statements are prepared primarily for shareholders, creditors and other interested parties outside the organization. In contrast to the above, in management accounting, accounting information are prepared for internal managerial purposes of trend analyses, planning, review and control. The major areas of management accounting are budgetary control, overhead allocation, investment appraisal, and break-even analysis. Hence, accounting information forms part of MIS. To determine the most relevant cost of decision making there is a need for information. It is mainly oriented towards internal management and control and it therefore closely identified with MIS. Thus, one can say that MIS is an extension of managerial accounting.

Information Technology

Familiarly known as IT includes the use of three electronic technologies, viz., computing, telecommunications and microelectronic, and the way they gather, store, process and manage the information. Originally computers were not planned for information processing, but now they are widely used. In fact the use of computers have added value to information/data. The way in which these technologies are used in the organization for information processing decides their success or failure. Hence, IT have give new face lift to the discipline MIS. Computer technology has been considered as a major factor in the development of MIS. The reason is its speed of processing, calculating, and retrieval of data.

Concept of MIS

The MIS consists of three individual terms namely, management, information and system. Management means planning and control of physical and personnel resources of an organization to reach its goals and objectives. Information is the processed data that have been retrieved, processed or otherwise, which helps the management to take decisions. System means order, arrangements, purposes, set or things joined together to achieve a decided objective.

The management Information System (MIS) is an integrated man-machine system that provides information to support the planning and control functions of managers in an organization. MIS can be seen as the combination of human and computer-based resources that results in the collection, storage, retrieval, communication and use of data for efficient management of business operations and resources. The MIS is something more than just a computer system. Before the evolution of computers, MIS techniques existed to supply users with information that would permit them to arrive at an effective decision. The computer has added new dimensions such as speed, accuracy, and processing of massive data that permit the consideration of more alternatives in a decision.

The scope and purpose of MIS is better understood if each component is discussed in detail. The MIS has three components as given in Fig. 2.2.

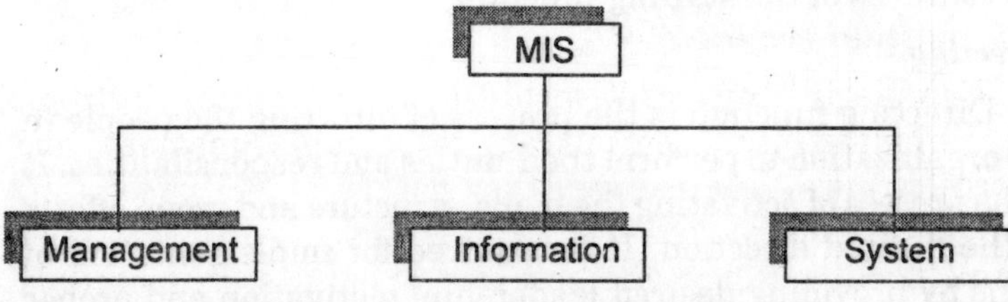

Fig. 2.2. MIS and its Components

Management

Management means manage men tactfully. Management has also been described as getting things done through others. Management is an art as well as a science. Management as a process encompasses activities or functions like planning, organizing, staffing, directing, and controlling. In fact, management is a process of achieving an organisation's goals and objectives by judiciously making use of resources of money, men, materials, machines, methods, messages and moments (the last two in the context of information being a vital resource to the manager for decision making).

Planning

Planning is the basic function of management. It is the process of seeing and deciding the future course of action to be undertaken by the organization. Planning gives answers to the questions: what is to be done? How is to be done? When is to be done? And so on. It is required for committing and allocating the available and limited resources of the organization for attaining its end results in the possible best way and anticipating the future business opportunities and threats.

Organising

Organising refers to the formal grouping of persons and activities to facilitate achievement of the organisation's end results. It is required for assigning responsibilities, jobs, and hierarchy among personnel based on the organization structure.

Staffing

Staffing function deals with the activities regarding staff members of the organization. Staff recruitment, selection, training and development, appraisal and welfare measures are the concerns of the staffing function.

Directing

Directing function is the process of directing the people in the organization to perform their duties and responsibilities. It is the process of activating the plans, structure and group efforts in the desired direction. It is required for implementation of plans by providing desired leadership, motivation and proper communication.

Controlling

Controlling is the function of checking the progress of plans and correcting any deviations that may occur along the way of executing the plans. A control is meaningful only when there are defined responsibilities for activities and results. Controlling techniques are there to control over the activities in the organization for effective use of resources and for corrective action.

The management can also be studied by grouping it into three hierarchical levels – top, middle and junior. Top management establishes the policies, plans and objectives of the organization as well as a budget framework under which various departments will operate. Middle management has the responsibility of implementing the policies and overall plans of the top management. Junior management has the responsibility of implementing day-to-day operations and decisions of the middle management to produce goods and services to the revenue, profit and other goals, which in turn will enable the organization to achieve its overall plans and objectives.

Information

Information can be defined as the data which is organised and presented at a time and place so that the decision maker may take necessary action. In other words, information is the result/product of processing data. The discussion on data and information has already been made in Chapter 1. Information contains an element of surprise, reduces uncertainty and triggers off action. It carries messages and when perceived by the recipients via any of the senses, it increases their state of knowledge or intelligence. The managers as decision makers may require three broad classification of information: environmental information, competitive information, and internal information.

Environmental Information

Environmental information can be of

(*i*) Government policies – required and may have a significant effect on future planning decisions;

(*ii*) Economic trends – includes information about economic indicators like employment, productivity, capital investment, price and wage levels, GNP level, trend and consumer disposable income;

(*iii*) Technological environment – information on technological changes or advancements and effect of such changes; and

(*iv*) Factors of production – information about source, cost, location, availability, accessibility and productivity of the major factors of production such as land, labour, material and capital.

Competitive Information

Competitive information requirement can be classified and described as:

(*i*) Industry demand – the demand forecast of the industry for the product manufactured;

(ii) Firm demand – assessment of the firm's capabilities, activities and potentialities to meet demand relative to the capabilities and actions of the competing firms;

(iii) Competition – information about competing firms for forecasting own product demand and making decisions.

Such information falls into past performance, present activity and future plans.

Internal Information

Internal information is the by-product of the normal operations of a business. Generally, it is historical or static in nature; it is after the fact data. Internal information is aimed at identification of the firm's strengths and weaknesses. It includes: sales forecast, the financial plan, supply factors and policies of the organisation.

System

Systems are diverse – economic system, computer system, decision-support system, communication system, transport system, educational system, solar system, etc. This means we live in an epoch of systems. But what exactly meant by a system? A system is a composite of subsystems or elements or components as group to fulfill certain functions. In a broader sense a system is an assemblage of process, procedures, methods, techniques, etc. A system consists of subsystems. A subsystem which may be composed of several sub-sub-systems. However, a system itself is part of a super system. The systems concept can be understood by Fig. 2.3.

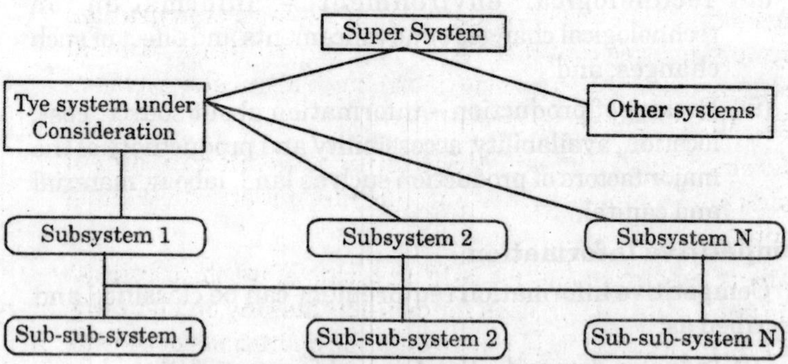

Fig. 2.3. System and its Components

A system can be schematically represented as below:

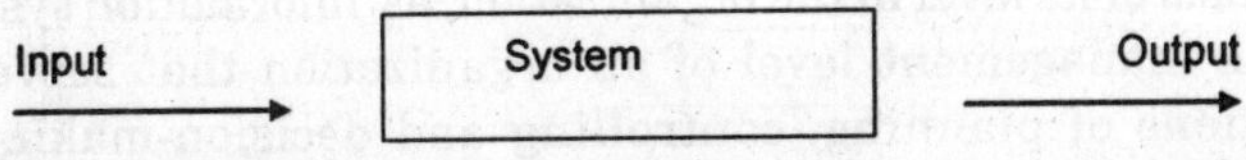

An expanded version of the system showing interaction between system entities is given below:

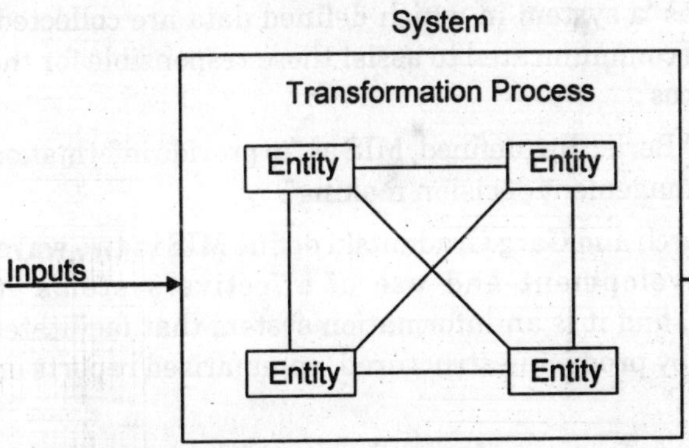

Definition of MIS

Various scholars have defined MIS by emphasizing its different use. The central theme of all these definitions is that MIS should make the organization more dynamic to the environment by providing necessary information for decision-making.

Gorden B. Davis defined MIS as 'an integrated user machine system for providing information to support operations, management, and decision-making functions in an organization. The system utilizes computer hardware and software; manual procedures; models for analysis, planning, control and decision-making; and database'.

Jarome Kanter defined MIS in terms of its role as a 'system that aids management in making, carrying out and controlling decisions'.

Robert G.Murdic defined MIS in terms of its objectives, as 'MIS is to provide information for decision-making on planning, initiating, organizing, and controlling the operations of the sub systems of the firm and to provide a synergistic organization in the process'.

Kenneth C. Laudon, and Jane P. Laudon defined MIS on the basis of its level in the organization, as 'information systems at the management level of an organization that serve the functions of planning, controlling and decision-making by providing routine summary and exception reports'.

The Institute of Costs and Works Accounts of USA has defined MIS as 'a system in which defined data are collected, processed and communicated to assist those responsible for the use of resources'.

James A.O Berien has defined, MIS as "to provide information to support management decision making".

Jojn G. Burch and Garg Gradmitski define MIS in two ways; "it is the development and use of effective systems in organizations, and it is an information system that facilitates management by producing structured, summarized reports on a regular basis".

"MIS is a set of organized procedures, which when executed provide information to support decision making" – Henry C. Lucas.

"A MIS is an organized set of processes that provide information to managers to support the operation and decision making within an organization" – Krober & Watson.

"MIS: The combination of human and computer-based resources that results in the collection, storage, retrieval, communication and use of data for the purpose of efficient management of operations and for business planning" – Kelly.

From the above definitions it can be said that MIS is nothing but an integrated system with transform the data (inputs) into report (outputs) through processing using various components of the computer system. Moreover, it is clear that MIS is a sub system in the organization, which is concerned with collection, processing, storing and transmission of relevant information to decision centres systematically.

Objectives of MIS

The principle objective of MIS is to facilitate the managers at different levels in the hierarchy of organization, so that they run the business more effectively and efficiently through:

1. Providing timely and cost effective information
2. Providing information relevant for decision-making at different levels of management
3. Providing information in right form and content, and
4 Developing a database.

Need for MIS

In the past managers faced the problem of paucity, accuracy and validity of information. Also, some times obtaining information was too costly and time consuming. Knowingly or unknowingly organizations did not paid much attention on the importance of information. But at present, decision-making in the organizations have become complex phenomenon due to:

1. Increase in volume of transactions due to growth of business.
2. Increasing competitions.
3. Information revolution.
4. Greater emphasis on total quality management.
5. Increasing awareness on cost of transactions.
6. Complexity of management problems.
7. Change in the structure of organizations.
8. Business diversifications and expansions.
9. The enormous capacity of computers to store, process and distribute the data / information, and
10. Increased availability of ready-made software packages and hardware peripherals for different functions of management.

These trends call for effective MIS in modern organizations.

Characteristics of MIS

Today the development in information revolution made MIS as inevitable part of any modern organization. According to Michael E. Porter and Vicbr E. Millar this revolution is effecting competition among organizations in three vital ways namely,

1 It changes industry structure and in doing so, alter the rules of competition.

2. It creates competitive advantage by giving companies new ways to out prefer their rivals.

3. It spawns whole new business often from within a company's existing operations.

Hence, without concise, accurate, timely and less costly information, organization's goals and objectives could not be achieved. For making correct decisions the organizations are very much interested in developing MIS. According to C.T. Bhunia a well-developed MIS will have the following characteristics:

1. It provides sufficient information to the managers. Less information may lead to an in appropriate decision taken.
2. It provides relevant information. Unwanted information may lead to take frustrated decision. Unwanted information is a king of noise.
3. It provides information with flexibility. This means that managers should be able to access information as per their desire and required fashion.
4. It provides accurate information. Inaccurate information may lead to take a wrong decision; more accurate is the information, more accurate will be the decision taken on the basis of it.
5. It provides timely information. Out of time and delay are negative aspects of today's management.
6. It supports managers' mobility.
7. It secures enough against intentional modifications and or deliberate destructions by opponents and or competitions.

The MIS is applicable to organizations, which are having:

1. Appropriate computer and communication systems.
2. Access to appropriate computer / data networks.
3. Less but quite skill full computer assistants; operators.
4. Managers with appropriate skill to use, operate, understand and interact with MIS.

While the first two demands 'improved machine system' and/or 'accessing facilities to computer networks', the later two demands improved human resources in the organization. Both the requirements are essential to the MIS.

Organizations across the industry have developed MIS indigenously. But the focus of developing MIS and the advantageous reaped out of it various among organizations. Some organizations give emphasis on the computerization of their routine transactions, while others interested on the strengthening of their communication system. At the same time it is to be ascertained that whether the purpose of MIS is achieved and whether MIS is developed towards which it ought to be developed? To answer this question basically a framework for understanding MIS is necessary.

Dimension of MIS

The characteristics of MIS may be of three dimensions.

Time Dimension:

Timeliness:	Information should be provided when it is required.
Currency:	Information should be up to date when it is provided.
Frequency:	Information should be provided as often as needed.
Time period:	Information can be provided about past, present, and future time periods.

Content Dimension:

Accuracy:	Information should be free from errors.
Relevance:	Information should be related to the information needs of a specific recipient for a specific situation.
Completeness:	All the needed information should be provided.
Conciseness:	Only the information that is needed should be provided.

Scope:	Information can have a broad or narrow scope, or an internal or external focus.
Performance:	Information can reveal performance by measuring activities accomplished, progress made, or resources accumulated.

Form Dimension:

Clarity:	Information should be provided in a form that is easy to understand.
Detail:	Information can be provided in detail or summary forms.
Order:	Information can be arranged in a predetermined sequence.
Presentation:	Information can be presented in narrative, numeric, graphic, or other forms.
Media:	Information can be provided in the form of printed-paper documents, video displays, or other media.

Framework for Understanding MIS

There are number of conceptual frameworks that standout in the area of MIS. A framework is a brief set of ideas for organizing a thought process about a particular type of thing or situation. It identifies topics that should be considered and shows how the topics are related and serves as guide maps to understand the kind of information system in the organization. Some of the available theoretical frameworks to understand the MIS are given in the Exhibit 2.1.

These frameworks focusing MIS, in different angles affect the need, structure, and operations of MIS in an organization. Designing MIS combining the advantages of these frameworks would help the modern organizations to reap maximum benefits (chart 2.1). The objective of any organization is to harvest maximum possible output with available inputs. This is possible through bugling organization's interest with the individual interest. MIS has greater role in bugling these two interests.

Exhibit 2.1
Framework for understanding MIS

Framework	*Focus*	*Advantages*
Nolan's Stage Hypothesis	Use of computer for data processing at different stages	It helps to understand current status of data processing in the organization
Robert Anthony's framework	Planning and control process	It helps to understand the nature and characteristics of information needed to support the planning and control process.
Simon's framework	Decision-making levels	It helps to understand the need of information in the stages of decision-making
Dickson's Systems Hierarchy	Levels of organization	It is useful to understand the structure of MIS, based on system approach
Zani's framework	Key success variables	Helps to design MIS, based on the key success variables of the organization
Stevan Alter's work centered framework	Work System	Decision can be taken on whether an information system needs to be created or improved

Prerequisites of an Effective MIS

- MIS should be able to meet the needs and requirements of the organization.
- Participation of both the operating managers as well as technical experts is necessary so that everyone knows how to install and use MIS.

Chart 2-1. Focus of MIS

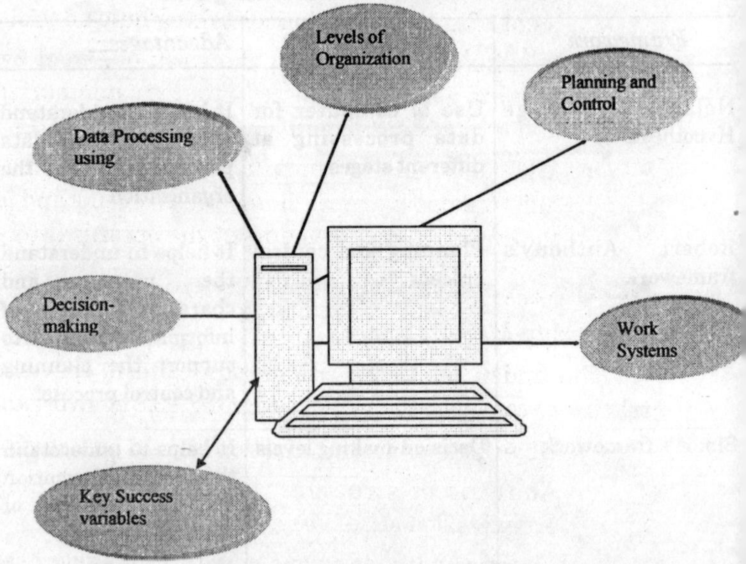

- MIS should be linked with every department and at all levels to facilitate better communication.
- MIS should be economical and must be able to provide the required information to the user.
- Pre-testing of MIS is necessary to avoid any problems during the course of work.
- An MIS should be flexible enough to accommodate the changing needs of an organization.
- An MIS should be reliable to avoid any misleading conclusions and wrong decisions.
- The flow of information should be continuous, meeting the desired needs.
- MIS should provide accurate results and assisting the users in all the areas.

Significance of MIS

The MIS is not only useful in taking decision but also in all other important aspects of organization. It has the significance as follows:

- MIS helps in the process of planning execution of the relevant, accurate, and timely information to the management of an organization for taking quick decisions.
- It is helpful in reducing the work overload by transforming a large number of data into summarized form and thus reduces confusion.
- MIS facilitates coordination and integration between different departments for solving problems and fulfilling the objective requirements of the organization.

MIS Design and Development Process

Designing MIS

The under-mentioned are certain criteria that should be taken into consideration while designing MIS of an organization.

- Objectives of an organization should be known.
- Analysis of structure, levels and functions of an organization should be determined.
- Functions and decisions made by managers should be known.
- The information requirements of different managers should be determined.
- Data should be transformed into information in such a way that it fulfills the need of the manager.
- If any shortcomings are found it the implementation of MIS, it should be removed immediately and preventive actions should be taken to avoid occurrences of such shortcomings in the future.

MIS Development Process

The development of MIS can be likened to the stages by which an architect designs a building. Firstly, he receives a design brief, which spells out what the building is expected to do. He then considers how to fulfill the objectives and produces a high level plan showing the overall perspective of the building. Lower level plans are then drawn each giving progressive more detail. This is a hierarchically structured approach, which is also used for the design of information systems (Fig. 2.1).

MIS Services

MIS provides the organization with a wide range of services, i.e., relevant information through reports for all levels and for all functional areas.

Routine Performance Reports: These are the scheduled summaries such as periodic sales reports, production reports, quality control reports, inventory control reports, etc.

Exception Reports: These reports are produced only when actual performance deviates from pre-determined standards.

On-Demand Reports: These are the occasional specialized reports that are requested by the management.

Predictive Reports: These are used mostly in strategic analysis and planning activities.

Benefits of Effective MIS

The benefits of MIS should be looked both at the macro and micro level. At the macro level the benefits of MIS in developing economy like India are high. It can be helpful both to the large organizations as well as the small and medium enterprises in increasing their production and productivity, which in turn will benefit the national economy and standard of living. Further optimum utilization of scarce resources are paramount importance for the countries like India. This can be achieved through effective MIS. At the organization level the benefits of MIS are:

1. The availability of accurate, cost effective and timely information for decision-making,
2. Accessibility to information according to levels in decision-making,
3. Delay in decision are avoided, and accuracy will be maintained,
4. Considerable savings in stationery,
5. Considerable savings in manpower and other resources, which can be productively used for some other purposes,
6. Management will be more effective and efficient,
7. Serves as an effective base for team work,

8. Reduction in wastage and cost and resultant increase in profit,
9. Establishment of database for future reference, and above all,
10. Increased morale among the human resource.

Functions of MIS

The functions of MIS are many folds. In fact new developments in management theory and science, management accounting and information technology add new dimensions to MIS. Generally the functions of MIS are:

1. Providing needed data/information relevant to the managers at different levels.
2. Reducing business uncertainties/risks by feeding correct information.
3. Helping the managers to expand their knowledge base.
4. Storing the relevant data and redundancy in data and overload in information is avoided.
5. Saving the time and cost in handling the information.
6. Helping to foresight the future and averts the crisis in business.
7. Identifying critical success factors and support key result areas of management.
8. Strengthening the reporting system in the organization.
9. Above all, with all these functions it aids in decision-making, which is the crux of management.

Limitations of MIS

Though MIS serves as an effective tool for decision-making it suffers from following limitations.

Managers Interest

MIS is only a tool for supplying information to management. It cannot replace manager's interest in particular decision.

Quality of data

MIS considers only quantitative aspects. Its quality depends upon the quality of input system. The process of decision-making needs not only quantitative data but also qualitative data / information.

Capability of MIS

In the fast changing environment MIS cannot provide tailor-made packages of information for decision-making. It can be effective in providing ready-made solutions to the repetitive problems.

Role of MIS

The role of MIS is only effective at the lower level, as the information requirements at this level are historical in nature. MIS has poor role at the top management level.

Effectiveness of MIS

MIS may loose its effectiveness where frequent changes / transfers are taking place at the top management level. Also, when organizations are tempted for frequent changes in organizational structures, MIS fails to function effectively.

Other limitations are:

- Due to the high cost of installation and maintenance, it is difficult for a small organization to go for MIS.
- MIS is less responsive to changing business environment and informational needs of the organization.
- There may be dangers of sabotage, computer viruses in the computerized information system, which can paralyze the system.
- Data redundancy, data inconsistency and data independence.
- Job requires one or more programs to be developed and interacted with one or more files.

The use of information system in the future will lead to significant improvements in the means of communicating. It will be more nearly paralled to the real flow of information within the organization. It will be flexible enough to incorporate the changes in the dynamics of management and business environment. Therefore, information must be made accessible to multiple users.

MIS is really revolution in the field of information technology for an efficient, effective and timely presentation of the reports. There has been an unprecedented opportunities of the application of MIS in the wide range of organizational problems. It will provide a linkage to a good quantity of life and certainly it will be a universal phenomenon in the time to come – 21st century – and would play a vital role in the success of any organization.

3

MIS and Management Levels

Management Levels

Each organization is made up of several levels. These could be classified broadly into three categories: Top, Middle and Junior or operational levels. In most cases, the top management performs strategic planning and the other two levels provide support in the form of processed information. The middle management performs tactical planning and control, and needs information so as to discharge managerial functions in the organization. The junior or operational level management is involved in day-to-day operations and control, needs information for its daily working. Exhibit 3.1 depicts a clear picture on the levels and functions, their tasks and location.

Exhibit 3.1

Management levels, tasks, location and functions

Task	*Location*	*Management functions*	*Level*
Strategic planning	Management	Management	Top
Management control	Office	Planning and Control	Middle
Operational control	Factory and Field	Execution	Lower

The top management performs the strategic planning as a management function at the management level; the middle management performs the task of management control as planning and control function at the office level; and the lower management performs operational control as execution function at the floor level. Figure 3.1 summarizes the interaction and role of these three levels of management in an organization.

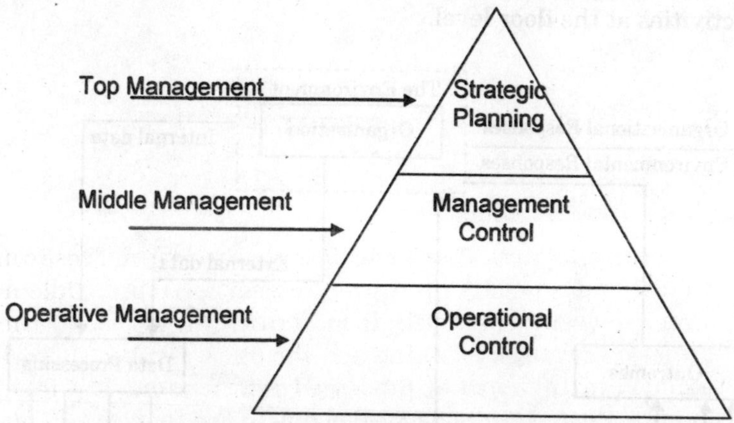

Fig. 3.1. Management Pyramid

The top management establishes the policies, plans and objectives of the organization as well as a budget framework under which various departments will operate. Middle management has the responsibility of implementing the policies and overall plans of the top management. Junior management has the responsibility of implementing the day-to-day operations and decisions of the middle management to produce goods and services to meet the revenue, profit, and other goals, which in turn will enable the organization to achieve its overall plans and objectives. The different levels of management are important for two reasons: (a) information needs tend to be different levels of management; and (b)amount of time required for any function varies considerably with each group.

MIS and Management Levels

Management information system provides selected decision-oriented information needed by management to plan, control, and evaluate the activities of the organization. It designed with a framework that emphasizes profit planning, performance planning, and control at all levels of management pyramid. It integrates all the business subsystems both financial and non-financial within the organization. An effective MIS needs current and future information on all respects and areas for evaluating the corporate objectives, strategic or long range planning, tactical or short range planning, and operational planning for routine activities at the floor level.

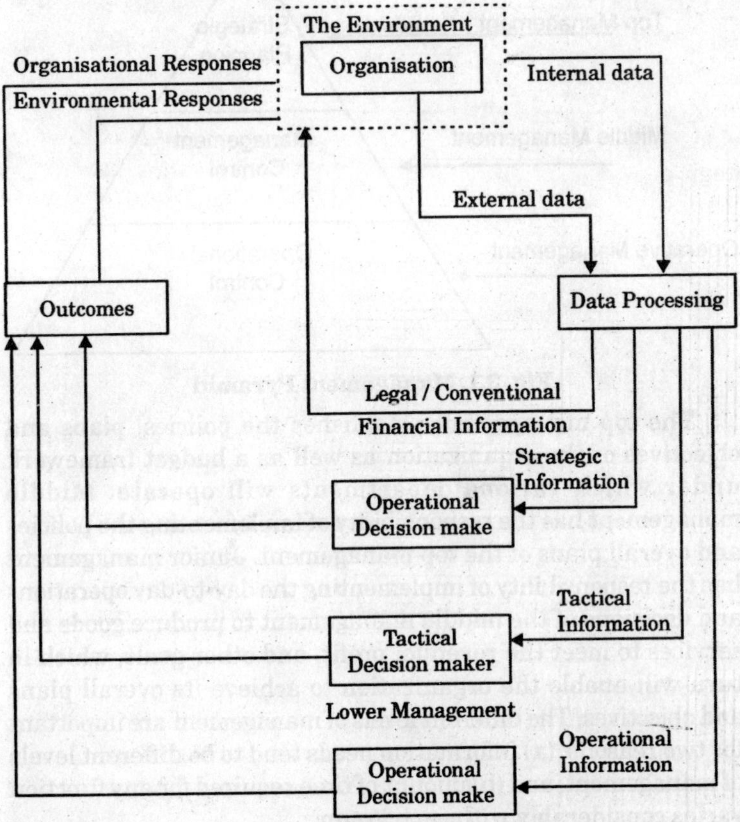

Fig. 3.2. MIS Framework

The MIS is an integrating, continuing and future oriented structure of all the resources of an organization ie., six M's – money, manpower, materials, machines, methods and management of information, designed to generate an orderly and integrated real time flow of information collected from internal and external sources, for use as the relevant bases for managerial decision making in any functional area of business organization.

Figure 3.2 presents the framework for MIS in a typical organization, works for collection, process and dissemination of information to the needy persons at all levels of management.

Data processing is the collection, transformation and retention of information. The organization and its environment generate data, which serves as the base (input) to data processing of internal and external data. Data processing ultimately provides strategic information for top level management the strategic planning; tactical information for middle management the management planning and control; and operational (technical) information for lower management the operational planning and control. It also provides the legal, conventional and financial information to the external users in the environment as and when required by them.

The action taken by the decision makers – top, middle and lower managers – as a result of the information they receive from MIS generate certain outcomes. These outcomes then stimulate organizational responses as well as environmental response. These responses now form the basis for the new data, or new input. The information system has input in the form of data received from internal and external sources. The process is in charge of transforming data into useful information. The output is the relevant information useful for planning, decision making and controlling the enterprise activities and operations. The controller is the decision maker who uses the information. The MIS provides necessary legal, conventional and financial information as well as that which is demanded by managers at strategic, tactical and operational levels of management. To manage business well is to manage its future. Management of future implies management of information as a resource of the organization – external and internal information. MIS is an integral part of decision making process at all levels of organization. Therefore, management must have well-designed and up to date MIS for making sound and timely business decisions at all levels of management on all problems in any area of the business.

Information needs of Levels of Management

The requirement of information at any level in the organization depends on the nature of activities performed at that level. At the operating level, the staff performs the operating activities of the organization leading to the production of goods and services. At lower levels of management, focus is on coordination and control of performance. The higher levels of management are engaged in planning. The information needs of planning consists of knowledge of current and past performance, forecasts on future performance, views of government policies, technological developments, market changes, and a feel for the political, social and economic climate. Control of performance against the plan involves three main stages: setting of performance standards, measurement of performance, and correction of deviations from the plan.

This requires detailed information on performance at the lowest level of the organization. Control may be exercised with the help of historical reports at the supervisory level or exception report at the middle level management. The historical report at worst, may be a complete printout of statistics going back over some period of time. Often it is produced by default, because the manager has been unable to define his real requirements. At best, it can be a comparison exercise; the period compared to the same period last year, classified on various parameters. In exception report, the computer sorts and selects only those items of information that the manager really needs. Obviously, rules have to be defined to establish what constitutes an exception. A significant deviation from the plan or standard may generally be considered as an exception.

Figure 3.3 depicts about the information for various levels of management in an organization.

The information needs of business organization at all levels of management are discussed below.

Operational information

At the operational level of the organization, staff handle operational transactions, such as orders, time-sheets, delivery notes, sickness notes, production work-sheets, inspection advices, stock records, etc. These documents are the working papers of the operational systems. The documents relating to business transactions are commonly referred to as "transaction documents". In fact, whenever a business transaction is executed, the parameters of the transaction are recorded in the form of a transaction document.

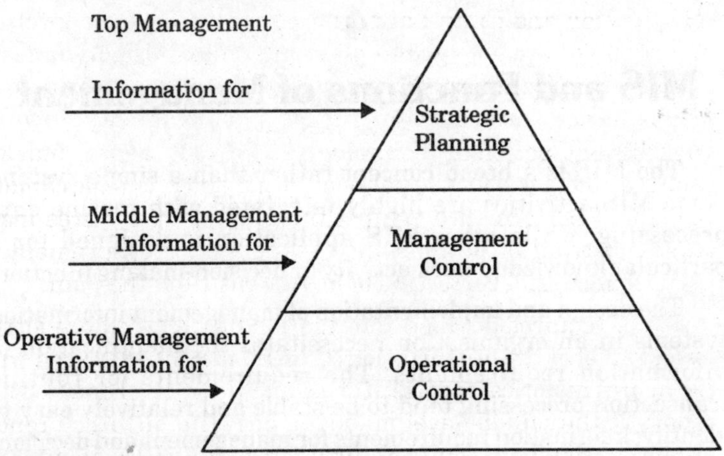

Fig. 3.3. Information for various levels of management

Tactical information

At the middle level the managers are responsible for implementation and control. They are in need of tactical information to implement and have control over the activities done by their subordinates.

Strategic information

At the top level the executives are concentrating on designing strategies to cope up with the changes in the environment so as to win the race by overriding the rivalries / competitors.

At the outset, the employees and managers at different levels of management pyramid need information to perform their tasks to achieve the organizational objectives. MIS plays a vital role in feeding information to all levels of personnel in an organization.

4

MIS and Functions of Management

The MIS is a broad concept rather than a single system. Some MIS activities are highly integrated with routine data processing, while other MIS application is designed for a particular knowledge work activity or decision-making function.

The design and implementation of management information systems in an organisation necessitates the identification of information requirements. The requirements for routine transaction processing tend to be stable and relatively easy to identify; information requirements for management and decision-making activities are more changeable and more difficult to define. For instance, the functions of management are pervasive to entire management team. But the level of intensity of these functions varies at different levels (see Chart 4.1).

Functions of Management

The five basic managerial functions are planning, organizing, staffing, directing and controlling.

Planning

Planning is basic to all managerial functions. It is a process of selecting one course of action, from different alternatives, for achieving the stated goals, objectives and targets. It is a decision making process determining in advance what to do, how to do, when to do and who is to do. Planning creates a frame of activity and events, which are to happen or a runaway for achieving corporate goals, objectives and targets. Planning process demands resource allocation through decision-making. The organisation may have a plan; but the question is how effective the plan is?

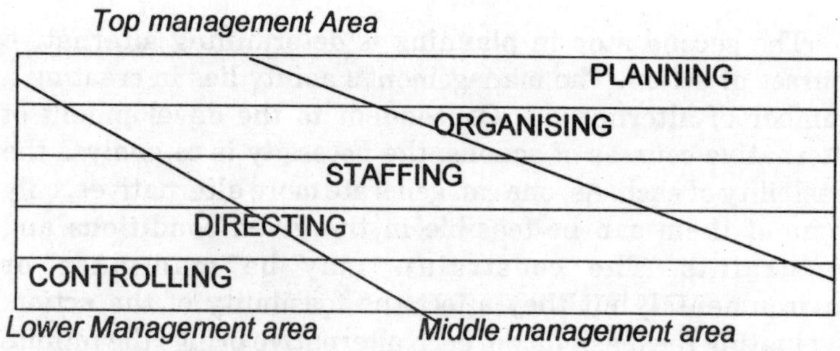

Chart 4.1. Relationship between levels and functions of Management

Planning is a continuous process. Koontz and O'Donnel rightly observed that like a navigator constantly checking where his ship is going in the vast ocean, a manager should constantly watch the progress of his plan. He must constantly monitor the conditions, both within and outside the organisation to determine if changes are required in his plans.

The efficiency of a plan is measured by the amount it contributes towards achievement of goals. The plan is efficient if it achieves the goals with less investment or with less resource. Therefore, efficient planning involves selecting a plan among several alternative plans. An efficient plan enables the management to handle uncertainty and risk in the business. It helps to make operations economical as it continuously evaluates the costs and outputs and forces optimum use of resources. It further helps to control business operations at all levels with common reference to goals, objectives and targets.

Steps in Planning

Planning is a step-by-step process. The first step in planning is forecasting the environment, in which the plan is to be made and operated. Forecasting provides information on population, growth, price trends, market changes, new opportunities, changes in technology and the external factors affecting the business. Forecasting provides the base on which the plan will be developed and implemented.

The second step in planning is determining alternative courses of action. The management's ability lies in creating a number of alternatives. Consequent to the development of alternative courses of actions, the necessity is to analyse the feasibility of each. As, one can generate more alternatives, only some of them can be feasible in the given conditions and constraints. The constraints may be man-made or environmental; but they affect the feasibility of the action. Evaluating the feasibility of each alternative brings the infinite number of alternatives to a limited number.

The third step in the planning process is to evaluate the best among all the feasible alternatives. The analysis and evaluation is done with reference to the objectives such as, minimization of cost, maximization of profit, yield and productivity etc. The right choice of an objective is a crucial factor in the selection process. The planning begins with the setting of goals and objectives and ends up in selecting the most rational course of action.

An organisation has a network of goals, objectives and structures. It is necessary to develop the network of plans corresponding to this network. The process leads to the development of corporate plans, area plans, functional plans, departmental plans and so on. For example, the organisation may have business plans, investment plans, marketing plans, and advertising plans. Normally, the corporate plans are for a longer period and the other plans are for shorter periods.

Organising

Organising is an important step in the managerial process and relates to the people in an enterprise. It deals with a quantitative and a qualitative aspect of manpower in terms of placement, the roles they play and the relations amongst them, with the aim that they work together effectively towards accomplishing the goals, objectives and the targets of the organisation.

The organisation could be formal or informal. The organisation is formal when the roles, the relation of the people and the objectives they should achieve are well defined. In an informal organisation, it is left to the people to understand and evolve suitable roles and relationships to achieve the objectives.

While creating the organisation, attention is given to an appropriate splitting of the enterprise activities, by way of function, and grouping them in such a way that they form a division, a department, a section or a formal group. The people heading these entities should have enough authority to decide, and should exercise a discretion in using the authority. The people should be put in such a structure of roles and relationship that it is designed to work effectively and the members of the structure are able to contribute substantially towards the achievement of goals. The structure would be productive, if it is manned properly. The process of manning involves people in right number and placing them in the appropriate levels.

Peter Drucker recommends three ways to determine the structure:

- Activity analysis,
- Decision analysis, and
- Relations analysis.

Organisation is a process by which a manager can bring a smoothness of operations, by way of conflict resolution, assigning work responsibility, and creating appropriate work environment.

Staffing

The functions of staffing deal with managing the enterprise as per the organisation structure so that the staff carryout the activities as per the plan. Staffing involves not only selection of persons but also their appraisal and development so that they perform the designated roles. The selection of a person is a difficult task. However, the chances of selecting a wrong person are very less if a proper method is used. Since people cannot be easily replaced because of socio- political and legal reasons, their selection, in terms of quality and quantity, is of paramount importance.

Staffing of enterprise should be for today's needs, as well as that of the future. The requirement of the future is difficult to predict in precise terms and this requirement needs to be forecasted for more than five to six years. So the purpose of staffing is not manning for the current plan of business but to create a manpower potential capable of undergoing development, so that the same manpower is able to perform the changed roles in the future.

Hence, the selection of a person in terms of age, qualification, and potential becomes an important task in staffing.

The selection of individuals for line functions is not that difficult because the role and the tasks are well defined and do not undergo any significant change over a period of time. The difficulty lies in the selection of management positions. The manager is a multi faceted personality. A person is said to have good managerial potential, if he has the following qualities apart from the functional knowledge:

- The person must have the desire to manage
- He must have the necessary drive and self-motivation to manage
- He must be able to identify himself with the corporate goals and be committed to them.
- The person must have the capability of applying knowledge to real life situations in the right perspective, locating the problem areas and generating a number of alternate courses of action.
- The person must be able to perform effectively. This is possible only if he has the ability to communicate effectively, i.e., the person must have a good command over the language in written and spoken form. Many times the person may have the skills, but due to the psychological barriers he cannot communicate. These barriers come to on account of personality conflict, power games and dissatisfaction on rewards and promotion.
- The manager must be a person of integrity.
- He should be honest, trustworthy and high achiever. This can be judged by the track record of the person and his work experience, the extra curricular activities he may be performing, and personal interview.

The staffing, therefore, deals with creation of human resource in the enterprise to achieve goals, objectives and targets set by the top management.

Directing

Direction involves the initiation of activities to achieve the goals of organisation. Koontz O'Donnel defines directing as.' the interpersonal aspect of managing by which subordinates are led to understand and contribute effectively and efficiently to the attainment of enterprise objectives'.

Directing function of management links other functions of management. Because planning, organizing and staffing are preparatory management functions. The purpose of controlling is to verify whether the goals are achieved or not. All managers who have subordinates undertake directing as a managerial function. To be effective, direction function must be undertaken continuously. Direction must be coordinated to achieve the results. This function consists of following elements:

- It includes the issue of orders that are clear, complete, and within the capabilities of subordinates to achieve
- It is a continuous training activity in which subordinates are instructed to carry out the task in the given situation
- It necessarily involves the motivation of workers to try to meet the expectations of the managers.
- It consists of maintaining discipline and rewarding those who perform properly.
- It consists of communication system, which makes the organisation live.

Direction is one of the most complex functions of management, which can be learned and perfected only through long experience. However, harmony of objectives, unity of command, direct supervision, efficient communication and follow-through will make this function more effective.

Controlling

Control is one of the important functions of management. The main object of control is to bring to light the variations between the standards set and performance and then to take necessary steps to prevent the occurrence of such variations in future. It is the process through which managers assure that actual activities conform to planed activities.

There are three basic steps in a control process:

1. Establish standards,
2. Measuring and comparing actual results against standards,
3. Taking corrective actions.

Establishing standards

Standards are criteria against which results are measured. They are norms to achieve the goals. Standards are usually measurable in terms of output. They can also be measured in non-monetary terms like loyalty, customer attraction, good-will, etc.

Measuring and comparing actual results against standards

After establishing standards the performance has to be measured in terms of the standards established earlier. Any deviations must be detected. Hence, measurement of performance has a future basis.

Taking corrective actions

If performance falls short, the manager must take the steps to correct the deviations. This can be done by means of altering the plans, reassigning the duties, employing more staff, etc.

Control Techniques

A variety of tools and techniques have been used over the years to help managers to control the activities of their organisation. Control techniques are broadly classified as budgetary and non-budgetary control techniques.

(i) Budget: A budget is a statement of anticipated results during a designated time period expressed in financial and non-financial terms. Budgets cover a designated time period – usually a year. At stated intervals during that time period, actual performance is compared directly with the budget targets and deviations are quickly detected and acted upon. On the basis of the purpose for which the budgets were prepared they are classified as sales budget, production budget, production cost

budget, capital expenditure budget, cash budget, master budget, etc.

(ii) Non-budgetary control devices: Non-budgetary control devices are statistical data, special reports and analysis, breakeven points, audit, standard cost, ratio-analysis, etc.:

1. *Statistical Data:* All needed and available data are collected and presented in tables, charts and graphs, through them performances are assessed.
2. *Special Reports:* To analyse particular problem areas, special staff are appointed to collect information.
3. *Breau-Even Point Analysis:* It involves the use of charts to depict the overall volume of sales necessary to cover costs. It is that point at which the cost and revenue of the enterprise are exactly equal. In other words it is the point where the enterprise neither earns a profit nor incurs loss.
4. *Audit:* The internal auditors, who are the employees of the organisation, conduct internal audit. An external auditor conducts external audit on the financial performance of the organisation. The audits check the financial health of the organisation and make the employees alert.
5. *Time-Event Network Analysis:* This is otherwise called as Programme Evaluation and Review Technique (PERT). Under this technique a project is divided into various units in a time sequence. For each event the 'critical path' is found, which is a sequence of events, which takes the longest time and which involves the least slack time. Summarized events are given for top management's perusal.
6. *Standard Costs:* Standard costs are prepared working out the cost of materials and labour for each unit of the product adding a standard overhead rate. Variations in costs could be found comparing the standard costs.
7. *Ratio Analysis:* It involves selecting two significant figures from a financial statement and expressing their relationship in terms of a percentage or ratio. There are various ratios are used to analyse financial statements. They are Liquidity ratio, Debt ratio, Profitability ratio, Operating ratio, etc.

Responsibility accounting: Responsibility accounting can be defined as a system of accounting under which each departmental head is made responsible for the performance of his department. Under this system, each department is made a semi-autonomous profit centre, i.e., a centre is responsible for the generation of profit. A department generates profits by 'selling' its outputs to the departments or profit centres in the same organisation.

MIS - A TOOL FOR MANAGEMENT FUNCTIONS

The present day business environment is more complex and challenging. Every day new companies are coming to the market and the strength of the existing companies are shackled. On other hand the information revolution have brought new identity and value to data/information. Every organisation is interested in harvesting the opportunities of the information revolution to strengthen their business. In this juncture the role of MIS have become more important in performing the management functions. The crux of management is decision making. Decision making though the part of planning process, the manager has to take decisions in all the functions of management. If the manager is not provided with the relevant data/information he will be put in to trouble. Here MIS plays key role. The role of MIS in the functions of management is given in the chart 4.2

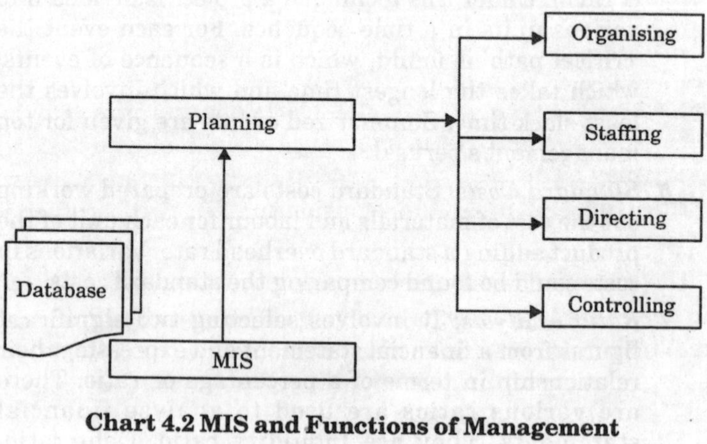

Chart 4.2 MIS and Functions of Management

MIS aids managerial functions through:

- Providing needed data/information relevant to the managers at different levels.
- Reducing business uncertainties/risks by feeding correct information.
- Helping the managers to expand their knowledge base.
  Storing the relevant data and redundancy in data and overload in information is avoided.
- Saving the time and cost in handling the information.
- Helping to foresight the future and averts the crisis in business.
- Identifying critical success factors and support key result areas of management.
- Strengthening the reporting system in the organisation.
- Above all, with all these functions it aids in decision-making, which is the crux of management.

Importance of MIS in Planning

Planning is the beginning of the process of management. A manager must plan before he can possibly organize, staff, direct and control. It is the basic function of management. Without planning other functions become mere activity.

Planning is an intellectual process, which requires a manager to think before acting. It is thinking in advance. It is by planning that managers of organizations decide what is to be done, when is to be done, how it is to be done and who is to do it. The decision-making is an integral part of planning. Decision-making may be defined as the process of choosing among best alternatives. Without plan decision-making will be futile exercise.

The manager must evolve a plan that is flexible i.e., the plan must be able to adapt to changing situations without undue cost. A plan must provide as many contingencies as possible. It needs to posses of built-in flexibility in atleast five major areas namely, technology, market, finance, personnel and organization.

Planning is important to all managers regardless of their level in their organization. Because, planning is a pervasive function.

The Management Information System have the goals, they are pre-specified and preplanned reporting to managers, interactive and ad hoc support for decision making to managers and critical information for top management.

Planning as a first function of management has its own significance. The paramount significance of MIS in planning is stated here under:

1. *Planning minimizes risk and uncertainty in business*: Today's business is more risky and complex. It has become challenging for the corporate man to seek more information so as to reduce the risk and uncertainty. It is the plan, which serves as the guide map in this respect with the support of MIS.
2. *Planning leads to success*: Planning cannot assure success. But experiences shows that without plan corporate success would not be feasible. Hence the managers must concentrate on the planning process itself to make the business success by means of establishing MIS.
3. *Planning focuses on the corporate goals*: It is the corporate goals, which decides the nature and form of business. The planning helps the manager to focus on the goals and thereby frame strategies to achieve the goals. It also enables the manager to chalk out in advance an orderly sequence of steps for the realization of corporate goals and to avoid the overlapping in efforts. For this MIS is required.
4. *Planning facilitates control*: The goals and plans set the standards for the organization functions. It is the control function ensures that the functions of the organization are confirmed to the goals and plans. Hence control can be exercised only if there are plans with the support of MIS.

As planning is the all-pervasive function all the managers regardless of the position in the organization have to plan in such a way that the corporate goals are achieved. Normally it is identified that there are three types of planning exercise are done in the organization. They are viz., strategic planning, management control and operational planning, the nature of these planning exercises are given in table 4.1.

Steps in Planning and MIS

Planning is a step-by-step process. MIS helps in all the steps involved in planning. The *first step* in planning is forecasting the environment, in which the plan is to be made and operated. Forecasting provides information on population, growth, price trends, market changes, new opportunities, changes in technology and the external factors affecting the business. Forecasting provides the base on which the plan will be developed and implemented. MIS supports the management in gathering needed information regarding forecasting.

The *second step* in planning is determining alternative courses of action. The management's ability lies in creating a number of alternatives. Consequent to the development of alternative courses of actions, the necessity is to analyze the feasibility of each. Though one can generate more alternatives, only some of them can be feasible in the given conditions and constraints. The constraints may be man-made or environmental; but they affect the feasibility of the action. Evaluating the feasibility of each alternative brings the infinite number of alternatives to a limited number. In this process MIS can feed information about the alternatives.

The *third step* in the planning process is to evaluate the best among all the feasible alternatives. The analysis and evaluation is done with reference to the objectives such as, minimization of cost, maximization of profit, yield and productivity etc. The right choice of an objective is a crucial factor in the selection process. The planning begins with the setting of goals and objectives and ends up in selecting the most rational course of action. For choosing the best alternative MIS provides valuable information.

Use of Computerized MIS in Planning and Control

The use of computerized MIS in the organization cannot be limited to planning and control. However, the following

Table 4.1. Types of Planning

Functions	*Strategic Planning*	*Management control*	*Operational Planning*
Planning levels	It is done at higher level of management	It is done at middle level of management	It is done at lower level of management
Term of Functions	Long-term planning	It is normally for 3-5 years	Short-term planning
Nature of Functions	It decides the goals and policies of allocation of scarce resources to achieve these goals	It decides detailed use of resources for achieving goals	It works out the modalities to use the resources to achieve goals
Bases of functions	It is generally based on long-term forecasts about socio-economic, technological and political etc., changes in the environment and therefore more uncertain	It is generally based on the cost benefit of each transaction. Hence partly certain and partly uncertain	It is based on routine and daily works and hence certain
Technicality	It is less detailed because it concerns with overall strategy of the organization	It is detailed because it concerns with execution of plans at each levels of organization	It is more detailed because it concerns with day-to-day operations at each section level

paragraphs identify certain use of computerized MIS for planning and control (Chart 4.3):

1. Planning needs information on corporate achievement, strength, weakness, market opportunities and threats. A well-established MIS with the use of computers can feed this information to the managers at right time.
2. Planning is an all-pervasive function. Hence, the coordination of mangers at all levels is necessary. The computers can link the work of all managers in the campus as well as off the campus.
3. As computerization reduces the work of the managers considerably, they can concentrate on devising strategies for achieving corporate plans.
4. Computerization can help the managers to forecast the future by using management tools and techniques, statistics, or techniques such as, PERT and CPM.
5. Computers can serve as the best control tool. The managers on their table itself can watch the performance of the workers and compare the results with the standards. Any deviations in the output can be corrected then and there.
6. As computerization will reduce the quantum of human resource required for the organization, span of control will become easy for the managers. Further excess human resources can be fully utilized where it is actually required.
7. Communication system serves as the nerve centre of the organization. The age-old filing, recording and reporting system in the organization demotivate the energetic managers. The managers are very often caught hold in the problems created by this system and procrastinate to plan for organization development. The computerization will help the managers to escape from all such nonsense and will give sufficient time for them to think on the organization goals.
8. E-commerce has generated more opportunities in business. The computerization can rightly help the managers to plan their e-commerce.

9. In nutshell the e-governance have proved success. The managers can make use of this technique to govern their enterprise so as to plan effectively and control the operations to achieve their goals.

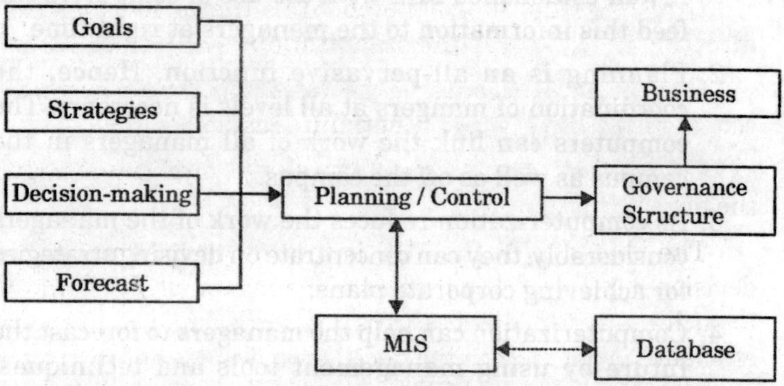

Chart 4.3. Use of MIS in Planning and Control

MANAGERIAL PROCESS AND INFORMATION SYSTEM

Management is the coordinating of resources to accomplish a goal or objective. Reaching the goal requires the managers to make decisions in order to plan, organize, staff, lead and motivate, and control. For which he requires information from within and outside the organization through various sources. An information system can retrieve and supply valuable information to make decisions in the management process planning, organizing, staffing, and leading and motivating, and controlling functions of an organization.

MIS: A Support of the Management

The management process is executed through a variety of decisions taken to each step of planning, organizing, staffing, directing, coordinating and control. The MIS aids decision-making. If the management is able to spell out the decisions required to be taken, the MIS can be designed suitably. The decisions required to be taken in these steps are here under:

Planning: A selection from various alternatives – strategies, resources, methods, etc.

Organization: A selection of a combination out of several combinations of the goals, people, resources, method, and authority.

Staffing: Providing a proper manpower complement.

Directing: Choosing a method from the various methods of directing the efforts in the organization.

Coordinating: Choice of the tools and the techniques for coordinating the efforts for optimum results.

Controlling: A selection of the exceptional conditions and the decision guidelines.

The objective of the MIS is to provide information for a decision support in the process of management. It should help in such a way that the business goals are achieved in the most efficient manner. Since the decision-making is not restricted to a particular level, the MIS is expected to support all the levels of the management in conducting the business operations. Unless the MIIS becomes a management aid, it is not useful to the organization.

The most frequent user of business information system is the business manager. Thus, thrust of the business information systems should be on the information needs of a manager. It is, thus, necessary to understand management and the managerial process. Management is what a manger does. What a manager does gives us an insight into the process of management. It is a universally accepted view that management is the art of getting things done through others to achieve certain objectives. This view of management focuses on the managerial process (i.e., the art) involved in achieving the desired results.

MIS: A Tool for Management Process

The process of management requires a lot of data and information for the execution of the plan. This requirement arises on account of the fact that in each step of management, a variety of decisions are taken to correct the courses of development. The decisions or actions are prompted due to the feedback given by the control system incorporated in the management system. The control of overall performance is made possible by way of budgets, summaries and reports. The summary showing sales, costs, profit and return on investment throws light on the direction the organization is moving to. The exception reports identify weaknesses in the system of management.

An effective management system is to be assured; it has to rest on business information. The management performance improves if the business risk and uncertainties are handled effectively. if the information provided is adequate, one can deal with these factors squarely. The information support improves tha lack of knowledge, enriches experience and improves analytical abilities leading to better business judgment. So, if efficient information support is to be provided, it calls for a system with the goals of generating management information. A good MIS must furnish information to the managers to expand their knowledge base. He must know the adverse trends in business, the shortfalls and failures in the management process.

The MIS should provide the support to act and to act decisively. It should support management in term of basic business information at the corporate level and meet the specific needs of the managers. It should highlight on the critical success factors and support key areas of management. MIS should have, wherever possible, decision support systems to help the manager in decision-making.

Modern management systems rely on MIS. The complexity of business management and competitive nature of business requires handling of business operations with skill and foresight to avert the crisis. Modern business management requires shift from the traditional controls to managerial control. The shift requires the manager to become more efficient in handling the tasks he is entrusted with. The manager becomes more efficient if he is well informed, made richer in knowledge, experience and analytical skills and is able to face the uncertainties and the risks of business. This is possible only if he is supported by MIS, in his specific tasks of management of business.

Modern business has become more technology-oriented wherein the manager is required to be up-to-date on technological advancement, not only in his field of operations but also in the other technologies. The emerging new technologies are posing threats to current business and are opening new opportunities for new business ventures. The manager has to keep himself abreast on the information of how these technologies affect his business prospects. A good MIS designed for such a support is absolutely essential. MIS, therefore, is a tool for effective execution of the management process.

Management Process and Information

Planning

Planning is the process of formulating objectives and determining how to achieve those objectives with available resources. A well-written plan is made up of two key components: (1) an objective specifying "what" is to be accomplished and "when" and (2) action statement telling "how" the objective is to be accomplished.

A planning process involves five steps, namely, (1) Analyze the environment, (2) Prepare a mission statement, (3) Set objectives, (4) Develop action plans and, (5) Establish control systems. Each of the aforestated steps in the planning process requires a lot of information regarding the internal and external environment in which the plans have to operate.

It may be note that each of the above steps in the planning process requires a lot of information regarding the internal and external environment in which the plans have to operate. The information regarding the external environment includes economic trends, technological changes, availability and cost of various resources, etc. The information regarding the internal environment includes sales forecasts, financial resources and plans, state of availability of resources in the company, etc. A manager also needs various tools for analysis of the information regarding the environment.

The planning process involves anticipation and forecasting. This requires information regarding the internal and external factors that are likely to influence the future state of affairs. The information regarding the relevance and relative impact of these factors is a critical input process of anticipation and forecasting of future events. Use of simulation, artificial intelligence techniques, neutral networks, fuzzy logic, etc. with the help of modern computer, have improved the predictive value of plans, as well as value addition to the planning information.

Organizing

Organization structure and information system are closely related to each other. If the organization structure is the body of the business enterprise, information system is its nervous system. The organization structure should be designed keeping in view the natural flow of information in the business enterprise. The performance measurement schemes must match the flow of information and the organization structure.

Ideally, any change in information systems should cause corresponding change in the organization structure; otherwise the information systems would not be able to reflect the plans of the business. For example, the advancements in data base technologies and use of distributed information systems are giving their own impact on the way organization structure are designed today. Conversely, if the organization structure changes, the information system must also change in order to cope up with the new realities of business processes. For example, in one organization, the changes in organization structure warranted by the increased competition necessitated redesigning of the information systems to offer not only information to managers with regard to the events in the enterprise but also the expertise in the business process. Information analysis tool and other artificial intelligence tools had to be incorporated into the information systems to strengthen the decision-making process.

Restructuring business organization could be painful and expensive if the information systems are not well developed. Efficient information systems can help managers cope up with the changes in their specific functions and activities. The information system that holds a part of the knowledge base of the enterprise can be of great help in handling situations that are new to a particular manager.

Staffing

With the increasing interdependence of various functions, appraisal of staff is becoming more complex. There is a need to use more advanced techniques of performance appraisal. These techniques can be applied with the hop of IT infrastructure. Well-designed information systems can gather information on various critical success factors for each managerial position and monitor the performance on regular basis. The advancement in multimedia technologies can help in automation of training and development systems.

Directing

Dissemination of information plays a crucial role in directing the efforts of people in the enterprise. In a business enterprise with operations spread over a wide geographical area, the personnel have to be mobile and are likely to be located far away from other members of the team and the immediate superior in the managerial hierarchy. Directing the subordinates, thus, becomes difficult because the communication may be quite expensive and may not reach the destination in time. Today, the information systems are the vehicles of formal communication. The facility of e-mail and use of the intranet has transformed the way formal communication takes lace in business enterprises. Seamless flow of information systems can also help in reducing the communication gaps that are many-a-time the main cause of employee dissatisfaction.

Controlling

The information systems play an important role in the control process. These systems not only help in measuring the performance of operations but also help in identifying deviations of performance from plans. The comparison between planned and actual performance is then analyzed with the help of information systems to identify reasons for deviations. The environmental information is used to identify such reasons.

Information regarding what actions are being taken or what is happening in the internal and external environments of business is essential for exercising control. Earlier, most of such information used to come by way of personal observation by the manager. Increasing size of the business enterprise has made personal observation a very difficult form of control. There is greater reliance on written reports. With the business becoming more knowledge intensive activity and composition of personnel of the enterprise getting dominated by knowledge workers, the measurement of performance is becoming more complex. Simple tabular reports with regard to achievement of quantified goals are not adequate for controlling.

Controlling function uses information regarding the planned performance and actual performance to arrive at deviations. Efficient information systems are only identify these deviations but also help in analyzing the deviations to pinpoint reasons for deviation. They also help in modifying the plans quickly in the light of the feedback.

The concept of flexible budgeting has become popular due to availability of better information processing facilities. With the availability of real time information system, the information regarding performance flows quickly. This helps in exercising control quickly, resulting in lower cost of managers in learning from the past experiences with minimum cost of mistakes. Detailed control information can be stored now for longer duration and analyzed as and when similar circumstances are observed to anticipate the changes in the environment. Modern information systems can help in handling complex control mechanisms almost automatically. The exception reporting is another aspect of controlling that has gained popularity due to advancements in information technology. Modern information systems enable managers get quicker access to information regarding the exception and help them take quicker decisions to mitigate the negative impact of the exceptional situations by revising plans immediately. An efficient information system can help in converting a disaster into a minor loss, as it would issue warning at the early stages of exceptional situations.

5
Functional Information Systems

This chapter provides more detail on how organizations use information systems from a functional perspective. Information systems can be classified by the specific organizational function they serve as well as by organizational level. The major organizational functions consist of sales and marketing, manufacturing, finance, accounting, and human resources. We now describe typical information systems that support each of these functions, showing functional application for each organizational level.

Sales and Marketing Information Systems

The sales and marketing function is responsible for selling the organization's product or service. Marketing is concerned with identifying the customers for the firm's products or services, determining what they need or want, planning and developing products and services to meet their needs, and advertising and promoting these products and services. Sales is concerned with contacting customers, selling the products and services, taking orders, and following up on sales.

Table 5.1 shows that information systems are used in sales and marketing in a number of ways. At the strategic level, sales and marketing systems monitor trends affecting new products and sales opportunities, support planning for new products and services and monitor the performance of competitors. At the management level, sales and marketing systems support market research, advertising and promotional campaigns, and pricing decisions. They analyze sales performance and the performance of the sales staff. Knowledge-level sales and marketing systems support marketing analysis workstations. At the operational level, sales and marketing systems assist in locating and contracting prospective customers, tracking sales, processing orders, and providing customer service support.

Table 5. 1. Examples of sales and marketing information systems

System	*Description*	*Organization Level*
Order processing	Enter, process, and track orders	Operational
Point-of-sale system	Record sales data	Operational
Sales region analysis	Analyze performance of sales territories	Management
Market analysis	Identify customers and markets using data on demographics, markets, consumer behavior, and trends	Knowledge
Pricing analysis	Determine prices for products and services	Management
Sales trend forecasting	Prepare 5-year sales forecasts	Strategic

A typical sales information system is one for recording sales using a point-of-sale device. A point-of-sales device captures data about each item sold at the time of the sale take place. For example, when a purchase is made at a Wal-Mart store, pint-of-sale terminals record the bar code of each item passing the checkout counter and send a purchase transaction directly to a central computer at Wal-Mart headquarters. The computer collects the sales data (which identify each item sold and the amount of the sale) and consolidates them for further management analysis. Wal-Mart managers examine these sales data to monitor sales activity and buying trends. The data are also used for placing orders to suppliers to replenish inventory of fast-selling goods.

Manufacturing and Production Information Systems

The manufacturing and production function is responsible for actually producing the firm's goods and services. Manufacturing and production systems deal with the planning, development, and maintenance of production facilities; the establishment of production goals; the acquisition, storage, and availability of production materials; and the scheduling of equipment, facilities, materials, and labor required to fashion finished products.

Table 5.2 shows some typical manufacturing and production information systems arranged by organizational level. Strategic-level manufacturing systems deal with the firm's long-term manufacturing goals, such as where to locate new plants or

Table 5.2. Examples of manufacturing and production information systems

System	*Description*	*Organization Level*
Plant scheduling	Schedule the production of a product by coordinating jobs, labor, supplies, and finances	Operational
Material movement control	Track purchases, receipts, and shipments	Operational
Machine control	Control the actions of machines and equipment	Operational
Computer-aided design (CAD)	Design new products	Knowledge
Production planning	Decide when and how much products should be produced	Management
Inventory control	Determine and maintain optimal level of stock for goods in process and finished goods	Management
Facilities location	Decide where to locate new production facilities	Strategic

whether to invest in new manufacturing technology. At the management level, manufacturing and production systems analyze and monitor manufacturing and production costs and resources. Knowledge manufacturing and production systems create and distribute design knowledge or expertise to drive the production process, and operational manufacturing and production systems deal with the status of production tasks.

Most manufacturing and production systems use some sort of inventory control system. Data about each item in inventory, such as the number of units depleted because of a shipment or purchase or the number of units replenished by reordering or returns are either scanned or keyed into the system. The inventory master file contains basic data about each item – the unique identification code for each item, the description of the item, the number of units on hand, the number of units on order, and the reorder point – the number of units in inventory that triggers a decision to reorder in order to prevent a stcockout. (Companies can estimate the number of items to reorder or they can use a formula for calculating the least expensive quantity of order called the *economic order quantity*.) The system produces reports such as the number of each item available in inventory that must be replenished.

Many firms are trying to create a seamless manufacturing process by integrating the various types of automated manufacturing systems using computer and communication technology. The data produced in one system are immediately available to be used by other systems. Leading-edge applications such as the computer-aided design/computer-aided manufacturing (CAD/CAM) system used by Odense Shipyards are even using the data from computer-generated designs to drive the actual fabrication and assembly of products. Before computer-integrated manufacturing, design engineers had to draft plans on paper and then hand them over to experts in manufacturing. The product development cycle was prolonged because the process requires so many manual steps in handoffs.

Finance and Accounting Information Systems

The finance functions is responsible for managing the firm's finance assets, such as cash, stocks, bonds, and other investments in order to maximize the return on these financial assets. The finance function is also in charge of managing the capitalization of the firm (finding new financial assets in stocks, bonds, or other forms of debt). In order to determine whether the firm is getting the best return on its investment, the finance function must obtain a considerable amount of information from sources external to the firm.

The accounting function is responsible for maintaining and managing the firm's financial records – receipts, disbursements, depreciation, payroll – to "account" for the flow of funds in a firm. Finance and accounting share related problems – how to keep track of a firm's financial assets and fund flows. They provide answers to questions such as: whet is the current inventory of financial assets? What records exist for disbursements, receipts, payroll, and other fund flows?

Table 5.3 shows some of the typical finance and accounting systems found in a typical large organization. Strategic-level systems for the finance and accounting function establish long-term investment goals for the firm and provide long-range forecasts of the firm's financial performance. At the management level, information systems help managers oversee and control the firm's financial resources. Knowledge systems support finance and accounting by providing analytical tools and workstations for designing the right mix of investments to maximize returns for the firm. Operational systems in finance and accounting track the flow of funds in the firm through transactions such as paychecks, payments to vendors, securities reports, and receipts.

A typical finance and accounting system found in all business is an accounts receivable system. An accounts receivable system keeps track of the money owed to the firm by its customers. Every customer purchase generates an "account receivable" – that is, the customer owes the firm money. Some customers pay immediately in cash, and others are granted credit. The accounts receivable system records the data from every invoice in a master file that also contains information on each customer, including credit rating. As the business goes on day after day, the system also keeps track of all the bills outstanding and can produce a variety of reports, both on paper and on computer screens, to help the business collect bills. The system also answers queries regarding a customer's payment history and credit rating. This system supplies information to the general ledger system, which tracks all cash flows of the firm.

Table 5.3. Examples of finance and accounting information systems

System	*Description*	*Organization Level*
Payroll	Produce paychecks and maintain payroll records	Operational
Accounts receivable	Track money owed the firm	Operational
Cash management	Track firm's receipts and Disbursements to determine funds available for investment	Operational
Portfolio analysis	Design the firm's portfolio of investments	Knowledge
Budgeting	Prepare short-term budgets	Management
Capital investment analysis	Evaluate the profitability of long-term capital expenditures	Management
Profit planning	Plan long-term profits	Strategic

Human Resources Information Systems

The human resources function is responsible for attracting, developing, and maintaining the firm's work force. Human resources identifies potential employees, maintains complete records on existing employees, and creates programs to develop employee' talents and skills.

Strategic-level human resources systems identify the manpower requirements (skills, educational level, types of positions, number of positions, and cost) for meeting the firm's long-term business plans. At the management level, human resources systems help managers monitor and analyze the recruitment, allocation, and compensation of employees. Knowledge systems for human resources support analysis activities related to job design, training, and the modeling of employee career paths and reporting relationships. Human resources operational systems track the recruitment and placement of the firm's employees (see Table 5.4).

Table 5.4: Examples of human resources information systems

System	*Description*	*Organization Level*
Employee record keeping	Maintain records of employee	Operational
Training and development	Track employee training, skills, and performance appraisals	Operational
Career pathing	Design career paths for employees	Knowledge
Compensation analysis	Analyze the range and distribution of employee wages, salaries, and benefits	Management
Contract cost analysis	Analyze the impact of projected changes in labor union contracts to the company's human resource costs	Management
Manpower planning	Plan the long-term labor force needs of the organization	Strategic

A typical human resources system is for employee record keeping. It maintains basic employee data, such as the employee's name, age, sex, marital status, address, educational background, salary, job title, date of hire, and date of termination. The system can produce a variety of reports, such as lists of newly hired employees, employees who are terminated or on leaves of absence, employees classified by job type or educational level. Or employee job performance evaluations. Such systems are typically designed to provide data that can satisfy federal and state record keeping requirements for Equal Employment Opportunity (EEO) and other purposes.

Applications of Operational, Tactical and Strategic Information Systems to Business Functions

The operational, tactical and strategic information systems can be applied into different business functions. This section of the present chapter discusses the application of operational, tactical and strategic information systems to various business functions like accounting and finance, marketing, production and human resource. Figure 5.1 presents a clear picture of these systems in a business organization.

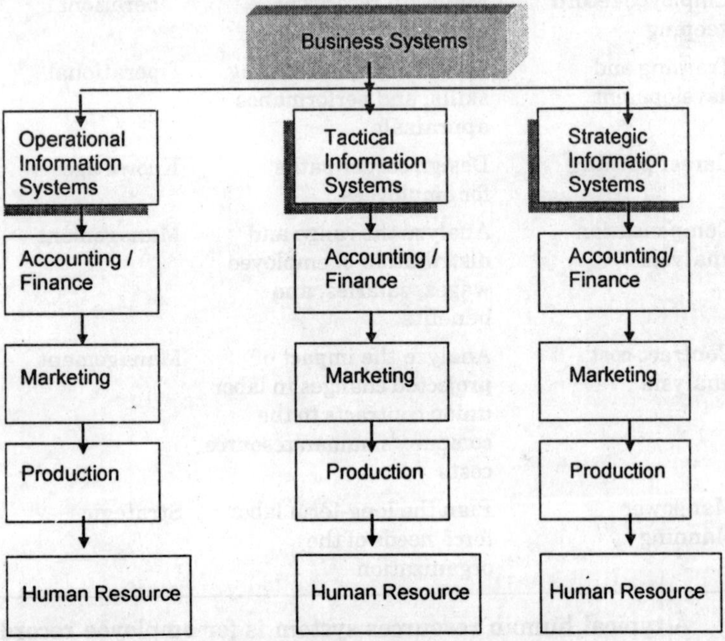

Fig. 5.1. Business systems in an organisation

Applications of Operational Information Systems

The information systems that perform or support the completion of tasks such as calculation, printing, distribution of paycheques, verification, calculation, mailing of sales invoices, purchase orders, vendors cheques, customer identification, tasks regarding employees, manufacturing activities, etc., are often referred to as operational information systems. Operational information systems record, process, and report all routine and

Exhibit 5.1
Activities – Operational Information Systems in Four Business Functions

Accounting / Finance	*Marketing*	*Production*	*Human Resource*
Fixed assets	Prospect leads	Purchasing	Position control
Sales order processing	Contact information	Receiving	Employee profile
Accounts receivable	Micromarketing and data warehousing	Quality control	Employee skills inventory
Accounts payable	Telemarketing	Shipping	Performance management
Inventory control	Direct mail	Automated materials handling	Government reporting
Purchase order processing	Point-of-sale	Computer aided design / manufacturing	Selection and recruitment
Payroll	Delivery tracking and routing	Image management	Training
Billing / invoicing	Electronic shopping	Material selection	
	Electronic advertising	Shop-floor scheduling	
		Mass customization	
		Shop-floor control	

repetitive activities. The information they produce is usually detailed, highly structured, accurate, derived from internal sources, and produced regularly. Exhibit 5.1 shows the details of operational information systems and activities that occur in all areas of business.

Operational Financial Accounting Information Systems

Operational financial accounting information systems are typically task oriented. They focus on processing financial transactions to produce the routine, repetitive information outputs that every organization finds necessary. These outputs include paycheques, cheques to vendors, customer invoices, purchase orders, stock reports, and other regular forms and reports. The following are the financial accounting system modules:

- General ledger
- Fixed assets
- Sales order processing
- Accounts receivable
- Accounts payable
- Inventory control
- Purchase order processing
- Payroll, etc.

These financial accounting systems are integrated. Each system receives data form various sources and processes, and disseminates output in the form of information to other systems.

Operational Marketing Information Systems

Operational marketing information systems consist subsystems such as sales systems, advertising systems, sales promotion systems, warehousing systems, and pricing systems. These systems collect data that describe marketing operations, process those data, and provide marketing information to the managers so as to make marketing decisions on time. Computer information systems have been widely applied to operational level marketing tasks. To be effective the marketing information systems should have linkage with other systems.

Operational marketing information systems may be:

(1) *Sales force automation systems* - that are designed to increase the productivity of sales force. The sales people may go for using prospect information systems to locate prospective customers. Electronic database and customer contact management systems may be useful in this activity;

(2) *Micro marketing and data warehouse systems* – Pitching sales or advertising campaigns to very narrowly defined customer targets is called micro marketing. It requires a large customer database, a data warehouse;

(3) *Telemarketing systems* – This usually include support for the automatic dialing of parties and / or delivering voice messages to the answering party under the control of a computer system. Telemarketers use electronic directories and online database on potential customers;

(4) *Direct mail advertising systems* – The organizations generate sales by mailing sales brochures and catalogues directly to customers using direct mail advertising systems;

(5) Point of sale systems – It is another facet of the order entry system. This system captures data about orders at the point of sale. It provides their customers with terminals that have direct access to the organisation's sales order system;

(6) Delivery tracking and routing systems – These systems are useful in delivering goods to customers on time by using tracking system software;

(7) Electronic shopping and advertising – Doing business online with the support of internet; virtual shopping by using electronic kiosks and internet advertising.

Operational Production Information Systems

Operational production information systems are diverse; they consist continuous flow production, mass production, job order production, and project production. Other operational information systems support the production function. Operational production information systems may be:

(1) *Purchasing systems* – This system is for maintaining and facilitating data and information on purchase of raw materials and production supplies. It includes receiving systems also;

(2) *Quality control systems* – These systems provide information about the status of production goods as they more from raw materials state, through goods in process, to finished goods. Quality control data may be collected by using shop floor data collection systems;

(3) *Automated material handling systems* – These systems track, control, and otherwise support the movement raw materials, work-in-process, and finished goods from the receiving docks to the shopping docks;

(4) *Computer aided and manufacturing systems* – These systems are useful in designing products/new products using software; and

(5) Image management systems, material selection systems, shop floor scheduling systems and mass customization and agile manufacturing systems are widely used at the operational production information systems to facilitate activities.

Operational Production Information Systems

Operational production information systems are diverse; they consist continuous flow production, mass production, job order production, and project production. Other operational information systems support the production function. Operational production information systems may be:

(1) *Purchasing systems* – This system is for maintaining and facilitating data and information on purchase of raw materials and production supplies. It includes receiving systems also;

(2) *Quality control systems* – These systems provide information about the status of production goods as they more from raw materials state, through goods in process, to finished goods. Quality control data may be collected by using shop floor data collection systems;

(3) *Automated material handling systems* – These systems track, control, and otherwise support the movement raw materials, work-in-process, and finished goods from the receiving docks to the shopping docks;

(4) *Computer aided and manufacturing systems* – These systems are useful in designing products / new products using software; and

(5) Image management systems, material selection systems, shop floor scheduling systems and mass customization and agile manufacturing systems are widely used at the operational production information systems to facilitate activities.

Operational Human Resource Information Systems

These systems provide managers with data to support the routine, repetitive human decisions that occur regularly in the organisations. There are many operational level human resource information systems such as:

(1) *Position control systems* – The purpose of position control systems is to identify each position in the organization, job title in which the position is classified, and employee currently assigned to the position;

(2) *Employee information systems* – this system maintains employee profile (name, gender, address, years of service, etc.) and skills inventory;

(3) *Performance management systems* – This system helps the organization to appraise employees' performance periodically. The data for performance appraisal is provided by these systems;

(4) *Selection and placement systems* – These systems help human resource staff members ensure compliance with employment laws. The data on selection and placement will be processed and disseminated by these systems;

(5) *Training systems* – Information on training of personnel at the operational level is available with these systems regularly.

Applications of Tactical and Strategic Information Systems

Tactical information systems support management decision making by providing managers with regular summary reports, regular exception reports, ad hoc reports and other relevant information helps them control their areas of responsibility and allocate their resources to pursue organization goals. In contrast, strategic information systems are goal oriented. That is, they are designed to support organizational goals and direction setting. Exhibit 5.2 presents about the activities of tactical and strategic information systems in four business functions.

Applications of Tactical Information Systems

Tactical Accounting and Financial Information Systems

The managers at tactical level make financial and accounting decisions with the support of tactical information systems. The tactical accounting and financial information systems are:

(1) *Budgeting systems* – They permit managers to track actual revenues and expenses and compare these amounts to expected revenues and expenses. It also allows the managers to compare current budget amounts with previous fiscal periods budgets;

(2) *Cash management systems* – The organization needs cash for two purposes: for working capital and for the acquisition of long term assets. Cash management systems help managers to manage cash by providing sufficient information;

(3) *Capital budgeting systems* – By using software managers can compute values and they can go for financial analysis and comparison;

(4) *Investment management systems* – Managers by computer information systems manage stock and bonds portfolios. They can maintain online database for this purpose.

Tactical Marketing Information Systems

Tactical marketing information systems differ from operational marketing information systems. In addition to

Exhibit 5.2

Activities – Tactical and Strategic Information Systems in Four Business Functions

Accounting / Finance	*Marketing*	*Production*	*Human Resource*
Tactical Information Systems			
Budgeting	Sales management	Materials requirement planning	Job analysis and design
Cash management	Advertising and promotion	Just in time	Recruiting
Capital Budgeting	Pricing	Capacity planning	Compensation and benefits
Investment management	Distribution channel	Production scheduling	Succession planning
	Competitive tracking	Product design and development	
		Manufacturing resource planning	
		Computer integrated manufacturing	
Strategic Information Systems			
Financial condition analysis	Sales forecasting	Site planning and selection	Workforce planning
Long term forecasting	Market research	Technology planning and assessment	Labour negotiations
	Product planning and development	Process positioning	
		Plant design	

producing information on a regular basis, they also generate ad hoc reports, create unexpected as well as expected output, produce comparative as well as descriptive information, provide summary information reports. Tactical marketing information systems include:

(1) *sales management systems* – The information systems that supply data about histories of each customer, salesperson, territory, product, and market segment;

(2) *Advertising and promotion systems* – These systems assist managers to decide advertising media and promotion devices, when to use media and devices, mix of promotional activities;

(3) *Pricing systems* – These systems provide information to managers that helps them set prices for products and services;

(4) *Distribution channel systems* – These systems provide cost of channels, reliability of channels in delivering goods and services, and market segment saturation provided by channels;

(5) *Competitive tracking systems* – gathering competitive intelligence is carried out through these systems in terms of competitive products, pricing, services, etc.

Tactical Production Information Systems

Tactical production information systems deal with all components of tactical production systems. These are:

(1) *Materials requirements planning systems* – These systems use software a set of programs that use data from the master production schedule, inventory files, and bill-of-material systems;

(2) *Just-in-time systems* – Just-in-time is not a tactical information system, but a tactical approach to production. These systems support the production systems based on the philosophy that operations should occur just when they are required to maintain production schedule;

(3) *Capacity planning systems* – Capacity planning decisions are tactical production decisions and include allocating

personnel and production facilities. This information is provided by capacity planning systems;

(4) *Production scheduling systems* – Information on production schedule to allocate the use of specific production facilities for the production of finished goods to meet the master production schedule is provided by these systems;

(5) *Product design and development systems* – many tactical decisions must be made to design and develop a new product. This is supported by software using these type of systems to ensure a good and competitive design of new products;

(6) *Manufacturing resource planning systems* – Manufacturing resource planning (MRP-II) software is available in the market, which extends the production information system to finance, marketing, human resource management, and other organization functions;

(7) *Computer integrated manufacturing systems* – It is a joint project system to integrate current production hardware and software products into systems.

Tactical Human Resource Information Systems

Human resource information systems include a number of tactical and strategic information systems. Tactical human resource information systems are:

(1) *Job analysis and design systems* – In developing job descriptions and specifications these systems support the organization;

(2) *Recruiting systems* – Tactical level managers need information on recruitment of personnel for the organization. The recruiting systems provide such data/information;

(3) *Compensation and benefit systems* – The information related to compensation and benefits to employees at tactical level should be known by the tactical managers and compensation and benefits systems provide the same to them to make decisions on such issues;

(4) *Succession planning systems* – Planning for the succession of key people is for identifying replacement employees and providing them appropriate training. Succession planning systems help human resource personnel with these activities.

Applications of Strategic Information Systems

Strategic Accounting and Financial Information Systems

Strategic accounting and financial information systems typically include several types of systems for information flow:

(1) *Financial condition analysis systems* – These systems support in reporting that automatically calculate and present the results of variety of analysis tools and ratios;

(2) *Long-range forecasting systems* – Strategic planners demand forecasts on a variety of factors that will affect organization performance in the future. In this context, they use long-range forecasting systems.

Strategic Marketing Information Systems

Strategic marketing information systems help strategic managers in strategic activities revolving around sales forecasting and product planning decision making. The subsystems of strategic marketing information systems are:

(1) *Sales forecasting systems* – Strategic sales forecasting systems include several varieties of forecasts like, forecasts of sales for industry as a whole, for the entire organization, for each product or service, for a new product or service, and for market segments. These information can be provided by sales forecasting systems;

(2) *Market research systems* – marketing research systems provide important input to strategic decision making. These systems are very important to know and assess the perception, taste, preferences, attitude of customers of different segments;

(3) *Product planning and development systems* – The major objective of these systems is to make information about consumer preferences obtained from marketing research systems for the development of new products and services.

Strategic Production Information Systems

Strategic production information systems provide support for top management level production decisions. These systems include:

(1) *Site planning and selection systems* – These systems rely on both internal and external sources for information and provide required information on site planning and selection;

(2) *Technology planning and assessment systems* – These systems support in identifying new technologies and assess them for strategic advantage, can help top management in many areas other than production;

(3) *Process positioning systems* – These systems provide information for making decisions on span of production process to perform for any given product or product line;

(4) *Plant design systems* – Designing and laying out a manufacturing plant is strategic decision and it requires information. This information is provided by plant design systems.

Strategic Human Resource Information Systems

Strategic human resource information systems are very much important at the strategic level management. These systems include:

(1) *Workforce planning systems* – These systems support the strategic managers in providing information on strategic human resource planning, and quality and quantity of workforce available to achieve organization goals;

(2) *Labour negotiations systems* – Negotiators need information from various sources both internal and external for negotiation. Labour negotiation systems provide such information for making right decisions during negotiations.

In addition to these systems, human resource information systems data also support other strategic decisions. These systems are useful in merger, downsize, sell off divisions, restructure, and workforce forecast strategically to negotiate for concessions from local governments when making decisions about organization locations.

6

Information System for Decision-making

Decision-making is a very important phase of not only planning, but also for the whole management. After alternative courses are discussed, a decision is taken about the right course of action. Drucker says,

> "A decision is something that takes place prior to the actual performance of the action that has been decided upon. It is a conclusion that the manager has reached as to what he or others should do at some later time."

Definition of Decision-making

Terry defined decision-making as 'selection of one behaviour alternative from two or more possible alternatives'. According to William Glueck 'decision-making is an act of choice by the managers from among two or more possible alternative courses in a given situation."

Decision-making in essence, is the important act of management. Decision-making permeates every part of management practice. Decision-making is an important round, which other management functions like organisation; directing and controlling are carried out. Drucker stresses the importance of decision-making as

> "whatever a manager does he does through making decisions. Those decisions may be made as a matter of routine. Indeed he may not even realize that he is making them. Or they may affect the future existence of the enterprise and require years of systematic analysis. But management is always a decision-making process."

Classification of Decisions

Decisions are classified into following categories:-

1. Environmental decisions,
2. Objective design decision,
3. Output evaluation decision,
4. Objective decisions,
5. Subjective decisions,
6. Programmed or routine decisions,
7. Non-programmed decisions,
8. Strategic decisions,
9. Organizational decisions,
10. Individual and group decisions,
11. Emergency decisions.

Principles of Decision-making

According to Louis Allen the following basic principles provide a sound basis for management decisions:

The Principle of Definition

A logical decision can be made if the real problem is first defined. Too often, time and effort are wasted because we do not think through what the problem or the objective is. We may not identify the real problem because we fall to take time to determine the basic factors that must be changed to arrive at a satisfactory solution.

The Principle of Adequate Evidence

A logical decision must be valid in terms of the evidence on which it is based. A manager expert in decision-making can back his conclusions with facts or reasonable inferences drawn from facts. When the facts underlying a problem are assembled and understood, the decision will often be obvious.

The Principle of Identify

Facts may seem to differ, depending on the point in time from which they are observed. From a different perspective, the same object will appear to be different to different people. A budget deficit means different things to the accountant, the salesmen, and the engineer. The relative importance of the same facts may differ from year to year.

To establish the validity of our facts, we must try to use the varying viewpoints involved and determine the significance of the time period during which the event happened.

Important Elements in Decision-making

The following are the important elements in decision-making.

1. **Intuition:** The element of intuition is useful in decision-making in view of time expediency and making purposeful use of decision-making ability. It is the outcome of the "inner feelings" of the decision maker.
2. **Facts:** Facts provide efficient and effective basis for making decisions. Before using facts, they are to be analyzed, classified and interpreted.
3. **Authority:** Authority means power to make decisions and to see that they are carried out. When a decision is acceptable to the organization, this lends authority to the decision maker.

Objectives of Decisions

The basic purpose of decision-making is to arrive a best possible solution for achieving desired results in the business. Hence, it has the following objectives.

1. One of the objectives of decisions is to help to reach, the desired result by the management. Objectives are standard guideposts any management has to fulfil.
2. Decision-making has to make all functions of management to be performed effectively and efficiently.
3. Decision-making has to clear conflicts that may creep in at every stage of planning function.
4. Decision-making is a human process. It involves interaction with many people at lower and higher levels.

Types of Decisions

There are two categories of decisions:

1. **Programmed decisions:** These are generally routine, repetitive, and applicable to known problems. These decisions generally handle well – structured problems, which are familiar, complete and easily defined and analyzed.

2. **Non – programmed decisions**: These decisions are unique and become necessary due to certain unexpected and unprecedented situations. These decisions are not simple and are generally necessary when confronting ill-structured problems.

Group Decision-making

The manager may make a decision himself or he may assign the responsibility to a task force or a group to look at the problem objectively and come up with a recommendation. The group decision would become particularly appropriate for non-programmed decisions because these decisions are complex and few individuals have all the knowledge and skills necessary to make the best decision. However, there are some factors to be considered when determining which approach to take in the decision-making. These factors are proposed by Vroom and Yetton as follows:

1. The importance of the quality of the decision.
2. The extent to which the manager possesses the information and expertise to make a high-quality decision.
3. The extent to which the subordinates have the necessary information to generate a high-quality decision.
4. The extent to which the problem is structured.
5. The extent to which acceptance or commitment on the part of subordinates is critical to the effective implementation of the decision.
6. The probability that the subordinates will accept the manager's decision.
7. The extent to which the subordinates will be motivated to achieve the organizational goals. Depending upon these considerations, some considerations would necessitate the decision-making-process to be initiated

by a team or a group, for the participation of subordinates would ensure the employee commitment to the implementation of.

Essentials of Group Decision-making

To make the group decision-making more effective there are certain conditions essential. These essentials make the group to be objective and have a team spirit while making decisions. The essentials of group decision-making are: -

1. Preliminary preparation needed to make the process more systematic and productive. Agenda setting becomes the focus of such planning.
2. The meeting atmosphere should be congenial and provide a backdrop for frank and free discussion. This is especially true for enhancing participation from among lower managerial levels.
3. Increased participation is a logical fall-out from the foregoing and all participants should be motivated to contribute meaningfully during meetings.
4. Presentation of ideas should not attract criticism or division of any kind.
5. Objectivity includes the feeling among the participants that the ideas presented would be purely based on merit.
6. Organization and evaluation of ideas within a laid-down time frame is an imperative, which calls for strict observance of the specific agenda.
7. Prioritization of alternatives in decision – making is an important fact and should draw upon ideas from all participants.
8. Documentation and achieving of ideas presented, alternatives and decisions, assist in continuity and information access at a later date.

Advantages of Group Decision-making

Compared to individual decision-making group decisions are having certain advantages. They are as follows.

1. Since the group members have different specialties, they tend to provide more information and knowledge. Also,

the information tends to be more comprehensive in nature and the group can generate a greater number of alternatives.

2. Implementation of the decision is more effective, since the people who are going to implement the decision also participate in the decision making process. This also increases the commitment of the people to see the implementation to success.
3. The participative decision-making process builds up groundwork as a training group for subordinates, who develop the skills of objective analysis and deriving conclusions.
4. The group decision-making is more democratic in nature while the individual decision-making is more autocratic in nature. The democratic processes are more easily acceptable and are consistent with the democratic ideals of our society.
5. The number of effective number of participants is enhanced and provides an equal opportunity for participants.
6. Few meetings with an overall decrease in duration are required for problem solving.
7. Creates an "organization memory" of the proceedings of various meetings. Also external information can easily be accessed.
8. Provides a well-structured and controlled mechanism for meetings.
9. Anonymity of participants improves participation and encourages a more open presentation of ideas.
10. Participants remain focused during meetings and behavior detrimental to the decision-making process is discouraged.
11. Permits participants to choose from a variety of structured and unstructured techniques and methods to perform the task.

Techniques of Group Decision-making

The prominent techniques of group decision-making are brainstorming, Delphi technique and nominal technique.

Brainstorming

Brainstorming technique involves, a group of people usually between five and ten sitting around a table, generating ideas in the form of free association. This generated a variety of solutions that can be later analyzed and the unpractical solutions discarded. The idea is to have as many ideas generated as possible and no idea is criticized no matter how absurd it sounds and no evaluation of any idea is made until the end of the discussion. This encourages freewheeling, and one idea sometimes generates – another. This free association and unrestricted thinking may generate some novel idea and a unique solution, which was not thought of before.

Delphi technique

It is a modification of the brainstorming technique and involves obtaining the opinion of experts physically separated and unknown to each other. All these opinions are handled by a central coordinator, who consolidates the opinions and this information is sent back to the experts for further analysis and opinion refinement. The Delphi technique is characterized by the following sequential steps:

1. The problem is identified and sets of questions are built relating to the problem so that the answers to these questions would generate solutions to the problem. These questions are consolidated in the form of a questionnaire.
2. Experts in the problem area are identified and contacted. The questionnaire is sent to each member who anonymously and independently answers the questions and sends it back to the central coordinator.
3. The results of this questionnaire are compiled and analyzed and on the basis of the responses received, a second questionnaire is developed, which is mailed back to participating members.
4. The members are asked again to comment, suggest and answer the questions, possibly generating new ideas and solutions.
5. The responses to this second questionnaire are complied and analyzed and if a consensus has not been reached,

then a third questionnaire is developed, pinpointing the issue and unresolved areas of concern.

6. The above process is repeated until a consensus is obtained. Then the final report is prepared.

One of the advantages of the Delphi technique is that the group members are totally independent and are not influenced by the opinion of other members. Also the members do not have to be present at one location, so that an expert who is geographically separated can also be asked for his opinion, so that the cost of bringing these experts together is avoided.

MIS and Decision making Process

The decision making process involved several stages. In all the stages the significance and role of MIS is admirable. MIS feeds required information at all the stages right from identification of the problem upto the implementation of the decisions and even in reviewing and evaluating the decisions after implementing them.

Defining the problem

Before a decision is taken the problem must be defined properly. It must be based upon experience rather than upon analysis. Drucker gives two steps in defining the problem namely 'finding the critical factor' and to determine the conditions for its solutions'. Critical factor means the crux of the problem, which must be found before defining a problem. 'This is the element (or elements) in the situation that has to be changed before anything has to be changed before anything else can be changed moved acted upon'.

The second step in defining the problem is to determine the conditions for its solution. To find solutions, the objectives for solution must be thought thoroughly. Drucker views that 'objectives should always reflect the objectives of the business, should always be focused ultimately on business performance and business results. They should always balance and harmonies the immediate and the long range future. They should always take into account both the business as a whole and the activities needed to run it'. Hence finding the right question, setting the objectives and determining the rules together constitute the first phase of decision-making. MIS helps in this regard.

Analyzing the problem

Analyzing the problem, according to Drucker, consists of classifying it and finding the facts. It is necessary to classify the problem in order to know who must make the decision, why must be consulted in making it and who must be informed. Without prior classification the effectiveness of the ultimate decision is seriously endangered; for classification alone can show who has to do what in order to convert the decision into effective action'. Drucker further gives four principles of classification namely, the futurity of the decision (the time span for which it commits the decision can be reversed); the impact of the decision on other areas and functions; the number of qualitative considerations that enter into it; and the thickness of or periodicity of the decision. After the problem is defined and classified the facts are to be found. Facts are found by considering the relevant data and committing the irrelevant data with the support of MIS.

Developing alternative solutions

For every problem alternative solutions must be found. Only through alternative solutions we can distinguish a right decision from wrong decisions. Drucker says that 'alternative solutions are the only means of bringing our basic assumptions up to the conscious level, forcing ourselves to examine them and testing their validity. Alternative solutions are no guarantee of wisdom or of the right decision. But atleast they prevent our making what we would have known to be the wrong decision had we but thought the problem through'. Information on the alternatives can be had from MIS.

Finding the best Solution

Among the alternative solutions the best one must be chosen. Drucker laid down four criteria for picking the best from among the possible solutions:

(a) The Risk: The manager has to weigh the risks ad gains of the course of action. 'What matters most is neither the expected gain nor the anticipated risk but the rates between them. Every alternative should therefore contain an appraisal of the odds it carriers'.

(b) ***Economy effort:*** The line of action, which can give greatest results with least efforts, is chosen.

(c) ***Timing:*** If the solution is to put into action quickly the organization must be geared for that. On the other hand if the solution has long time for action, a slow start can be given.

(d) ***Limitations of Resources:*** As human resources are important among all resources, their limitations and competence must be properly assessed. If additional men are needed they can be added.

MIS supports the management to choose the best alternative by feeding proper information to decide the best alternative.

Making the Decision Effective (Action/Implementation)

This implies the conversation of a solution into action. Motivation is needed to get things done. 'It required that any decision become 'over decision' to the people who have to convert it into action. This in turn means that they have to participate responsibly in making it'.

Decision-making & Areas of Application – The role of MIS

According to the nature of problem different techniques can be used:

1. **Market analysis:** Market analysis can be used for market strategy planning, preventive maintenances, programme planning, and manpower training programme design.
2. **Linear programming (LP):** For product mixes decisions, oil refinery operation, and capital structure planning, capital budgeting, advertising media assignment, Linear programming would be very useful.
3. **Assignment and transportation models:** These models are useful for physical distribution planning, production planning, manpower assignment, and machine assignment and space allocation.
4. **Goal programming:** Advertising decisions, economic predictions, investment analyses, etc., needs goal programming.

5. **Inventory models:** This is specialized model for raw material inventory planning, retail sales and inventory planning.
6. **Network models:** This model is useful for project scheduling, project budgeting, traffic control, pipeline routing, and commissioning communication networks.
7. **Dynamic programming:** For complex systems analysis, sales distribution, planning production and inventory planning dynamic programming will be useful.
8. **Decision theory:** Investment decisions, military strategy planning, medical decisions, gambling (football, basketball, betting), etc., needs decision theory.
9. **Game theory:** Collective bargaining decisions, bidding strategy planning, and military strategy planning, needs game theory.
10. **Simulation:** For complex systems analysis, stochastic systems analysis, shop scheduling and planning, and inventory policy planning, simulation techniques will be useful.
11. **Waiting line models (queues):** These models make the service facility planning, road and freeway design, and plant layout planning makes more effective.

MIS and Management Decisions

Decision-making is a process of using formal procedure, tools and techniques to ensure that decisions are arrived in organization in an objective manner. Here MIS plays an important role. The role of MIS in managerial decision-making is decided by the levels at which decision are made as the nature of functions of levels are different but dependent on each other. Strategic planning finalizes the objectives of the organization and determines the courses of action needed to achieve these objectives. Hence, the information needs of this level is highly external and non programmable. Whereas the management control involves taking decision with regard to converting objectives set by strategic planning in to workable actions and set standards to measure the performance of operations level and providing exception report to strategic planning. Hence, the information requirements at this level are partly programmable and partly non programmable. In the case of operation management or transaction processing their information requirements are highly historical, routine, repetitive, short term in nature and fully internal.

Hence, the relevance of computer applications is high at lower level than at the higher level. This is attributed to the fact that the data / information at the operational level are highly structured hence, can be easily programmed. At the higher level the information requirements are moving towards qualitative in nature and derived from external environment, therefore less programmable. Further at the higher-level information requirements are very complex as they are extremely depending on external environment and the involvement of too many variables. Therefore the nature of information requirements at different level for different purposes demands separate information support system for effective decision-making. This led to the emergence of Transaction Processing System (TPS), Decision Support System (DSS), Executive Information System (EIS), Geographical Information System (GIS), and Expert System. Except the TPS other systems are also called as Intelligent Support System.

MIS can provide information for the followings:

Decisions in management functions

Management Function	*Typical decisions (managers)*
Planning	• What are the organization's long term objectives • What strategy will best achieve the objectives • What should be the organization's short term objectives
Organizing	• How many subordinates should report directly to me • How much centralization should be there in the organization • How should jobs be designed • When should the organization implement their products

Leading	• How do I handle employees • Who appear to be low in motivation • How will a specific change affects work productivity • When is the right time to stimulate conflict
Controlling	• What activities in the organization need to be controlled. How should these activities should be controlled • What type of MIS should the organization have

What type of information is needed for decision-making?

What type of information is needed for decision-making?

Managers	*Required information for decision-making*
Accounting	• What accounting firm should be used • Who should process our payroll • Should we give customer credit
Finance	• What bank should be used • Should we sell bonds or stocks • Should be buy back some of our company stock
HRM	• Where should we recruit our employee • Should we setup a testing program
Production	• Which supplier should we use • Should we build the new plant • Should we buy the new machine
Sales	• Which sales representative should we use in this district • Should we start the advertising campaign

Comparing programmed and non-programme decisions

	Programmed decisions	*Non-programmed decisions*
Type of decision	Programmable/ Routine/Generic	Non-programmable/ Unique
Nature of decision	Procedural/Periodical/ Well defined information and decision criteria	Novel/Unstructured/ Incomplete channels
Strategy for making decision	Reliance on rules and computation	Reliance on principles/ General problems – Solving process

Decision-making techniques

Types of decision	*Programmed decisions*	*Non-programmed decisions*
General nature of the situation	Relatively unchanging	Rapidly changing
Decision-making techniques	Management science/ Capital budgeting/ Computerized solution	Judgement/Creativity

MIS Pyramidal Structure and Decision-making

The MIS is an integrated man/machine system for providing information to support the operations, management and decision making functions in an organisation. The MIS utilizes computer hardware, software, manual procedures, management and decision models and data base. The MIS has a pyramidal structure: bottom layer provides information for transaction processing, the next level provides information resources to support routine operations, the third level offers information resources to help tactical planning and decision making for middle management planning and control, the top level provides information resources in support of strategic planning and policy making by top management group. If the information is better, more complete, more reliable and timely, it is easier for the manager to make a final decision and to exercise effective control.

Lower management is interested in technical and operational information. Operational and technical decisions are programmed decisions for controlling routine operations, e.g., production scheduling, inventory control, timely execution of orders. Control-oriented detailed reports are needed for such decisions. MIS is eminently suited for this (Fig. 6.1).

Middle management is interested in tactical information, e.g., comprehensive reports basically planning and control-oriented for taking tactical decisions. Tactical decisions are related to the implementation of plans and policies approved by top management.

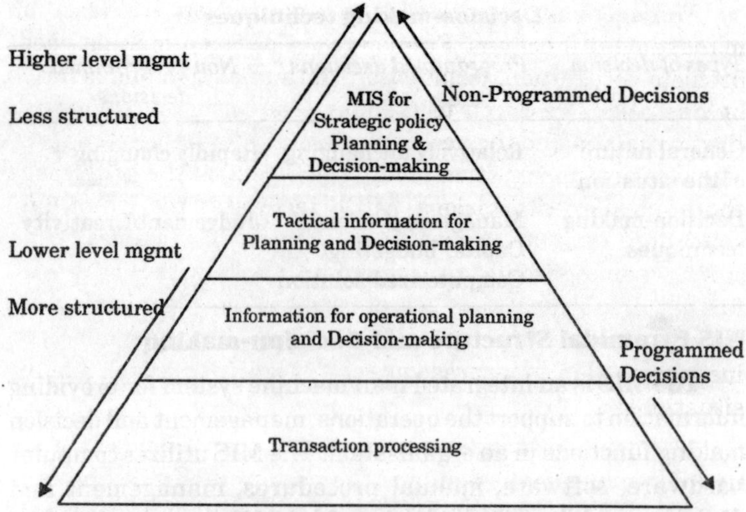

Fig. 6.1. MIS and Planning, Decision making and Control

Top management requires strategic information, eg., overall reports fundamentally planning oriented for strategic or unprogrammed decisions. The decisions at higher level are much less structured. They are forward-looking. They need more external information from various sources. Reliance on fixed rules is bound to decrease as management moves upward in the organization and it has to deal with more and more unstructured decisions. Computerised information is of greatest use at the operational level. It has lesser use at strategic level and this must be clearly recognized.

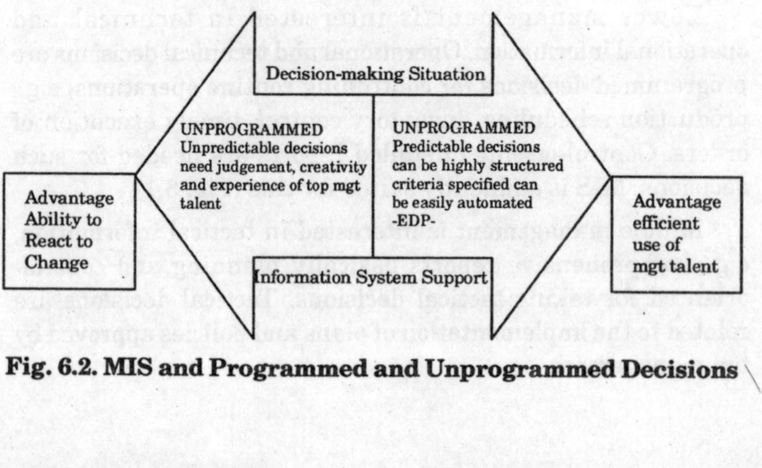

Fig. 6.2. MIS and Programmed and Unprogrammed Decisions

Management activities in an organization are based on management functions. Framework of decision-making needs problem recognition, formulation, data collection and solution by operations research techniques. The optimum solution is then validated and the decisions are made for implementation. The decision maker must monitor and control the progress of the implemented decisions. MIOS facilitates the job of data collection, estimation and forecasting of parameters. Once the decision is made to implement the solution, the MIS further aids in tracking key parameters and monitoring the progress towards the goal. The MIS development has been instrumental in widespread use of O.R tools in decision making situations.

Management desires a trade off between efficiency in the use of management talent and the need to retain flexibility to react to change (see the Fig. 6.2). Feasibility of EDP or ADP will be only with reference to programmed decision situation. In unprogrammed decision situation, uncontrollable factors both internal and external are able influence the alternatives available to the managers. The management cannot rely on EDP totally in such decision situations. MIS must recognize these vital differences. Automated data processing on computerized information system is eminently suitable only for tactical and operational decisions – not for strategic decisions.

7
Business Management Support Systems

Business Management Support Systems

A business enterprise may establish diverse information systems for meeting the information needs of managers at various levels. An information system will be based number of target users, scope of its applications, and whether it serves a specific or general function. The latter system would offer a variety of facilities for processing of information and may be useful for unplanned and unexpected decision making situations. The present chapter discusses the business management support systems at various levels of management in a detailed manner. Primarily business management support systems may be classified into three broader categories: Operations Support Systems, Management Support Systems, and Office Automation Systems. Each category may have sub categories of support systems. They are discussed hereunder.

Operations Support Systems

The operations support systems focus on operations of the enterprise and the prime objective is to improve operational efficiency through processing data primarily for managers at the lower levels. This system may be classified into: Transaction processing Systems (TPS), Management Information Systems (MIS), and Enterprise Resource Planning (ERP). These support systems are discussed hereunder.

Transaction Processing System

A system which processes predefined transactions, one at a time, with direct, on-site entry of the transactions into a terminal, and which produces predefined outputs and maintains the necessary data base. A *Transaction Processing System* (TPS) is a type of *information system*. TPSs collect, store, modify, and retrieve the *transactions* of an organization. A transaction is an event that generates or modifies *data* that is eventually stored in an information system. To be considered a transaction processing system the computer must pass the ACID test.

There are varieties of transactions taking place in an organization. They may be internal and / or external to the organization. The primary function of TPS is to record all those transactions, process and store them in a programmed manner. The primary objective of this system is to store the data for future use and report to management for decision-making. Railway Reservation System is an example of TPS. When a passenger place a request for ticket reservation, the data given by the passenger through his application, is fed to the computer, where processing and validation of data is taking place. The reservation agent enter query in to the computer, which displays all the details about the availability of train, birth / seat position, ticket price, distance, time of departure, etc., When the ticket is booked the information is made available to other officers concerned to check your ticket. All these transactions are taking place though a set of programmes, which specifies the mode of recording, processing, storing and retrieval of data. This system is called TPS. TPS is most useful sub system in our daily life. Front Office Operation of Hotels, Reservation Centres, Information Kisoks, Automatic Teller Machines in Banks, On-line course enrollment systems of colleges and universities, On-line stores are some of the best examples.

The functions of TPS are data entry, data processing and validation, storage, output generation and query support. TPS is considered as primary system, which generates data on the transaction of the organization for management control system and strategic planning.

The traditional TPS was centralized around mainframe computer. But the development of low cost PCs and web technologies replaced costly mainframe computers through new form of computing called Client Server Computing. One of the main advantages of Client Server applications are their front end and back end solutions.

The front end is the Client sub system, where you enter the data. The front end prepares data and send back to back end. The back end is a powerful computer and even may be mainframe. After receiving the data, the back end processes it and sends the results for the query made by Client Server. Then the Client presents the data to the end user. The back end sub system is more powerful and may be complex. There may be several Client Server attached to one back end.

TYPES OF TRANSACTION PROCESSING SYSTEMS

Batch Processing

Batch processing is a transaction where information is gathered and stored but not processed immediately. Advantages of batch processing is being able to share information among users and avoiding idling computer systems by processing transactions when the computer's resources are less busy. Examples include cheques in a banking system or the billing of a credit card where you receive one bill for a month's worth of purchases.

Real-time Processing

Real-time processing is a transaction where information is processed immediately and the operator has access to an online catalogue. Real-time processing is mostly used in *Online transaction processing*. For example a withdrawal from a bank account or library loans.

Features of Transaction Processing Systems

The following features are included in real time transaction processing systems:

- **Good Data Placement**: The database should be designed to access patterns of data from many simultaneous users.
- **Short transactions**: Short transactions enables quick processing. This avoids concurrency and paces the systems.

- **Real-time backup**: *Backup* should be scheduled between low times of activity to prevent lag of the server.
- **High normalisation**: This lowers redundant information to increase the speed and improve concurrency, this also improves backups.
- **Archiving of historical data**: Uncommonly used data is moved into other databases or backed up tables. This keeps tables small and also improves backup times.
- **Good hardware configuration**: *Hardware* must be able to handle many users and provide quick response times.

In a TPS, there are 5 different types of files, the TPS uses the files to store and organise its transaction data:

- **Master file**: Contains information about an organisation's business situation. Most transactions and databases are stored in the master file.
- **Transaction file**: It is the collection of transaction records. It helps to update the master file and also serves as audit trails and transaction history.
- **Report file**: Contains data that has been formatted for presentation to a user.
- **Work file**: temporary files in the system used during the processing.
- **Program file**: Contains the instructions for the processing of data.

Management Information Systems

Before one can explain management information systems, the terms *systems*, *information*, and *management* must briefly be defined. A *system* is a combination or arrangement of parts to form an integrated whole. A system includes an orderly arrangement according to some common principles or rules. A system is a plan or method of doing something.

A system is a scientific method of inquiry that is, observation, the formulation of an idea, the testing of that idea, and the application of the results. The scientific method of problem solving is systems analysis in its broadest sense. Data are facts and figures. However, data have no value until they are compiled into a system and can provide information for decision-making.

Information is what is used in the act of informing or the state of being informed. Information includes knowledge acquired by some means. In the 1960s and 70s, it became necessary to formalize an educational approach to systems for business so that individuals and work groups and businesses who crossed boundaries in the various operations of business could have appropriate information. Technical developments in computers and data processing and new theories of systems analysis made it possible to computerize systems. Much of this computerization of systems was an out growth of basic research by the federal government.

Management is usually defined as planning, organizing, directing, and controlling the business operation. This definition, which evolved from the work of Henri Fayol in the early 1900s, defines what a manager does, but it is probably more appropriate to define what management is rather than what management does. Management is the process of allocating an organization's inputs, including human and economic resources, by planning, organizing, directing, and controlling for the purpose of producing goods or services desired by customers so that organizational objectives are accomplished. If management has knowledge of the planning, organizing, directing, and controlling of the business, its decisions can be made on the basis of facts, and decisions are more accurate and timely as a result.

Management information systems are those systems that allow managers to make decisions for the successful operation of businesses. Management information systems consist of computer resources, people, and procedures used in the modern business enterprise. The term *MIS* stands for management information systems. MIS also refers to the organization that develops and maintains most or all of the computer systems in the enterprise so that managers can make decisions. The goal of the MIS organization is to deliver information systems to the various levels of corporate managers. MIS professionals create and support the computer system throughout the company. Trained and educated to work with corporate computer systems, these professionals are responsible in some way for nearly all of the computers, from the largest mainframe to the desktop and portable PCs.

Management information systems are be coming more important, and MIS personnel are more visible than in the 1960s and 1970s, when they were hidden away from the rest of the company and performed tasks behind closed doors. So remote were some MIS personnel from the operations of the business that they did not even know what products their companies made. This has changed because the need for an effective management information system is of primary concern to the business organization. Managers use MIS operations for all phases of management, including planning, organizing, directing, and controlling.

Types of MIS

Management information systems can be used as a support to managers to provide a competitive advantage. The system must support the goals of the organization. Most organizations are structured along functional lines, and the typical systems are identified as follows:

Accounting management information systems

All accounting reports are shared by all levels of accounting managers.

Financial management information systems

The financial management information system provides financial information to all financial managers within an organization including the chief financial officer. The chief financial officer analyzes historical and current financial activity, projects future financial needs, and monitors and controls the use of funds over time using the information developed by the MIS department.

Manufacturing management information systems

More than any functional area, operations have been impacted by great advances in technology. As a result, manufacturing operations have changed. For instance, inventories are provided just in time so that great amounts of money are not spent for warehousing huge inventories. In some instances, raw materials are even processed on railroad cars waiting to be sent directly to the factory. Thus there is no need for warehousing.

Marketing management information systems

A marketing management information system supports managerial activity in the area of product development, distribution, pricing decisions, promotional effectiveness, and sales forecasting. More than any other functional area, marketing systems rely on external sources of data. These sources include competition and customers, for example.

Human resources management information systems

Human resources management information systems are concerned with activities related to workers, managers, and other individuals employed by the organization. Because the personnel function relates to all other areas in business, the human resources management information system plays a valuable role in ensuring organizational success. Activities performed by the human resources management information systems include, work-force analysis and planning, hiring, training, and job assignments.

The above are examples of the major management information systems. There may be other management information systems if the company is identified by different functional areas.

Enterprise Resource Planning

The increasing relevance of flexibility in the process to reorient them to the changing business environment, have made the MIS less relevant. With the business process re-engineering becoming the buzz word of today, there is a need to change the entire approach towards business processes. The new approach should consider the following premises to develop the information systems:

- Business processes influence;
- Communication systems – inter departmental;
- Integration of different business functions.

With the advancement of networking technology, Enterprise Resource Planning (ERP) has emerged. ERP system integrates business processes and functions at all levels of the organization. It concentrates on customer satisfaction and management of resources of an enterprise.

The entire process begins with sales prospecting and once it is successful sales order maintenance process takes over. The sales order is directly linked to the inventory system, work order maintenance and accounts receivable modules, thereby integrating marketing function with production as also with finance. In ERP system all the functions and processes are linked and integrated together.

Management Support Systems

Decision Support System

When MIS have become useful sub system for making decisions the concept of Decision Support System emerged as an outcome of MIS. DSS is a sub system, which support the process of decision-making at different levels in the organization. DSS as a sub system was originally coined by G. Anthony Gorry and Michael S. Scott Morton and they developed a grid familiarly known as Gorry and Scott Morton Grid. This grid was the fusion of Simon's concept of programmed and non-programmed decisions and Antony's concept of management levels.

In an organization manager needs variety of information. They may be generated from within the organization and outside the organization. All these information are gathered, processed, analyzed and send to managers in a form they require them. A programme developed to gather, analyze data, especially unstructured data, from many sources are called as DSS. For example, economic forecast based on Government's New Economic Policy may be used to device new marketing plan for next five years. The population growth in rural areas may be used for developing market segmentation plan.

A system that supports technological and managerial decision making by assisting in the organization of knowledge about ill-structured, semistructured, or unstructured issues. A structured issue has a framework comprising elements and relations between them that are known and understood. Structured issues are generally ones about which an individual has considerable experiential familiarity. A decision support system (DSS) is not intended to provide support to humans about structured issues since little cognitively based decision support is generally needed.

Emphasis in the use of a decision support system is upon provision of support to decision makers in terms of increasing the effectiveness of the decision-making effort. This support involves the systems engineering steps of formulation of alternatives, the analysis of their impacts, and interpretation and selection of appropriate options for implementations. *See also Systems engineering.*

Decisions may be described as structured or unstructured, depending upon whether or not the decision-making process can be explicitly described prior to its execution. Generally, operational performance decisions are more likely than strategic planning decisions to be prestructured. Thus, expert systems are usually more appropriate for operational performance and operational control decisions, while decision support systems are more appropriate for strategic planning and management control. *See also Expert systems.*

The primary components of a decision support system are a database management system (DBMS), a model-base management system (MBMS), and a dialog generation and management system (DGMS). An appropriate database management system must be able to work with both data that are internal to the organization and data that are external to it. Model-base management systems provide sophisticated analysis and interpretation capability. The dialog generation and management system is designed to satisfy knowledge representation, and control and interface requirements. *See also Decision theory.*

An information and planning system that provides the ability to interrogate computers on an *ad hoc* basis, analyze information and predict the impact of decisions before they are made.

An Integrated Solution

Database management systems (DBMSs) let you select data and derive information for reporting and analysis. Spreadsheets and modeling programs provide both analysis and "what if?" planning. However, any single application that supports decision making is not a DSS. A DSS is a cohesive and integrated set of programmes that share data and information. A DSS might also retrieve industry data from external sources that can be compared and used for historical and statistical purposes. An integrated DSS directly impacts management decision-making.

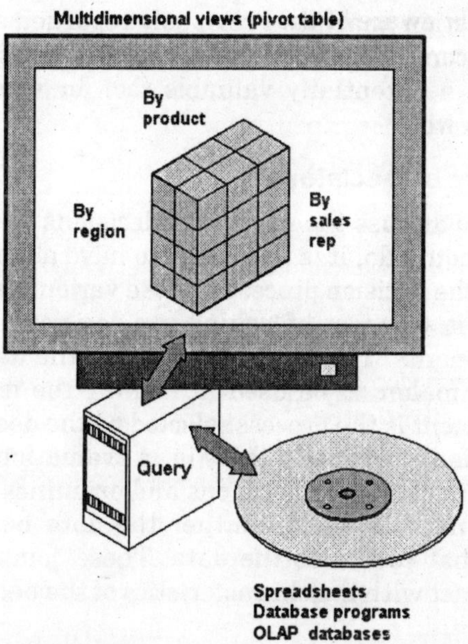

Decision Support

Decision support systems increasingly use OLAP databases, which provide rapid access to multidimensional views of the data. A user can quickly flip from "by product" to "by region" with a multidimensional database.

Decision Support

Decision support systems increasingly use OLAP databases, which provide rapid access to multidimensional views of the data. A user can quickly flip from "by product" to "by region" with a multidimensional database.

Broadly speaking, decision support systems are a set of manual or computer-based tools that assist in some decision-making activity. In today's business environment, however, decision support systems (DSS) are commonly understood to be computerized management information systems designed to help business owners, executives, and managers resolve complicated business problems and/or questions. Good decision support systems can help business people perform a wide variety of functions, including cash flow analysis, concept ranking, multistage fore-casting, product performance improvement, and resource allocation analysis. Previously regarded as primarily a tool for big companies, DSS has in recent years come to be recognized as a potentially valuable tool for small business enterprises as well.

The Structure of Decisions

In order to discuss the support of decisions and what DSS tools can or should do, it is necessary to have a perspective on the nature of the decision process and the various requirements of supporting it. One way of looking at a decision is in terms of its key components. The first component is the data collected by a decision maker to be used in making the decision. The second component is the process selected by the decision maker to combine this data. Finally, there is an evaluation or learning component that compares decisions and examines them to see if there is a need to change either the data being used or the process that combines the data. These components of a decision interact with the characteristics of the decision that is being made.

Structure decison

Many analysts categorize decisions according to the degree of structure involved in the decision-making activity. Business analysts describe a structured decision as one in which all three components of a decision—the data, process, and evaluation—are determined. Since structured decisions are made on a regular basis in business environments, it makes sense to place a comparatively rigid framework around the decision and the people making it.

Structured decision support systems may simply use a checklist or form to ensure that all necessary data is collected and that the decision making process is not skewed by the absence of necessary data. If the choice is also to support the procedural or process component of the decision, then it is quite possible to develop a program either as part of the checklist or form. In fact, it is also possible and desirable to develop computer programs that collect and combine the data, thus giving the process a high degree of consistency or structure. When there is a desire to make a decision more structured, the support system for that decision is designed to ensure consistency. Many firms that hire individuals without a great deal of experience provide them with detailed guidelines on their decision making activities and support them by giving them little flexibility. One interesting consequence of making a decision more structured is that the liability for inappropriate decisions is shifted from individual decision makers to the larger company or organization.

Unstructured decison

At the other end of the continuum are unstructured decisions. While these decisions have the same components as structured ones—data, process, and evaluation—there is little agreement on their nature. With unstructured decisions, for example, each decision maker may use different data and processes to reach a conclusion. In addition, because of the nature of the decision there may only a limited number of people within the organization that are even qualified to evaluate the decision.

Generally, unstructured decisions are made in instances in which all elements of the business environment—customer expectations, competitor response, cost of securing raw materials, etc.—are not completely understood (new product and marketing strategy decisions commonly fit into this category). Unstructured decision systems typically focus on the individual or team that will make the decision. These decision makers are usually entrusted with decisions that are unstructured because of their experience or expertise, and therefore it is their individual ability that is of value. One approach to support systems in this area is to construct a program that simulates the process used by a particular individual. In essence, these systems—commonly referred to as "expert systems"—prompt the user with a series of questions regarding a decision situation. "Once the expert system has sufficient information about the decision scenario, it uses an inference engine which draws upon a data base of expertise in this decision area to provide the manager with the best possible alternative for the problem," explained Jatinder N.D. Gupta and Thomas M. Harris in the *Journal of Systems Management.* " The purported advantage of this decision aid is that it allows the manager the use of the collective knowledge of experts in this decision realm. Some of the current DSS applications have included long-range and strategic planning policy setting, new product planning, market planning, cash flow management, operational planning and budgeting, and portfolio management."

Another approach is to monitor and document the process that was used so that the decision maker(s) can readily review what has already been examined and concluded. An even more novel approach used to support these decisions is to provide environments that are specially designed to give these decision makers an atmosphere that is conducive to their particular tastes. The key to support of unstructured decisions is to understand the role that individuals experience or expertise plays in the decision and to allow for individual approaches.

Semi-structured Decisions

In the middle of the continuum are semi-structured decisions, and this is where most of what are considered to be true decision support systems are focused. Decisions of this type are characterized as having some agreement on the data, process, and/or evaluation to be used, but are also typified by efforts to retain some level of human judgement in the decision making process. An initial step in analyzing which support system is required is to understand where the limitations of the decision maker may be manifested (i.e., the data acquisition portion, the process component, or the evaluation of outcomes).

Grappling with the latter two types of decisions—unstructured and semi-structured—can be particularly problematic for small businesses, which often have limited technological or work force resources. As Gupta and Harris indicated, "many decision situations faced by executives in small business are one-of-a-kind, one-shot occurrences requiring specifically tailored solution approaches without the benefit of any previously available rules or procedures. This unstructured or semi-structured nature of these decisions situations aggravates the problem of limited resources and staff expertise available to a small business executive to analyze important decisions appropriately. Faced with this difficulty, an executive in a small business must seek tools and techniques that do not demand too much of his time and resources and are useful to make his life easier." Subsequently, small businesses have increasingly turned to DSS to provide them with assistance in business guidance and management.

Key DSS Functions

Gupta and Harris observed that DSS is predicated on the effective performance of three functions: information management, data quantification, and model manipulation: "Information management refers to the storage, retrieval, and reporting of information in a structured format convenient to the user. Data quantification is the process by which large amounts of information are condensed and analytically manipulated into a few core indicators that extract the essence of data. Model manipulation refers to the construction and resolution of various scenarios to answer 'what if' questions. It includes the processes of model formulation, alternatives generation and solution of the proposed models, often through the use of several operations research/management science approaches."

Entrepreneurs and owners of established enterprises are urged to make certain that their business needs a DSS before buying the various computer systems and software necessary to create one. Some small businesses, of course, have no need of a DSS. The owner of a car washing establishment, for instance, would be highly unlikely to make such an investment. But for those business owners who are guiding a complex operation, a decision support system can be a valuable tool. Another key consideration is whether the business's key personnel will ensure that the necessary time and effort is spent to incorporate DSS into the establishment's operations. After all, even the best decision support system is of little use if the business does not possess the training and knowledge necessary to use it effectively. If, after careful study of questions of DSS utility, the small business owner decides that DSS can help his or her company, the necessary investment can be made, and the key managers of the business can begin the process of developing their own DSS applications using available spreadsheet software.

DSS Uncertainties and Limitations

While decision support systems have been embraced by small business operators in a wide range of industries in recent years, entrepreneurs, programmers, and business consultants all agree that such systems are not perfect.

Level of "User-friendliness"

Some observers contend that although decision support systems have become much more user-friendly in recent years, it remains an issue, especially for small business operations that do not have significant resources in terms of technological knowledge.

Hard-to-quantify factors

Another limitation that decision makers confront has to do with combining or processing the information that they obtain. In many cases these limitations are due to the number of mathematical calculations required. For instance, a manufacturer pondering the introduction of a new product can not do so without first deciding on a price for the product. In order to make this decision, the effect of different variables (including price) on demand for the product and the subsequent profit must be evaluated. The manufacturer's perceptions of the demand for the product can be captured in a mathematical formula that portrays the relationship between profit, price, and other variables considered important. Once the relationships have been expressed, the decision maker may now want to change the values for different variables and see what the effect on profits would be. The ability to save mathematical relationships and then obtain results for different values is a feature of many decision support systems. This is called "what-if" analysis, and today's spreadsheet software packages are fully equipped to support this decision-making activity. Of course, additional factors must be taken into consideration as well when making business decisions. Hard-to-quantify factors such as future interest rates, new legislation, and hunches about product shelf life may all be considered. So even though the calculations may indicate that a certain demand for the product will be achieved at a certain price, the decision maker must use his or her judgment in making the final decision.

If the decision maker simply follows the output of a process model, then the decision is being moved toward the structured end of the continuum. In certain corporate environments, it may be easier for the decision maker to follow the prescriptions of the DSS; users of support systems are usually aware of the risks associated with certain choices. If decision makers feel that there is more risk associated with exercising judgment and opposing the suggestion of the DSS than there is in simply supporting the process, the DSS is moving the decision more toward the structured end of the spectrum. Therefore, the way in which a DSS will be used must be considered within the decision-making environment.

Processing model limitations

Another problem with the use of support systems that perform calculations is that the user/decision maker may not be fully aware of the limitations or assumptions of the particular processing model. There may be instances in which the decision maker has an idea of the knowledge that is desired, but not necessarily the best way to get that knowledge. This problem may be seen in the use of statistical analysis to support a decision. Most statistical packages provide a variety of tests and will perform them on whatever data is presented, regardless of whether or not it is appropriate. This problem has been recognized by designers of support systems and has resulted in the development of DSS that support the choice of the type of analysis.

Executive Information System (EIS)

Executive Information System an information system that consolidates and summarizes ongoing transactions within the organization. It provides top management with all the information it requires at all times from internal and external sources.

The greatest problems manager faces every day is to 'know what is going on' in the organization. But the time factor limits the flow of information and managers may not receive the information on which they are most interested. Very often they are overloaded with information, papers and files. They find it very difficult to sort out the important from unimportant and relevant from irrelevant. Here the technique of Management by Exception over comes this problem to certain extend. According to this technique only significant deviations from planned results are reported upwards. Here EIS is serving as more powerful tool to help the managers for decision making by overcoming the problem of overload of information. EIS gives emphasis on graphical presentation of data than printouts. EIS may be defined as set of computer based tools, which support the managers to have exception information through graphs, charts, touch screens and natural language interactions. The characteristics of EIS are:

1. It is a top down approach
2. Graphical presentation of data helps the user to easily identify the trends and relationships among variables, and
3. Managers are escaped from the problem of overload of information and above all,
4. Only significant deviations from plans are reported.

EIS Vs. DSS

The terms EIS and decision support system (DSS) are often used synonymously; however, an EIS implies more of a war room style graphical interface that overlooks the entire enterprise. A decision support system (DSS) typically provides a spreadsheet style "what if?" analysis capability, often for only one department or one product at a time. LightShip and Forest & Trees are examples of EIS software that popularized the concept. The EIS systems in the 1980s were the progenitors of the business intelligence (BI) software in the 1990s.

An *Executive Information System* (EIS) is a computer-based system intended to facilitate and support the information and *decision making* needs of senior executives by providing easy access to both internal and external *information* relevant to meeting the strategic goals of the *organization*. It is commonly considered as a specialized form of *Decision Support System* (DSS).

The emphasis of EIS is on graphical displays and easy-to-use *user interfaces*. They offer strong reporting and *drill-down* capabilities. In general, EIS are enterprise-wide DSS that help top-level executives analyze, compare, and highlight trends in important *variables* so that they can monitor performance and identify opportunities and problems. EIS and *data warehousing* technologies are converging in the marketplace.

For the past few years, the term EIS has been little-used. A more common term used to describe this domain area is Business Intelligence (sub areas of reporting, analyitics, dashboards).

Today, the application of EIS is not only used in typical corporation hierarchies, but also installed at the personal computer levels or workstation levels on a *local area network*. EIS now cross computer hardware platforms and integrate information stored on mainframes, personal computer systems, and minicomputers. As some client service companies adopt the latest enterprise information systems, employees can now use their personal computers to get access to the company's data and decide which data are relevant for their decision makings. This arrangement makes all users capable to customize their access to the proper company's data and provide relevant information to both upper and lower levels in companies

EIS Applications

EIS enables executives to find those data according to user-defined criteria and promote information-based insight and understanding. Unlike a traditional management information system presentation, EIS can distinguish between vital and seldom-used data, and track different key critical activities for executives, both which are helpful in evaluate if the company is meeting its corporate objectives. After realizing its advantages, people have applied EIS in many areas, especially, in manufacturing, marketing, and finance areas.

Manufacturing

Basically, manufacturing is the transformation of raw materials into finished goods for sale, or intermediate processes involving the production or finishing of semi-manufactures. It is a large branch of industry and of secondary production.

Manufacturing operational control focuses on day-to-day operations, and the central idea of this process is effectiveness and efficiency. To produce meaningful managerial and operational information for controlling manufacturing operations, the executive has to make changes in the decision processes. EIS provides the evaluation of vendors and buyers, the evaluation of purchased materials and parts, and analysis of critical purchasing areas. Therefore, the executive can oversee and review purchasing operations effectively with EIS. In addition, because production planning and control depends heavily on the plant's data base and its communications with all manufacturing work centers, EIS also provides an approach to improve production planning and control.

Marketing

In an organization, marketing executives' role is to create the future. Their main duty is managing available marketing resources to create a more effective future. For this, they need make judgment s about risk and uncertainty of a project and its impact on company in short term and long term. To assist marketing executives in making effective marketing decisions, an EIS can be applied. EIS provides an approach to sales forecasting, which can allow the market executive to compare sales forecast with past sales. EIS also offers an approach to product price, which is found in venture analysis. The market executive can evaluate pricing as related to competition along with the relationship of product quality with price charged. In summary, EIS software package enables marketing executives to manipulate the data by looking for trends, performing audits of the sales data, and calculating totals, averages, changes, variances, or ratios. All of these sales analysis functions help marketing executives to make final decisions.

Financial

A financial analysis is one of the most important steps to companies today. The executive needs to use financial ratios and cash flow analysis to estimate the trends and make capital investment decisions. An EIS is a responsibility-oriented approach that integrated planning or budgeting with control of performance reporting, and it can be extremely helpful to finance executives. Basically, EIS focuses on accountability of financial performance and it recognizes the importance of cost standards and flexible budgeting in developing the quality of information provided for all executive levels. EIS enables executives to focus more on the long-term basis of current year and beyond, which means that the executive not only can manage a sufficient flow to maintain current operations but also can figure out how to expand operations that are contemplated over the coming years. Also, the combination of EIS and *EDI* environment can help cash managers to review the company's financial structure so that the best method of financing for an accepted capital project can be concluded. In addition, the EIS is a good tool to help the executive to review financial ratios, highlight financial trends and analyze a company's performance and its competitors.

Advantages and Disadvantages of EIS

Advantages

- Easy for upper-level executives to use, extensive computer experience is not required in operations
- Provides timely delivery of company summary information
- Information that is provided is better understood
- Filters data for management
- Improves to tracking information
- Offers efficiency to decision makers

Disadvantages

- Functions are limited, can not perform complex calculations
- Hard to quantify benefits and to justify implementation of an EIS
- Executives may encounter overloaded information
- System may become slow, large, and hard to manage
- Difficult to keep current data
- May lead to less reliable and secure data

- Small companies may encounter excessive costs for implementation
- No mames XOR

Future Trends in EIS

The future of executive info systems will not be bound by mainframe computer systems. This trend allows executives escaping from learning different computer operating systems and substantially decreases the implementation costs for companies. Because utilizing existing software applications lies in this trend, executives will also eliminate the need to learn a new or special language for the EIS package. Future executive information systems will not only provide a system that supports senior executives, but also contain the information needs for middle managers. The future executive information systems will become diverse because of integrating potential new applications and technology into the systems, such as incorporating *artificial intelligence* (AI) and integrating multimedia characteristics and *ISDN* technology into an EIS.

Expert Systems (ES)

A programme that uses available information, heuristics, and inference to suggest solutions to problems in a particular discipline. Methods and techniques for constructing human-machine systems with specialized problem-solving expertise. The pursuit of this area of artificial intelligence research has emphasized the knowledge that underlies human expertise and has simultaneously decreased the apparent significance of domain-independent problem-solving theory. In fact, new principles, tools, and techniques have emerged that form the basis of knowledge engineering systems.

Researchers in this field suggest several reasons for their emphasis on knowledge-based methods rather than formal representations and associated analytic methods. First, most of the difficult and interesting problems do not have tractable algorithmic solutions. This is reflected in the fact that many important tasks, such as planning, legal reasoning, medical diagnosis, geological exploration, and military situation analysis, originate in complex social or physical contexts, and generally resist precise description and rigorous analysis.

The second reason for emphasizing knowledge is pragmatic: human experts achieve outstanding performance because they are knowledgeable. If computer programs embody and use this knowledge, they too attain high levels of performance. This has been proved repeatedly in the short history of expert systems. Systems have attained expert levels in several tasks: mineral prospecting, computer configuration, chemical structure elucidation, symbolic mathematics, chess, medical diagnosis and therapy, and electronics analysis.

The third motivation for focusing on knowledge is the recognition of its intrinsic value. Traditionally, the transmission of knowledge from human expert to trainee has required education and internship periods ranging from 3 to 20 years. By extracting knowledge from humans and transferring it to computable forms, the costs of knowledge reproduction and exploitation can be greatly reduced. At the same time, the process of knowledge refinement can be accelerated by making the previously private knowledge available for public test and evaluation.

Most of the knowledge-engineering applications fall into a few distinct types, summarized in Table 7.1..

Table 7.1. Generic categories of knowledge engineering applications

Category	*Problem addressed*
Interpretations	Inferring situation descriptions from sensor data
Prediction	Inferring likely consequences of given situations
Diagnosis	Inferring system malfunctions from observables
Design	Configuring objects under constraints
Planning	Designing actions
Monitoring	Comparing observations to plan vulnerabilities
Debugging	Prescribing remedies for malfunctions
Repair	Executing a plan to administer a prescribed remedy
Instruction	Diagnosing, debugging, and repairing students' knowledge
Instruction	Weaknesses
Control	Interpreting, predicting, repairing, and monitoring system
Instruction	Behaviors

The ideal expert system contains: a language processor for problem-oriented communications between the user and the expert system; a blackboard for recording intermediate results; a knowledge base comprising facts plus heuristic planning and problem-solving rules; an interpreter that applies these rules; a scheduler to control the order of rule processing; a consistency enforcer that adjusts previous conclusions when new data or knowledge alter their bases of support; and a justifier that rationalizes and explains the system's behavior.

Agents are autonomous programs; programmes that communicate with an agent communication language (for example, KQML); mobile programs that can travel from one computer to another; or programs that collaborate with humans in solving tasks, offloading tedious tasks, and acting as monitors and liaisons with other agents. Agents can also be viewed as higher-level architectural components, providing distributed open architectures in which the agents can be registered, requests can be brokered, and different organizational structures can be used to solve higher-level tasks. In this architectural view, they are distinguished from objects by their persistence, autonomy, communications capabilities, and behavior. Another key aspect of most agent definitions is the agent's dynamic and uncertain environment. Agents also may or may not have graphical representations, commonly called avatars or personas.

Agents can vary from simple programs, lacking knowledge, to sophisticated autonomous real-time control systems that provide both deliberative reasoning (for example, including sophisticated planning and scheduling) and fast real-time response. The vast majority of simple utilitarian agents, such as off-line browsers that automatically download Web sites, or agents that monitor Web pages for changes, are not knowledge-based. Most knowledge-based agents are still experimental.

An AI application that uses a knowledge base of human expertise for problem solving. Its success is based on the quality of the data and rules obtained from the human expert. In practice, expert systems perform both below and above that of a human.

It derives its answers by running the knowledge base through an inference engine, which is software that interacts with the user and processes the results from the rules and data in the knowledge base.

Examples of uses are medical diagnosis, equipment repair, investment analysis, financial, estate and insurance planning, vehicle routing, contract bidding, production control and training.

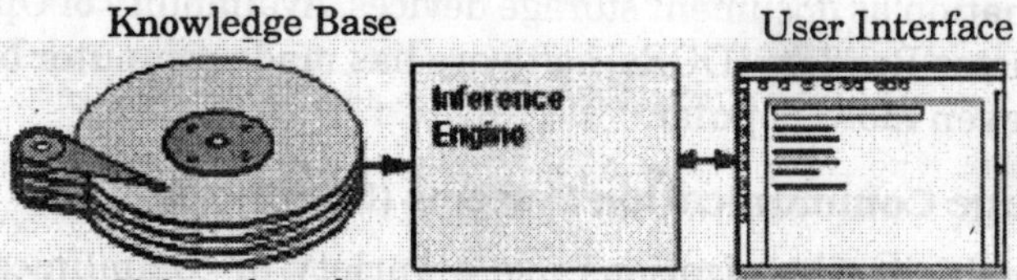

Expert System

Office Automation Systems (OAS)

It is a sub system in the organization, which uses electrical and electronic devices to strengthen the communication system in the organization. The objective of OAS is to enhance the efficiency of workforce and increase their productivity through better communication. The invasion of computer-based tools in communication system enhanced the efficiency of OAS. OAS include word processing, e-mail, Internet, audio/video conferencing system, Facsimile transmission, phones, etc. This system is supporting system for TPS. These systems may be: Text Processing Systems (TePS), Document management Systems (DMS), Message Communication Systems (MCS), and Tele and Video Conferencing Systems (TVCS).

Text Processing Systems (TePS)

TePS are the most commonly used components of the office automation systems. This is due to large proportion of office communication takes place using text processors. These systems can be assisted by dictation systems. These systems consist of voice recognition systems "trained" to recognize the voice of the executive. These text processing or processor may be simple word processing systems or desk top publishing systems. TePS may be shared or may be part of personal information systems.

Document Management Systems (DMS)

The computer based DMS aim at gathering information contained in documents, stored for future reference and usage to communicate the same to users when required. These systems are linked with other office automation systems. The storage devices are used widely in these systems to store information as document storage devices. Availability of Optical Character Readers (OCRs) software has made computer based DMS even more popular.

Message Communication Systems (MCS)

Business organizations use a variety of communication systems to pass and exchange message. They include, telephone, email, voicemail, facsimile (Fax), etc. The computer based message communication systems offer services economically in terms of time in sending or receiving message, reliability of the message and cost of communication.

Tele and Video Conferencing Systems (TVCS)

Tele and video conferencing is widely used by business enterprises for conducting meeting and conferences. These systems help in reducing time and cost of meeting, as participants do not have to travel to attend meetings. At present these systems are very popular among large-scale multi-national companies.

8

System Design and Development

Information system should not be allowed to grow as it grows. This will result in complete mess. MIS may not provide what is needed and what is provided by it may not be needed for management, when the MIS is allowed to grow irrelevant or unplanned manner. Information system serves as a nerve system for an organization. The hurdles in the flow of information may certainly disturb working system and demoralize the workforce. This calls for scientific approach in designing MIS.

Approaches for MIS Development

Organizations across the industry follow different approaches for developing MIS. It is all based on their nature of business, levels in the organization, the level of importance and interest shown by the organization for MIS development and above all the management ethics. Generally there are three basic approaches (See table 8.1) followed across the industry viz., (1) top down approach, (2) bottom up approach and (3) integrated approach.

Table 8.1. MIS Approaches

Process → / *Approach ↓*	*Participation of Management levels*		
	Design	*Implementation / control*	*Operations*
Top down	Top	Middle	All
Bottom up	Top	Middle	All
Hybrid	All	Middle	All

Table clearly presents the participation of management levels in MIS approach in different tasks of designing, implementation and control, and operations of MIS in an organization. The approaches are discussed hereunder.

Top Down Approach

Top down approach is a form of bureaucratic approach. Here the top management decides the goals of the organization and determines the courses of action for achieving goals. An information system is developed to communicate the plan of top management to middle and lower management. This approach may be useful for organizations established to carryout a project during short span of time. The main deficiency of this approach is it may loose the cooperation and coordination of the employees who actually involved in the work.

Bottom up Approach

Here the top management restricts role in deciding the company wide objectives, policies and programmes. Keeping these in mind, the functional area wise plans are set by middle management and lower management and finally the organizational design for MIS is drawn. The bottom up approach gives importance for reporting system, while top down approach insist on target and achievement. The merit of bottom up approach is the involvement of all the levels of management in deciding the design for MIS. The demerit of this approach is it is a time consuming process as the designing process involves the support of all the levels of management. By the time many changes may take place in the hardware and software requirements of the MIS.

Integrated Approach

It is the fusion of the merits of top down and bottom up approaches. Here the top management gives importance to the opinions of the middle management and lower management in designing MIS. On the basis of wide discussions only the required design is finalized. The merit of this approach is the involvement of the all the stakeholders of the MIS with in the organization.

Prerequisites for Good MIS

From the foregoing analysis one could understand that there are certain factors prerequisites for good MIS. Both the organization and the human resource associated with the organization exhibit these factors. Organization provides the mission, structure and the resources of the organization. By using this structure and resources it is the human resources, which work for the realization of the mission of the organization. Based on this assumption the following factors are identified as the prerequisites for good MIS.

1. Institutional factors: Institutional factors are branching out from organization's vision. They are:

1. Well-defined organizational mission and the objectives to be achieved
2. Organizational structure clearly showing the authority and responsibility relationship and the reporting system
3. Resources of the organization, and
4. The degree of autonomy in taking decisions regarding the above.

2. Individual factors (Human Resource): This is concerned with the employers and employees.

1. Educational status
2. Length of service in the field
3. Knowledge on organization mission, objectives and information system
4. Ability in managing information during
   - Transfers
   - Peak hours
   - Handling additional responsibility
5. Perception on
   - Organizational goal
   - Organizational structure
   - Importance of team work
   - Importance of information
   - Knowledge on computers.

The MIS is *sin quo non* for modern business organization. The developments in the information technology have widened the horizon of MIS. Modern business organizations cannot be silent spectator of the developments in this field. Especially the changing environment, due to globalization, has posed critical challenges before modern organizations. In this context organizations should think of whether to strengthen their MIS or to develop new one? A detailed study based on the mission (purpose for which the organization has been established) of the organization alone would answer for this question.

Designing and Implementing MIS

Irrespective of the type of organization care must be taken while designing MIS. As communication is lifeblood for the organization, MIS provides a structure for the flow of information. Further though good MIS may not give guarantee for business success but poor MIS may weaken the strength of the organization. This calls for greater care and vision on the part of organization in designing MIS. Another tug up war always reported while designing MIS are the continuance of conflict between organization's requirements and system capabilities. MIS designer first should understand the following realities.

1. Organization's objective is superior to the MIS objectives
2. MIS can support for decision-making cannot supplant the process
3. End users coordination is must to make the MIS effective
4. Organization must always be dynamic to the changes in the environment, and
5. MIS has life cycle

Therefore what is required is utmost diligent in designing MIS. There are several steps involved in designing MIS. As per Robert G Murdick conventional design step of MIS are:

1. A initial survey and defining the problems thereon
2. A conceptual design and defining methodology
3. A principle design
4. A practical design
5. Final design and implementation

According to David A. Wilson there are five main stages in an information systems project. They are:

1. Feasibility study,
2. Business analysis,
3. System design,

4. Implementation,
5. Maintenance.

After discussing various factors than can be used for overall assessment of the MIS function, Versha Mehta identified the following stages of MIS development.

1. Planning for MIS,
2. Structure for MIS,
3. Implementation of MIS,
4. Impact of MIS,
5. Evaluation of MIS.

Generally the following steps are followed while designing MIS for organizations:

1. Feasibility study, which includes drawing organization's structure based on the objectives of the organization and defining the duties and responsibilities of all the employees as per job chart
2. Set up steering committee consisting of all stakeholders
3. Match the reporting system with the information requirements at different levels, which includes analyzing the reporting system and find out the redundant/irrelevant/over loan problems of information
4. Define the information needs in consultation with the users, which includes segregating the information as statutory and non-statutory and developing procedures on access and use of information
5. Commissioning the project, which includes placing orders for hardware and software requirements and other peripherals.
6. Review and monitoring

These stages are explained through the following flow Chart 8.1.

Evaluation of MIS

Evaluation of MIS is a continuous process. As the commissioning of MIS is a costlier project every organization

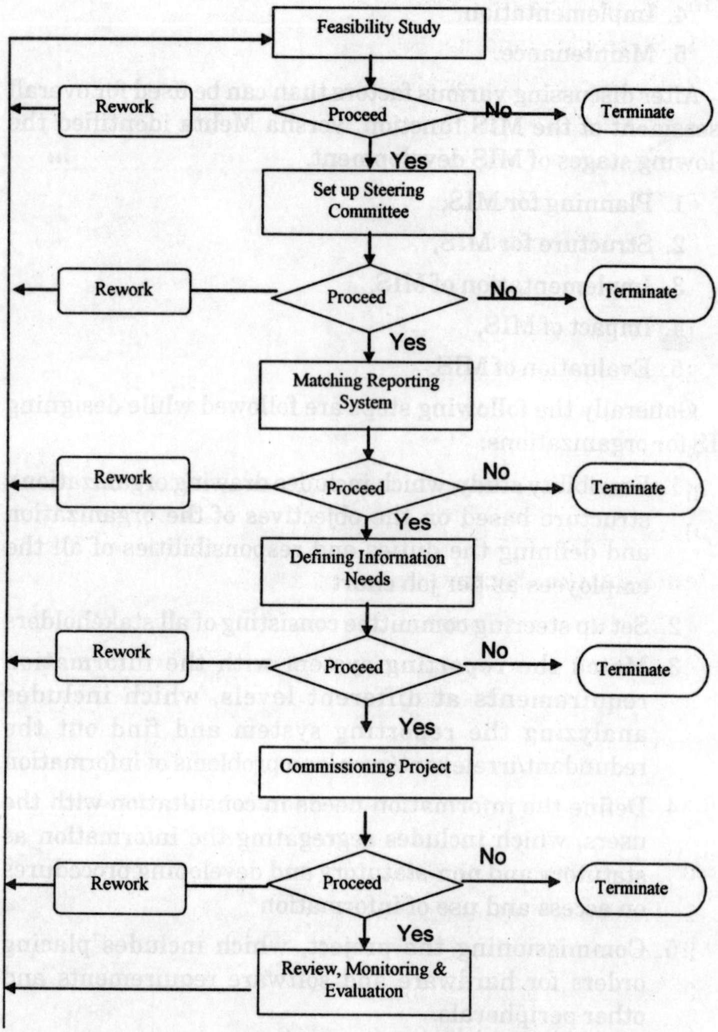

Flow Chart 8.1. MIS Design and Implementation

indents to analyze the impact of MIS on the management. Based on the criterion given by Kanter, Dickson and Wetherbe, Versha Mehta has developed the following criterion for evaluating the success of different stages of MIS.

Planning: Factors included are:

1. Strategic Planning,
2. Corporate Plan for MIS,
3. Top Management Interest,
4. Information requirement analyses,
5. Resource allocation,
6. Project planning.

Structure: Factors included are:

1. Hardware components,
2. Software components,
3. Procedures,
4. Personnel,
5. Data Communication,
6. Centralized vs decentralized system.

Implementation: Factors included are:

1. Application software,
2. Sources of Hardware & Software,
3. Site of MIS,
4. Training Personnel,
5. Operations Research Techniques,
6. Corporate Database.

Impact: Factors included are:

1. Impact on top management,
2. Impact on individuals,
3. Impact on organization,
4. Impact on financial performance.

Evaluation of MIS: Factors included are:

1. Timeliness of reports,
2. Reliability and accuracy of reports,
3. Relevance of reports,
4. Information availability etc.

These parameters will be helpful for the analysts to analyze the impact of MIS on management at different stages. Impact evaluation helps the designers to redesign the MIS according to the changing requirements.

System Development Life Cycle

The system development life cycle (SDLC) can be described in a different way also. The SDLC is discussed elaborately in this section. The SDLC is presented in the Fig. 8.1.

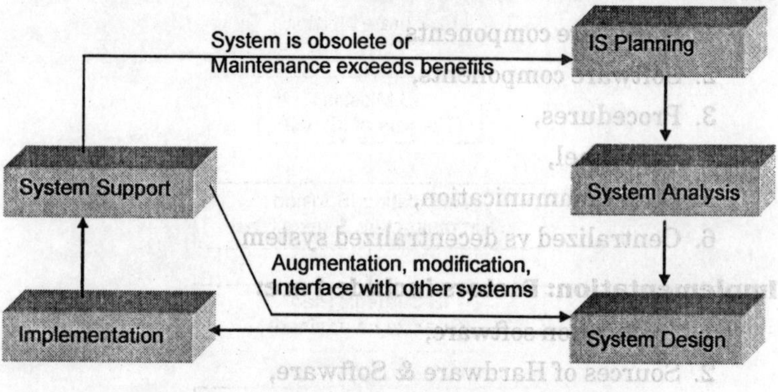

Fig. 8.1. System Development Life Cycle.

Stage 1: Information System Planning

The information systems planning can be done in two ways: a) goal driven; and b) problem driven. Goal driven as an approach adopts top down approach for IS planning, whereas the problem driven as an approach adopts bottom up and critical success factors planning approach. The modern IS planning is integrated into the overall organizational strategic plan. There are pre-requisites for IS planning. They are:

- Recognize IT as an indispensable resource;
- Understand that IT is a complex resource that must be planned and controlled;
- Regard IT as owned by the entire organization and not just by the IS unit;
- Regard IT as a source for gaining strategic goals; and
- View IT as a tool to control power.

IS plan starts with a vision statement and a long-term vision. Planning then set goals and objectives. They outline the strategic plan for IS resources and the tactical steps to attain strategic goals. Then they get down to the more specific details of operations: projects, priorities, staffing, purchasing of hardware and software, and funding. In the latter effort, planners consider several factors: flexibility of the hardware and software in supporting a variety of business needs, compatibility, connectivity of equipment, and scalability. The IS planning process is given in Fig. 8.2.

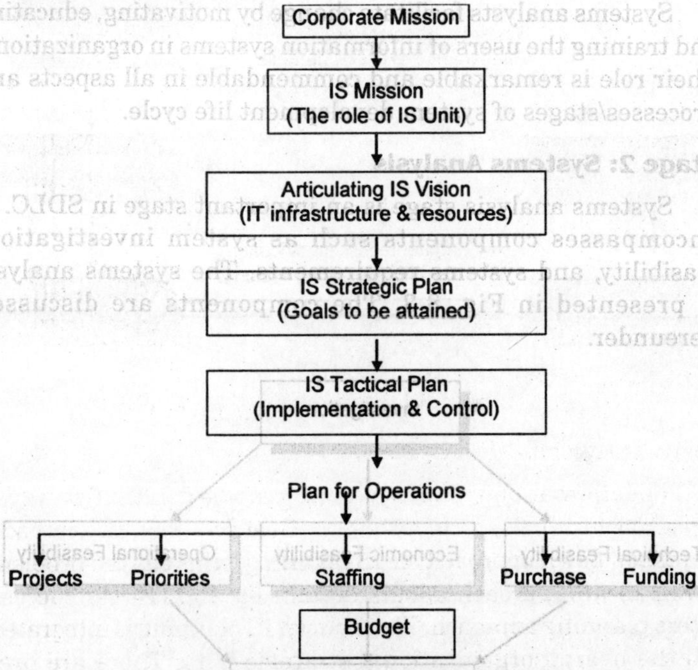

Fig. 8.2. IS Planning Process

All the persons in the organization may trigger discussions of needs that may result in the addition of new elements to the IS plan. The system analysts play an important role as agents of change, in addition to their technical performance as system developers. IS and IT professionals have a great impact on planning, building, and maintaining information systems. The role of systems analysts can be presented as follows:

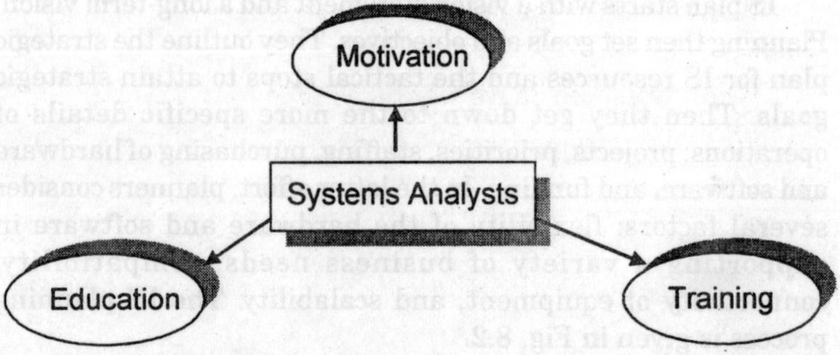

Systems analysts facilitate change by motivating, educating and training the users of information systems in organizations. Their role is remarkable and commendable in all aspects and processes/stages of system development life cycle.

Stage 2: Systems Analysis

Systems analysis stage is an important stage in SDLC. It encompasses components such as system investigation, feasibility, and systems requirements. The systems analysis is presented in Fig. 8.3. The components are discussed hereunder.

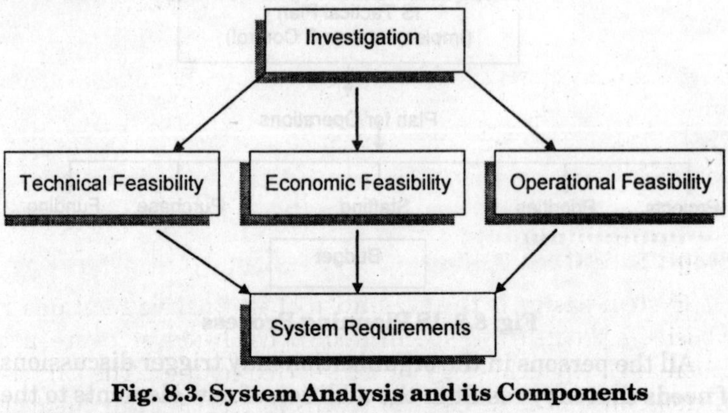

Fig. 8.3. System Analysis and its Components

At this stage for each component we have to ask certain question and we have to get the answers.

Investigation

How does the existing system work?

What business opportunity do we want the system to seize?

What problems do we want it to solve?

What directive must we fulfill ?

Technical Feasibility

Is there technology to create the system we want?

What about the availability of technical professional and resources?

Economic Feasibility

What resources do we need to implement the system?

Will the system's benefit outweigh its costs?

Operational Feasibility

Will the system be used appropriately by its intended users?

Will the system be used to its full capacity?

Systems Requirements

What features do we want the system to have?

What interface will the system have with other systems?

These and other related questions are to be asked and we have to find answers for these questions by observation, questionnaire, interview and examination of documents, etc. This system analysis stage is crucial stage to find out and analyse possible ways to go for new system design and development process.

Stage 3: System Design

System design is the evaluation of alternative solutions to a business problem and specification of hardware, software, and communication technology for the selected solution. The purpose of this phase is to devise the means to meet all the business requirements detailed in the systems requirements report.

Steps involved in System Design Stage

System design stage involved several steps: Logical design, physical design, construction, and system testing.

Logical design: It is a translation of the user requirements into detailed functions of the system. During this step, the system designers determine the following components:

Flow charts: These use graphical symbols to illustrate a system's logical operations.

Data Flow Diagrams (DFDs): These are used to describe the flow of data in a business operation, using universally accepted symbols for elements such as entities, process, data store, direction in which data flow. The symbols are given below:

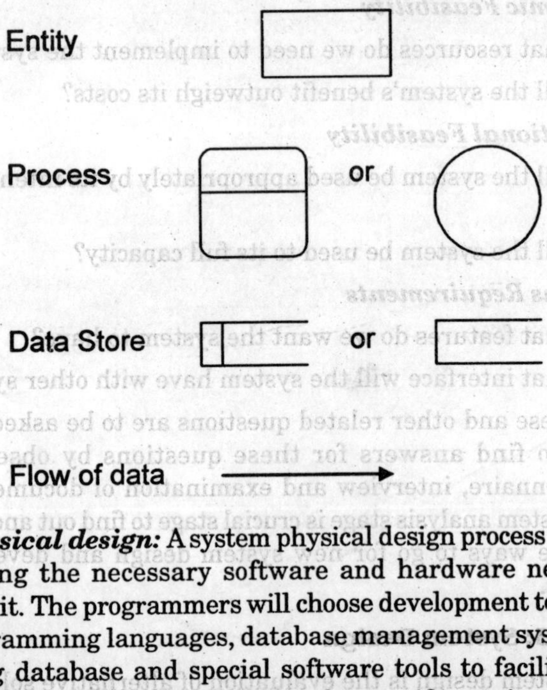

Physical design: A system physical design process includes specifying the necessary software and hardware needed to support it. The programmers will choose development tools such as programming languages, database management systems for building database and special software tools to facilitate the development effort. As with hardware, if certain software development tools are the standard at the organization, only these tools will be used. Unlike construction workers, programmers tend to be inventive and overly optimistic.

System Construction: Once the software development tools are chosen, the construction of the system begins. System construction is predominantly programming. Professional programmers translate input, output and process, as described in flow charts and DFDs, into programmes. When a program module is completed, it is tested by simulation.

System testing: Although simulation with each module provides some testing, it is important to test the entire integrated system. The system is checked against the system requirements originally defined in analysis phase by running typical data through the system. The quality of output is examined, and processing times are measured to ensure that the original requirements are met. Testing should include attempts to get the system to fail, by violating processing and security controls. If the new system passes the tests, it is ready for installation in the business units that will use it.

Stage 4: System Implementation

The implementation of a new IS, also called delivery, consists of two steps: training and conversion or installation as given in the figure 8.4. Although training usually precedes conversion, if training is done on the job it may occur after conversion.

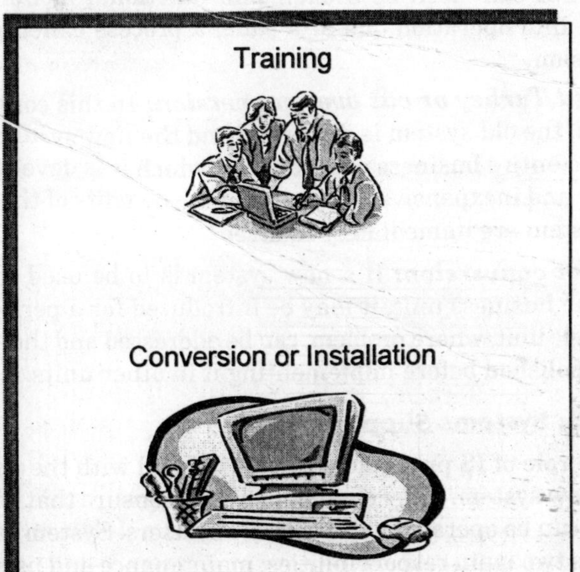

Fig. 8.4. System Conversion / Implementation Process

Training: To operate the new system, the staff must be trained. People can be trained in several ways. The most common methods are in classes or on the job. Multimedia technology and other training software can be used. This approach frees syatem analysts to attend to other business while employees train themselves and also allows each trainee to learn the system at his /her own place.

Conversion: Conversion takes place when as operation switches from using an old system to using a new system. Conversion can be a difficult time for an organization. Operators need time to get used to new systems, and although every effort may be made to thoroughly test systems, conversion can hold some unpleasant surprises of certain bugs or problems have not been discovered earlier. There are four conversion strategies designed to manage the transition.

Parallel conversion: In this process, the old system is used along with the new system for a predetermined period. It minimizes risks but costlier to run two systems.

Phased conversion: Information systems especially large ones can often be broken into functional modules and phased into operation one at a time, a process called phased conversion.

Cold Turkey or cut over conversion: In this conversion process, the old system is discarded and the new system takes over the entire business operation for which it is developed. It is risky and inexpensive; if successful the benefits of the entire new system are immediately realized.

Pilot conversion: If a new system is to be used in more than one business unit, it may be introduced for a period time in a single unit, where problem, can be addressed and the system can be polished before implementing it in other units.

Stage 5: Systems Support

The role of IS professionals does not end with the delivery of the new system. They must support and ensure that the new system can be operated satisfactorily by users. System support includes two main responsibilities: maintenance and user help. Maintenance consists of post-implementation debugging and updating (changes and additions also). *Debugging* is the correction in programs of bugs or problems that were not discovered during tests. *Updating* is revising the system to comply with changing business needs that occur after the implementation phase. Time and again changes and additions shall be made according to the requirements. The people who work at an organisation's *help desk* must be familiar with new system so that they can provide advice and guidance to users.

The system design and development process is done by the systems analysts and professionals along with the users in organizations. The users are expected to work with the IS professionals so that they can design and effective and efficient system for their organization in compliance with the organizational goals and objectives.

9

IT Infrastructure and its Applications

NETWORKING CONCEPT

Evolution of Internet

The Internet traces its origin back to 1960, when it grew out of an experiment conducted by the US department of Defense. They wanted to create a computer network that could continue to function in the event of a disaster, such as a nuclear war. Even if a part of the network was damaged or destroyed the rest of the system would continue to work. That network was known as ARPANET (advanced Research Projects Agency Network), which linked US scientific and academic researchers. It was the forerunner of today's Internet.

By 1970s ARPA helped in the development of a new protocol known as TCP/IP (Transmission Control protocol/Internet Protocol) for transferring data between the networks. The TCP/IP is the core of Internet. Internet really took off in the year 1980s when the National Science Foundation (NSF) used ARPANET to link its five regional super computer centers at major universities so that many users could share their work. Later on, NSF created NSFNET (NSF Network), a series of net works for research and education communication. This network was based on ARPANET protocols and it was provided free to any US research and educational institution.

In the 1980s, Usenet newsgroups and Electronic Mail came into picture. To keep track of the information on the Internet, indices such as Archie and the Wide Area Information Server (WAIS) were also created in this decade. To give users an easy to use interface to work with the universities created Gopher, a simple menu driven system for accessing files. Internet really becomes popular in the 1990s after the development of World Wide Web (WWW). Before that it was opened to a handful of sites only. It is amazing that as recently as June 1993, there were only 130 web sites but now there are millions.

In 1991,CERN (Conseil Europeen pour la Recherche Nucleaire) released World Wide Web, also known as 'the Web'. With the growth of Internet, the quantity and quality, and variety of information also grew. The Internet today is a repository of every consumable type of information. Now days, an Internet users can get information on all sorts of activities ranging from how to add to the design of a functional spaceship to choosing a product for personal use.

Internet is a worldwide system of computer networks, which allows the participants to share information. It enables the users to use applications such as E. Mail and the World Wide Web. A Web page is a document, which is created with HTML (Hyper Markup Language). The web pages are linked together through hyperlinks, which enable the users to jump from one web page to another by clicking on a link. A web site is a set of related (linked through hypertext) web pages, published by an organization or individual. It is an area on the web, which is accessed by its own Internet address.

So, Internet is a group of two or more networks, there are three obvious reasons. They are; Get information, Provide information, and Compile information.

Getting Information on the Internet

The amount of information available through the Internet is staggering. To make all of it more easily available to users, programs such as the gopher were developed to help present material in some logical fashion. The most recent and very successful attempt at presenting information over the Internet is the WWW. You could get information about people, products, organizations, research data, electronic versions of the printed media etc from the Internet.

Providing Information on the Internet

Most of what you want to provide could be considered advertising. While that may sound somewhat commercial, it is the best and most inexpensive way to let people know who you are, what you are doing/ have done, and how. For an organization or institution, setting up a home page is a good way to let the world know what its products and services are.

Compiling Information from the Internet

This is obviously a special case of 'getting' information. The distinction is that it is possible to get specialized information from the web. For instance, if you wanted to poll the readership for a magazine or conduct a survey to detect the pulse of a selected community, the web provides you with the ideal platform and opportunity. Using forms, email, etc, you can conduct surveys; get opinion of people across the world.

Internet Software

To connect to the Internet, a computer requires mainly three different kinds of software: They are.

TCP / IP: TCP/IP or Transmission Control Protocol/ Internet Protocol is the basic communication protocol of the Internet. It allows programs on user's computer communicate properly over the Internet. Usually when you are set up with direct access to the Internet, your computer is provided with a copy of the TCP/IP program. Similarly every other computer that you may send messages to or get information from also has a copy of TCP/IP.

Dialer Software: This software is provided by the ISP to instruct the modem to dial the phone number, and to identify the users machine to the access providers system for access to the network.

Browser: To use the Internet, a web browser is essential. This program allows the user to view the information available on the World Wide Web.

Internet Application

Nowadays, an Internet user has access to a wide variety of services such as electronic mail, file transfer, vast information resources, Internet group membership, interactive collaboration, multimedia displays, real time broadcasting and much more. The important services are:

World Wide Web (WWW): The World Wide Web is one of the most popular services available on Internet. It is a subset of the Internet and it presents text, images animation, video, sound and other multimedia in a single interface. Although the WWW is often referred to as the Internet, they are actually two different concepts. The internet is the decentralized global network of computers that transfer information and the wiring that make all this possible, whereas the web is a collection of documents or web sites, that users can access using the internet and a web browser. The web is a part of the Internet and it refers to a system of Internet services that supports hypertext using a specific Internet protocol called HTTP. In addition almost every protocol type available on the Internet is accessible on the web. This includes E. Mail and Usenet News. Since the WWW is a subset of the Internet, it stands to reason that the web could not exist without the Internet.

Electronic Mail (E.Mail): Internet was developed mainly to communicate and interchange knowledge irrespective of distance limitation. Hence, from the very beginning, users used Internet primarily for sending and receiving messages. Even today communicating through the Net is the main application of the Internet. Since these messages are communicated electronically, they are known as Electronic Mali or Email. Electronic mail can be defined as the " process of exchanging messages electronically, via a communications network, using the computer." Email allows users to communicate with each other in less time and for less money as compared to traditional services. Emails can be sent anywhere in the world using your computer and a modem.

Electronic mail or Email is a fast, easy, and inexpensive way to communicate with other Internet users around the world. It is one of the basis and earliest services of the Internet and the most used application on the Internet too. Email overcomes most of the problems and delays of getting a physical·document from one person to another person. Each user of Email has a mailbox address to which messages are sent and the mailbox can be accessed from anywhere any time in the world. One can receive and send Email from all systems whether it is a windows PC or a Unix machine. Email can also be used to send documents, images, audio, video, etc as an attachment along with the mail.

How E. Mail Works?: The electronic mailing system works in similar fashion as the postal service. Just as the postal service uses letters in envelops with addresses on them, mailboxes and post offices, electronic mailing system completes the same operation with the help of computers. To send E. mail one needs a connection to the Internet and success to a mail server, which forwards the mail. The standard protocol used for sending Email is called SMPT (Simple Mail Transfer Protocol). The SMTP server then connects a DNS (Domain Name Service) server, and asks for the location to theirdomain.com. The DNS server sends the address back to the SMTP server. The SMTP server then sends the E. mail message to the SMTP server where theirdomain.com is located. This SMTP server delivers the Email message to someone else's account.

E. Mail Name and Address: Email allows information to be sent between computers and people on the Internet. It is the most widely used Internet resource. Just as a written letter can be sent to multiple recipients, an electronic mail message can be sent to one or more email address. An email address means, it identifies a person and the computer for purposes of exchanging electronic mail messages.

Advantages and Disadvantages

Advantages

1. The delivery of messages is very fast, sometimes almost instantaneous.
2. The cost of E. mailing is very cheap and it costs just few seconds of phone time.
3. Multiple copies of the same can be sent to a group of people at the same time.
4. Pictures, documents and other files can also be attached to messages.

Disadvantages

1. The slightest error in the address or a failure in one of the links between sender and the receiver is enough to prevent a delivery.

2. Although E. mail is delivered instantly, the recipient may or may not read his/her mail on time.
3. Since E. mail passes through a network, therefore it may be intercepted in between.
5. Electronic mailing system depends on the electricity and telephone system. Thus failure of any one of them can prevent the user from sending or receiving E. mail.

ELECTRONIC COMMERCE (E-COMMERCE)

Today business is taking place through electronic telecommunication media. Now days various organization offer the facility of shopping online. This type of business model is known as Electronic Commerce or E-Commerce. E-commerce refers to buying and selling goods and services online. It integrates communication, data management and security capabilities, which allow organization to exchange information about the sales of goods and services. It is the end-to-end digital exchange of information needed to conduct business including Electronic Data Interchange (EDI) and Electronic Funds Transfer (EFT). EDI is the computer-to-computer exchange of routine business transactions including payments, information exchange and purchase order requests. EFT is a technology that allows the transfer of funds from the bank account of one person or government organization.

The development of E-Commerce, the Internet has established an electronic global worldwide market that operates 24 hours and 365 days a year. Organizations and individuals are able to market goods and services, while purchasing is supported by secure facilities such as digital signatures.

E-commerce is changing the shape of competition, the speed of action, and the streamlining of interaction, products and payments from customers to companies and from companies to supplier. E-commerce is just buying and selling products online. It encompasses the entire online process of developing, marketing, selling, delivering, serving and paying for products and services worldwide network of business partner.

IT INFRASTRUCTURE AND IT RESOURCES

Information Systems and Information technology have closer relationship. They have to move together in the information environment. Information systems are on analyzing the demand and information technology is on analyzing the supply. In other words, information systems they need the support of information technology and its resources to gather data, process and disseminate information to various levels for making decisions on time.

IT Infrastructure

IT infrastructure is necessary for the managers at different levels of the management pyramid of an organization. The following points are in support of IT infrastructure in an organization:

- To be able to meet information needs of the managers, it is necessary that a suitable IT infrastructure be created in the enterprise;
- It is important to design and develop IT infrastructure (architecture) in the light of needs and priorities.

The advantages of IT infrastructure are: easy and speedy access to information; contributing database and maintenance; and exchange of information. The elements of IT infrastructure are:

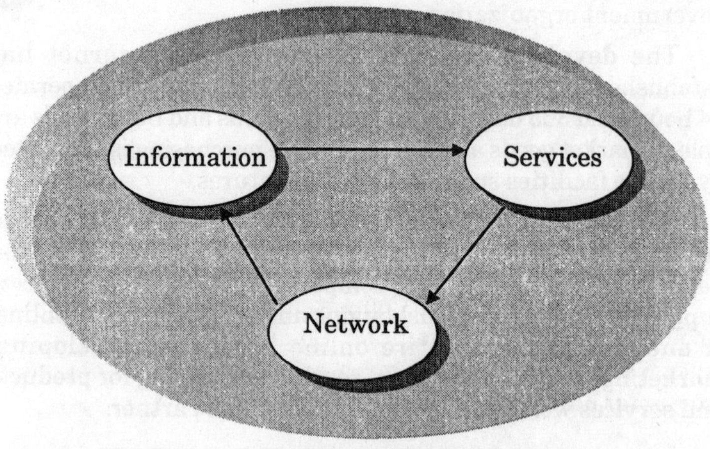

Information	–	The stock of information
Services	–	Facilities for generation of information on a regular basis

Network – Physical system for linking users of information with the stock of information and services ie., process of generating information.

IT Resources

IT resources are as important as IT infrastructure. They are the major components of computer based information systems that serve the best for generation of information for making timely decisions. The IT resources are: Computer hardware, software, data and people. The following figurc 9.1 presents a clear picture on these IT resources and their relationship in generation of information in an organization.

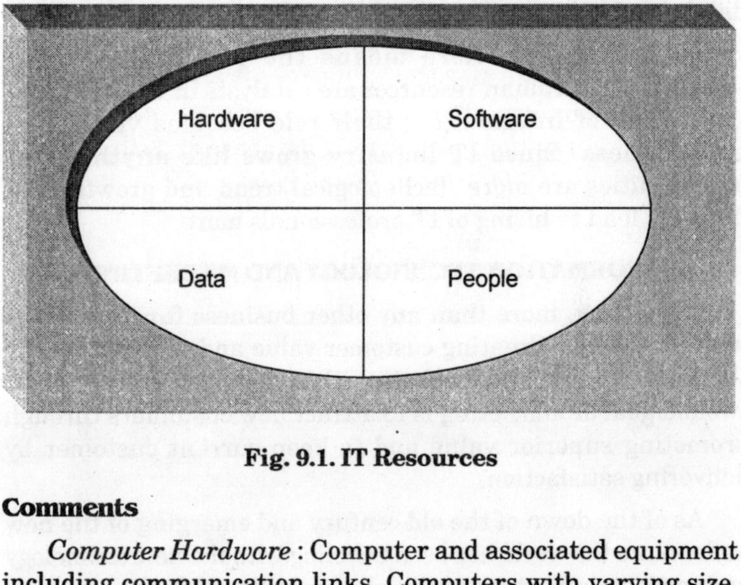

Fig. 9.1. IT Resources

Comments

Computer Hardware : Computer and associated equipment including communication links. Computers with varying size, speed and functional features are available. To determine computer hardware it is necessary:

- To properly assess the nature of IT needs;
- The volume of data to be processed;
- Sources of data;

- Complexity of data analysis; and
- Impact of other related factors.

Software: It is a set of inter-related computer programs and lifeline of IT infrastructure. It determines what the hardware does and makes the hardware perform. Software can be operating software, programming software and applications software.

Data: data may be in the form of symbols, digits, alphabets, pictures, diagrams, facts, figures, graphs, etc. capturing, processing, and storage of data are the essential functions of IT infrastructure. Data are the basic raw material in the process of generation of information. The sources of data may be internal and external. Proper integration of internal and external data is essential for generation of quality information. In this regard, database should be maintained.

People: People here means the IT personnel and professionals. Human resources are catalysts in the process of generation of information; their role becomes vital in its effectiveness. Since IT industry grows like anything job opportunities are more. Technological trend and growth of IT industry lead to hiring of IT professionals more.

INFORMATION TECHNOLOGY AND MARKETING

Marketing, more than any other business function, deals with customers. Creating customer value and satisfaction are the heart of modern marketing thinking and practice. The twofold goal of marketing is to attract new customers through promoting superior value and to keep current customer by delivering satisfaction.

As of the down of the old century and emerging of the new millennium the world has been bubbling with the new technology and modern infrastructure in all the fields. With the new way of technology it has brought fundamental changes in all sectors like banking, finance, trading, marketing, communication, information, management, administration, etc. The evolution of information technology has brought in many changes in the business activity and it is needless to say that those who have not yet reaped the benefits are lagging behind 'Electronic

Commerce'/'E-marketing'/'Online marketing' is the latest concept in the modern business world which helps executives to take broader view and to understand that technology will redefine the very rules of business. All the businesses are discovering the global networking and other technological innovations to use as a competition and other market forces and consumer demands for high service and improved quality. These demands are forcing companies to integrate previously 'isolated islands of automation' into coherent weapons.

The development in IT has affected every industry and every profession. A recent research predicts that by the year 2010, business conducted through electronic commerce will be more than $1000 billion.

IT and Marketing System

Marketing is concerned with identifying the customers for the firm's products or services, determining what they need or want, planning and developing products and services to meet their needs, advertising and promoting these products and services, contacting customers, marketing the products and services through market network, taking orders, and following up on marketing. IT is helpful for marketing managers with respect to sales monitoring and control, market share monitoring and analysis, developing marketing mix alternatives, logistics planning, media mix planning, sales force deployment, marketing cost analysis, market surveys and other market research studies and product launch, planning and control. IT infrastructure can be entrusted with the activities done through the marketing sub-systems like, sales, stock accounting, finance, and distribution sub-systems.

E-marketing, an internet based business opportunities include marketing and promotion, customer support, product research and development, buying and selling products. E-marketing can be divided into four categories:

Business to Business (B2B) – just normal business done over the net. Suppose if one company wants to strike a business with another, it can be done by using the net. Links with dealers, warehouse and manufacturer can be established online;

Business to Customers (B2C) – sales and service around the world through web sites. These sites are meant for selling goods directly to customers through the internet and it has led to direct access to customers' preferences and buying trends;

Consumer to Business (C2B) – a unique way of how e-marketing empowers the customers and changes the way in which one does business; and

Consumer to Consumer (C2C) – the cyber version of good old auction houses. If one wants to sell off anything, he can just post his message on the site and the buyer will get in touch with him through the internet and would close the deal.

Basic IT Applications in Marketing

There are four basic IT applications / functions in marketing. They are,

(1) Communication;

(2) Process Management;

(3) Service Management; and

(4) Transaction Capabilities.

The communication function is basically the delivery of information and/or documents to facilitate business transactions through e-mail. The process management includes process improvement functions, which covers the automation and improvement of business processes through marketing network. Service management is the third function of the application of technology to improve the quality of service through federal express web site. It permits customers to track shipments and schedule pick-ups 24 hours a day world wide without having to talk to a customer service representative. Customer service is greatly enhanced due to the capabilities of the site. The final basic function is transaction capabilities, which provides the ability to buy / sell on the internet or some other on-line service. It allows fast and flexible execution and response to market opportunities. The web enables a company to introduce a new product, get immediate customer reaction, refine and perfect it, all without incurring huge investments in a physical distribution infrastructure.

IT and Channel Partners

Business is extended to customers, partners and suppliers. The internet alone cannot transform business relationships and bring about the electronic or IT based market place. It takes the web+IT to equal e-business. Combined, the web, IT and flexible supply-chain management solutions extend the business across company locations and retail stores through intranets to partners, suppliers, distributors, and banks through extranets to the world over the internet with IT infrastructure.

Distributors: Through the extranet, distributors access the information they want, such as commissions and merchandising programmes, whenever they require.

Trading partners: By extending a business to trading partners through an extranet, value net (a network of partners, each selected for its core competency along the value chain) can be built.

Suppliers and manufacturers: The internet makes it easier to find suppliers with the best products, prices and delivery methods. Many companies use EDI to place orders with manufacturers and suppliers. Product data is always on tap. Information flows back and forth. Orders, payments fulfillment and services are transacted in real time, resulting in major efficiencies and cost reductions.

Customer service centers: For customers, the web will be helpful 80 percent of the time. But, 20 percent of the time, customers will want to interact with a human being,. E-business can easily integrate a Call Centre into a Web site, enabling them to deal more effectively with customers' inbound e-mail; explain offerings in greater depth; and help them with buying decisions.

Retail stores: Intranets tighten communication lines between a headquarters location and retail stores branches. To provide universal access for customers, suppliers, partners, and distributors requires platform and divice independence. It is advisable to build an electronic commerce platform fully equipped with IT infrastructure using industry tested and open standard technologies so that it can easily link to business systems.

The role of IT in marketing in connection with the attraction of new customers and keeping the current customers is discussed here under.

To attract new customers: IT infrastructure helps the marketers to *identify the potential customers*, designed as a highly proactive approach. The key is to move qualified information into a marketing database and doing it such that it is clearly identified and understood by anyone viewing the data. A wide variety of sources can provide the information required for this database with the support of IT application. In the overall customer development programme the *cultivation of database* is done continuously. Strategies are developed to market consistently a company's products and services to specific segments of the database. Monitoring and review of cultivation is the next phase in which a regular review of the information is essential for translating potential customers into active customers. This would include moving potential customers from one category to another at the current moment.

To keep current customers: IT helps the marketers in keeping the current customers through *customer database*. The customer database is maintained by the marketing manager of a company as also by the channel partners. For strengthening customer database the marketing managers can refer to *dealers database, suppliers database, distributors database, budget database and production / inventory database*. The relationship from personal to international level can be built by integrating various networks with the support of IT infrastructure.

To sum up, marketing conducted through interactive online computer systems, which link consumers with sellers electronically can bring the several benefits to the companies which includes, customer services, reduced distribution cost, global reach of its product and product and services and marketing of product more quickly, etc. IT brings the mobility of technology, skills, know-how and information to producers, traders and consumers. It will provide speed, transparency and user-friendliness in business transactions. Business orders can be placed electronically but actual delivery of goods and services can be done physically. The ultimate goal of an organization is to make available products and services to the customers as quickly as possible in the most economic way. Time management, cost effectiveness and logistics are the responsible factors to speedup the actual delivery of goods. Therefore, the concept of marketing would be 'sky marketing', 'delighted customers', 'solution marketing', mail-marketing'.

Relationships are important for a marketer because nothing sells like a testimonial does. With increasing improvements in Information Technology (IT) networking between the marketers and customers has become very effective. It relies on computer based information system, because analyzing the demand is information system and analyzing the supply is IT. The IT infrastructure, by building a market network, enables to attain the twofold goal of marketing namely, (1) to attract new customers (identification of potential customers, cultivation of database, monitoring of cultivation); and (2) to keep current customers (customer database, budget database, production / inventory database). IT helps the marketing of products by all sectors in building a lasting relationship with its customers, distributors, dealers and suppliers. The infrastructure and the strategic initiation of IT usage in the organization can only bring about higher productivity, collaborative framework, lower cost and faster response to customer needs. It has to use it in all the segments from shop floor automation, to designing of distribution network support from internal communications to online needs.

10
Software Packages, Applications and Management Support

The Need for Packages

Developing software is a major cost item for any organization. High-level programming languages enable computer programming without the difficulties of machine language, and further-generation languages make programming much easier and faster. But software packages are intended to remove the need for programming altogether; they are programs designed and written by specialists for customers who buy them 'off the shelf' and ready to use. Some users have highly specialized requirements and may commission a specialist software house to develop a package for them. But many organizations share similar computing needs, for example to process payroll data and basic accounts, and to type letters. The package suppliers have therefore moved in to supply an enormous market for standard software. Because the software vendor usually hopes to sell the same software product to many customers, the price for each unit can be very much less than the total cost of designing and producing the software. Some packages, such as the more popular word processing and spreadsheet packages, have sold hundreds of thousands of copies world wide. Micros and PCs are often used by people who do not have programming skills, or do not wish to spend time developing their own programs; thus the market for micro packages is truly enormous, and represents a major growth area. To a large extent, software packages have removed the need for specialist programming staff for micros and have opened the way to the very wide range of applications for which they are now used. Because of the breadth of software available, there is now less of a demand for software houses to create bespoke software for individual organizations; instead the trend is increasingly towards standardized, commercial packages.

Packages and Applications

Software packages can be considered to fall into two main groups: dedicated and general purpose. General-purpose packages include world processors, spreadsheets and databases. They can be used for a wide range of different applications and are very popular on PCs and small business machines. Dedicated packages address one particular business application. There are dedicated packages available to do just about any business function; the following list shows some of the enormous range of business-orientated topics now covered.

airline reservations
banking
basic accounting: sales, purchases and nominal ledger
budgeting
computer aided design (CAD)
computer aided learning (CAL)
computer aided manufacture (CAM)
decision analysis
decision support systems (DSS)
desk-top publishing (DTP)
executive information systems (EIS)
expert system shells
financial analysis and management
forecasting
investment appraisal
linear and integer programming
management science techniques
mathematical modeling
market research
operational research techniques
payroll
pension planning
personnel records
production scheduling and control
sales analysis
sales order processing
simulation
statistics
stock control
systems modeling

These dedicated packages range in price from one to two hundred pounds for an elementary payroll system through to hundreds of thousands of pounds for a sophisticated DSS package. In addition to the more usual business functions, there are business-specific packages designed for the specialized work of doctors, dentists, solicitors, stockbrokers, estate agents, insurance agents and travel agents.

The three most popular application areas for dedicated business packages are payroll, basic ledger accounting and stock control. Payroll was one of the first business applications to be computerized in the early 1950s; payroll calculations are intricate and repetitive and it is hardly surprising that it is the most popular package for the business micro. A typical payroll package suitable for a small business costs somewhere around £300, plus annual maintenance charges.

The functions of the payroll package include:

- calculation of gross and net pay for employees including hourly, weekly and monthly paid staff;
- incorporating PAYE deductions, national insurance and pension contributions, and any other special amounts;
- printing pay-slips, cheque lists and/or bank giros, and coin analysis;
- maintaining constant, current and cumulative data on each employee, and updating these records;
- printing information for end-of-year, periodic and special tax forms, such as P60, P11 and P45;
- providing postings to the nominal ledger for PAYE, insurance, cash and wages accounts;
- producing organizational and divisional summaries of payments made on a current and year-to-date basis for management.

Payroll packages are provided by a number of vendors. More than perhaps with any other package, it is important that the user can count on ongoing vendor support. While computer problems which cause system failure may be a nuisance on some systems, failure to pay employees correctly and on time would be a disaster. The support takes two forms. Firstly, answering queries by telephone in emergency, which helps to overcome any unexpected difficulties that might arise. Secondly, the automatic provision of changes and amendments to the software to dope with legislative changes which affect tax rates and other items. The support is usually provided as part of an annual contract which attracts a fee.

ACCOUNTING APPPLICATIONS

Accounting packages are designed to cope with records for the principal account ledgers: sales, purchases and nominal. Although these can be acquired as separate packages, most users buy them as an integrated accounts package. The package is usually designed to facilitate entries between the purchase and sales ledgers, and the nominal ledger.

The sales ledger has the following functions:

- invoicing customers for goods or services, including allowing discounts and calculating appropriate VAT charges (although invoicing is not strictly part of the sales ledger, most integrated packages include this facility);
- crediting customers for returns or errors;
- accepting payments received from customers;
- maintaining sales ledger accounts for each customer: file maintenance such as adding new customer records, deleting unwanted records if zero balance, updating records for changed names and addresses and other constant data;
- printing statements of each customer's account;
- management information: sales day book, aged debt analysis, monthly sales analysis.

Most packages allow coding of customer and product transactions to facilitate later analysis. The better packages maintain open-item accounts, whereby transactions are retained on file until fully allocated against cash or credit. Simpler balance-forward systems transfer summarized balances at the end of each period.

The purchase ledger operates in much the same way as the sales ledger, except that the accounts refer to suppliers and not customers, and the purchases statement which is sent out to the supplier is usually accompanied by a cheaue rather than a demand for payment! In other respects the functions and operations of the packages are very similar.

The nominal ledger holds those nominal accounts specified by the user as being necessary for analyzing the financial transactions of the firm. Most firms have the following nominal accounts; fixed assets, current assets, current liabilities, long-term liabilities, revenue, expenditure and trading accounts. These accounts may be further divided or detailed to show specific groups of sales or puchases for example. In order to achieve the automatic posting of entries from the other ledgers (sales and purchases) transactions entered onto these ledgers must be coded with the corresponding nominal account codes. As well as receiving entries from the other ledgers, journal entries are made directly within the nominal ledger for other financial transactions, such as heating and lighting, rent and rates, and depreciation. The nominal system produces a trial balance, listings of the nominal accounts, a profit and loss statement and a balance sheet.

Last, but by no means least, the accounts package has to provide system controls, an acceptable audit trail, and back-up security routines to provide a means of recovery in the event of failure of other disaster. System controls are calculated by the package to check that the data held is internally consistent; for example, the sales ledger total debt should equal the debtor's balance in the nominal ledger. These internal checks should 'prove' that the system is functioning correctly and that records and files are in a valid state. Control totals are printed which can be checked against the system's output, and can be used to check that all input data has been successfully processed and that each system run is consistent with the next.

An audit trail is essentially a means whereby the auditor can follow the progress of a transaction throughout the system. One problem with computerized systems, from the auditor's point of view, is that data is held invisibly on magnetic media and cannot be readily examined. Another is that the system operates according to a complex set of rules embodied in a computer program, the details of which are almost certainly incomprehensible to the auditor. The audit trail consists of printouts which identify the origin and progress of all transactions through the system, and shows how they make up balances and control totals in the various parts of the system.

There are many reasons why a system can fail. These range from physical disasters such as fire and flood, through human error and deliberate fraud, and include hardware and software failures. The purpose of back-up is to retain one or more complete copies of the system and its files so that there is a recovery route in the event of disaster, whether it be of a major or minor degree. (The very important question of security is covered in more detail in Chapter 16). The integrated package should provide a straightforward means of taking regular security copies of key files. This usually consists of routine coping of files onto floppy disks which can be stored securely and reused as part of a back-up cycle.

STOCK CONTROL

Recording accurate stock levels is an essential business activity, and vitally affects many other functions, including accounting, sales, purchasing and production. Computerized stock recording essentially involves receiving data on all stock movements in and out and maintaining a balance for each product item. The physical stock level quantity is often a more useful piece of information to sales staff when reduced by known customer demand,, giving the free stock level, i.e. the amount that can be allocated for sales from stock. When the stock balance has reduced to some predetermined level, a replenishment order must be produced. Monitoring stock levels in order to trigger replenishment is a normal feature of stock control systems. Some packages also provide routines for the supply side of the systems, in the form of orders on suppliers' schedules and suppliers' records.

It is an accepted maximum of stock control that 80 per cent of the total stock value is usually made up of only 20 per cent of the products, and it is to this important 20 per cent that most management attention should be given. A more elaborate scheme is known as Pareto analysis, or ABC analysis, which indicates three groups to which different levels of management attention should be directed. The stock control package will produce a listing of products in each category. Such an analysis might yield the following groups of products:

Class A items: 80 per cent of value; 20 per cent of items; review constantly

Class B items: 15 per cent of value; 30 per cent of items; review less frequently

Class B items: 5 per cent of value; 50 per cent of items; review rarely

The maintenance of stock holdings at an optimum level which balances stock holding costs against the risks of stock-out (and hence lost sales) is a crucial management problem. Mathematically, the optimum stock reorder level, the economic order quantity (EO) is given by Where Co is the ordering cost, D is the demand and Cs is the stockholding cost. Management science techniques have been developed which can forecast future demand from past sales. One technique is exponential smoothing, a mathematical forecasting procedure which can take into account seasonal and random fluctuations in order to provide estimates of likely future demand based on past history. By taking into account physical stock, customer demand (actual and forecast), together with orders on suppliers, the stock controller can calculate when and how much stock to order from a supplier or from the production department. Clearly, the calculations involved are lengthy and tedious and made an ideal computer application.

Many firms manufacture items from several components or subassemblies. Calculating stockholding requirements requires analyzing demand for finished products in terms of their component parts. Enumerating the components and their subcomponents and their sub-subcomponents results in a parts explosion exercise, which becomes immensely complex. Computer-based techniques for handling the extensive calculations involved are known as material requirements planning (MRP), or bill of materials processing (BOMP) systems. Routines to handle MRP or BOMP are available either as part of a stock or production control package, or as a separate system.

COMPLETE BUSINESS PACKAGES

Several packages are currently marketed which aim to provide many general business functions. Pegasus has modules, which include payroll, accounts, order processing and invoicing, stock control, job costing and bill of materials. Another popular package called Tetra plan contains payroll, accounts, cash book, order entry, invoicing and sales analysis, purchase order scheduling, bill of materials, job costing and fixed assets. The Sage business package contains payroll and accounts, word processing, spreadsheet and database, communications software, and a 'desk-top organizer' with automatic telephone, alarm and diary features. The modules of these packages can usually be bought individually, depending on the requirements of the business; but the linkages between the modules should be more straightforward than if the user had bought separate packages from separate suppliers, and the advantages of similarity of format and consequent ease of use may offset problems due to parts of the package not matching user needs exactly.

Advantages and Disadvantages of Applications Packages

Make or buy: which is the best choice? Because the availability of a software package removes the necessity for costly and time-consuming programming it might be thought that there is little point in ever developing software in-house if a suitable commercial package is available. Indeed for many small businesses that lack any internal systems development capability, packaged software may represent the only way of implementing computer systems. But, in practice, packages can have their drawbacks and it is worth considering with some care the advantages and disadvantages when compared with purpose-built software.

ADVANTAGES OF PACKAGED SOFTWARE

Reduced Costs

A package should cost less, overall, than the real cost of developing the software in-house. A commercial programmer may command a salary of £20K p.a. or more, with overheads on top, and a typical system may take the equivalent of 6 months to develop; a package to do the same job may cost only £ 1000 or so.

In practice it may be hare to measure the real costs of an internal programming project; also, commercial software often comes with annual licence and maintenance fees, which make direct cost comparisons awkward. Packages often need modifying and updating, and certainly need reviewing and understanding, and user will need training. A key point is that the full costs of implementation are always greater than just the initial cost of the software.

Reduced Time for Implementation

In theory a package should be ready to run; there is no need to wait for the in-house development cycle of systems design, programming and testing to occur. (But there is still the problem of evaluating and choosing the package.) Where the organizational IS development team is tied up for months or years ahead with priority projects, then packaged software may be the only way to proceed.

Inbuilt Expertise

Hopefully experts in the topic have developed the package, be it stock control, sales forecasting or a system for airline seat reservations. This enables the built-in expertise in the package to be tapped by the user, and reduces the need to develop technical application expertise in-house. For example, acquiring a stock control package with a demand-forecasting option provides the forecasting without the need for the user to become expert in the mathematics of exponential smoothing.

Error-free Package

Hopefully the package has been fully tested. If it is one of the more popular commercial packages, then many thousands of other clients will have already run the software and most of the bugs should have been found (by somebody else) and disposed of. The moral here seems to be: 'first in gets the worst deal'. In practice, no software can ever be regarded as entirely bug-free.

DISADVANTAGES OF PACKAGED SOFTWARE

Inexact Fit on User Requirements

Rarely will a package do everything in exactly the way required by the users. Sometimes packages can be tailored to user requirements, by the vendor or internally; either way this adds greatly to the costs and time involvement, and if extensive modifications are needed then the point of using a package may be obviated. Some organizations are prepared to change their procedures to fit the package. More usually a compromise is arrived at, with changes made to procedures and to the package.

Dependence on the Software Supplier

Some organizations will not be prepared to delegate crucial information systems to an outside organization; the systems may be especially sensitive, or with high security requirements such as those associated with national defence. In these circumstances system development by outsiders represents an additional security risk. Even without these factors some organizations will prefer to do crucial systems development themselves in order to ensure that they have full control.

Ongoing Maintenance and Support

Information systems never stand still; changes in legislation and trade practices require changes in operational procedures. Also, organizations are forever changing in response to internal and external pressures, and user needs are therefore changing too. Maintaining internally produced software is bad enough; maintaining packaged software can be a major problem area. The larger software vendors can provide training, support and the modifications that are needed for all their clients, and this facility is often built into an annual maintenance charge. But where a client requires special modifications, the vendor may decline to undertake the work or may charge enormous fees. A very real problem arises with the smaller software houses; as with any small business, the risk of ceasing to trade is large and if this occurs clients are left high and dry with no sure way of getting help or of changing their systems. In these circumstances, companies may be forced to abandon their systems and start a fresh with a new software house.

General-purpose Packages

These packages include word processing, spreadsheet and database. They are highly flexible and can each perform a wide variety of different business functions. Because of this they are used very extensively on business PCs and we will consider them in detail.

WORD PROCESSING

Word processing is one of the most popular of business micro applications. The ability to manipulate text and to store, print and modify it at will represents a crucial advantage not only for professional typists and secretaries but increasingly for managers, professionals and information workers generally. (This book was written on a word processor; it was typed directly by the authors and the output sent to the publisher for typesetting.) A complete word-processing system essentially consists of a CPU, VDU display, keyboard, printer and disk storage, together with one or more software packages. The software can be very basic, giving typewriter-like effects such as bold, italic and underline, or it can be very sophisticated indeed with a wide range of fonts and special effects and can include automatic spelling check and thesaurus, automatic section numbering and indexing facilities, context-sensitive help, plus much, much more.

The basic characteristics of word processors include the facility to type text freely on the keyboard, an immediate display on the VDU screen, and automatic adjustment of end-of-line and word-wrap. Errors can be seen and corrected easily on-screen, and sections of text can be moved about or copied or deleted. Most packages have the ability to search for chunks of text and to replace sections with new text automatically. The more sophisticated packages tend towards the detailed control of printing associated with desktop publishing (DTP). Achieving different fonts and special effects requires not only the software but also the printer, which can physically reproduce the effects, such as a laser or ink-jet type.

One of the crucial features of a word-processing system is its ability to present WYSIWYG (pronounced Wizzywig), which stands for 'what you see is what you get'. This means that the screen display shows how the typing will appear on the printed page, including font size, italic, bold and any special effects. This is very difficult to achieve in an absolute sense, and requires exceptional computing power on a PC, together with an expensive screen and associated electronics. The more recent and sophisticated word-processing packages, running on powerful 16-or 32-bit PCs, can produce something approaching WYSIWYG. If it is necessary to manipulate the print layout in absolute detail, then a desktop publishing package may be more suitable. The Apple MAC is ideally suited to this kind of work and for a long time has been the main contender for sophisticated text creation.

Context-sensitive help is a facility found on some of the more sophisticated packages. For example, using WORD to print a report involves selecting the print menu and making suitable selections about pagination, number of copies and so on. If the user does not understand or has forgotten what the commands mean he can enter a special function code-Alt H-and look at a display of help information which relates directly to the command he is considering. This saves considerable time looking through manuals, searching indexes and so on, and provides a relatively painless way of learning more about the package. It also means that help information does not clutter up the working display or slow down the experienced user who does not need it. Context-sensitive help is not restricted to word processing and is found on other types of package too.

An important facility for a business is the ability to reproduce standard letters, which have been personalized with a customer name or other special insert, for marketing or other purposes. The standard part of the text is called 'boilerplate', and the technique has become so common with junk mailers that not many of us are impressed with these so-called 'personal' letters any more. Some packages offer this feature as a special facility called mail merge; the technique involves the user producing a file of names, which the package automatically merges with the boilerplate text to produce complete letters. Similar techniques are used to produce address labels and self-addressed envelopes.

No one commercial word-processing package has captured a lion's share of the enormous market recently; instead, the market is currently shared widely among many contenders. In terms of the installed customer base, WordStar (in its several different versions) is the leader. Some of the other popular packages are: WordPerfect, MultiMate, Word craft, DisplayWrite and Word.

DESK-TOP PUBLISHING (DTP)

Packages for DTP take word-processed textual materials and combine them with graphics, artwork and other non-textual materials to produce a complete, printed document, the format and layout of which can be controlled in great detail. The professional publishing world has already been revolutionized by the advent of computer-based publishing systems. DTP places the facilities of the professional publisher on the desk of any businessman or professional.

DTP gives business the opportunity of developing printed materials to high standard in-house without the need to send out to professional printers. This can represent substantial savings in time and costs. Effectively the sequence of author's drafts, proofing, checking an correcting can be reduced or eliminated. Examples of the kind of work which can be done include advertising materials and brochures, headed notepaper and notices, newsletters and internal reports, books and pamphlets. Figure 12.1 is a typical example.

A DTP system consists of similar elements to a word-processing system, except that in order to achieve the more sophisticated effects of professional printers, more powerful software and equipment are needed. A reasonably sophisticated system might consist of the following components:

- Apple MAC or IBM PC/AT compatible PC
- 20 MB (or larger) hard disk
- Laser printer with Postscript printer-driver
- PageMaker DTP software

The market for DTP packages is much more recent than for word processing and two products-Ventura and PageMaker-currently lead the market. Other popular packages include: Fleet St Editor, Fontasy and MacAuthor. A DTP software packages will offer similar facilities to the more sophisticated word-processing packages, but in addition to this there are some special features, which can distinguish the two types. These extra features include the following:

- Multi-column and block-text presentation: this is seen in newspapers and journals, it is usually difficult to achieve with ordinary word processors;
- Fonts: additional, and special fonts and print sizes; some common fonts are:

Courier abcdefghijklmnopqrstuvwxyz

Dutch Roman abcdefghijklmnopqurstuvwxyz

Swiss Roman abcdefghijklmnopqrstuvwxyz

Bookman abcdefghijklmnopqrstuvwxyz

Although the facilities available in DTP packages made page layout and design technically easy and place a wide range of special effects at the user's disposal, it is still by no means certain that the end result will be pleasing to the eye, or more effective as a means of communication. It is still necessary to supply artistic and creative skills in order to create pleasing results. This was dramatically demonstrated recently in a university department, where the internal news-sheet was first produced using an advanced word processor. The new new-sheet appeared in a plethora of type styles and special effects, which had clearly been chosen 'because they were there'. The result looked amateurish and was not at all pleasant to read. After a time, some discipline returned and a more restrained approach resulted in an improved effect.

SPREADSHEETS

The electronic spreadsheet has become the standard working tool for many managers, accountants and professionals. The essential, and very simple, concept behind the spreadsheet is the data matrix. This consists of an area marked out by numbered rows and columns, and in which the user enters numbers. The junction of each row and column is referred to as a cell, and cells can be filled with numbers (values), text (labels) or formulae. The part of the matrix shown on the screen is not the limit of the spreadsheet; most modern packages allow hundreds of rows and columns to be addressed, giving many thousands of cells. The spreadsheet effectively continues to the right and below the visible portion; to see these parts the user moves the cursor, and the spreadsheet automatically scrolls sideways or up and down to bring the new parts of the sheet into view. The screen can be thought of as a window onto the much larger electronic piece of paper lying behind it.

Initially the spreadsheet is empty and shows only the row and column headings. The user then moves the cursor to a cell and enters data (in the form of numbers, text or formulate). In Fig. 10.2 the word "Sales' has been entered into cell B2 and the number 3208 into cell B3. Cells C2 and C3 and D2 have also been filled. No number is entered into cell D3, where we want to see the profit figure appearing.

SOFTWARE PACKAGES. APPLICATIONS AND MANAGEMENT SUPPORT

	/ A /	B /	C /	D /	E
1	[cursor]				
2		Sales	Costs	Profits	
3		3208	2943	(B3-C3)	
4					
5					

Fig. 10.1. Spreadsheet data matrix

Here, we can command the spreadsheet to calculate the answer for us by entering a simple cell formula, which tells the spreadsheet what to do. In this case we want it to subtract the figure in C3 from that in B3 and put the answer in D3, so we enter the formula (B3 – C3). The brackets tell the system that this is a formula rather than ordinary text or label. The formula disappears from view and is instantly replaced by the answer, which the spreadsheet calculates for us. The formula has not been lost; it sits invisibly 'behind' the cell and guides the contents of that cell continually until the formula is changed or deleted. So changing the data in cells B3 or C3 results in a new answer appearing in D3 with no effort from us. It is important to grasp the different between the background of the spreadsheet, into which the formulae are placed, and the foreground, which displays the results. Good spreadsheet model building requires the modeler to think primarily in terms of the background.

In this way the spreadsheet performs elementary calculations on columns and rows of data. There are few limits on the complexity of the formulae, which can be used. For example, a command such as (F2* G2 + E2/26% + SUM(Z3..Z10)) has the symbols *,/and % which act as multiply, divide and per cent, respectively, and SUM is a function code which tells the package to add up all the cells between Z3 and Z10 inclusive. Most spreadsheets also have a range of inbuilt special functions including financial, mathematical and statistical operation. So the calculations performed can be very complex and sophisticated indeed.

A key point is that once data and formulate have been entered it is very easy to change one figure and see what effect this has on all the others. For example, Fig. 10.2 shows a slightly extended version of the previous spreadsheet; in this latter

	/ A	/ B	/ C	/ D	/ E
1		John Smith's Ltd	Sales in £000s		
2		Sales	Costs	Profits	
3	Product A	3208	2943 /	265	
4	Product B	2209	1307 /	902	
5	Product C	4966	4998 /	-32	
6	Totals	10383	9248	1135	

Fig. 10.2. Extended version of Spreadsheet

version the spreadsheet will calculate all the figures below and to the right of the dotted line. Now suppose we ask: what if costs for one product change? Let us say we want to see the effect on the totals if the costs for product B go up. To do this we simply alter the figure in cell C4, and all the affected totals will change immediately and automatically as the spreadsheet recalculates its formulate. This what if capability is a very powerful and effective feature of spreadsheets and enables an enormous range of business problems to be studied quickly and easily.

The spreadsheet is both simple and short; but simple and short; but supposing there were 100 products to be evaluated, would this not represent a lot of keying-in of formulae? In practice, spreadsheets offer clever ways of speeding the process of entering formulae. In the above example the profit formula would be entered once only in cell D3; this cell would then be reproduced in the other 99 cells with a single replicate command: the spreadsheet itself calculates the relative formula values required for each cell. In this way quite large and complex spreadsheets can be developed and evaluated very rapidly.

The first spreadsheet packages were Visicalc and Supercalc, developed in the late 1970s. Since that time hundreds of packages have appeared on the market, each based on the original concept but offering more in the way of featueres and enhancements. Currently the market is led by Lotus 1-2-3 and Supercalc, which hold aobut 80 per cent of the market between them. These two packages represent the industry standard for business users. Both offer an extensive range of facilities, including extensive graphics capabilities in addition to the ordinary spreadsheet features (the 1-2-3 of the Lotus title refers to the three features of spreadsheet, graphics and database). Other popular packages include: Multiplan, Excel, Quattro and VP Planner.

The graphics capability of the modern spreadsheet is most important and enables columns of figures to be displayed by histograms, pie charts or line graphs. Choosing the right sort of graphical presentation is not always straight-forward, and the following guidelines may be helpful.

1. The series: showing data which changes over time. Use bar charts of line graphs. Multiple data sets require careful labeling and/or colour differentiation.
2. Proportions: showing data as a part or percentage of the whole. Use a pie charge. Significant portions can be shown very effectively as exploded segments. Where several data sets are involved, stacked bar charts can be an effective alternative.
3. Comparing values. Use bar charts, either horizontal or vertical.
4. Relationships between variables. Use line graphs with sample data points which can make an effective display, as can bar charts.

The use of colour, both in the highlighting of negative numbers in tables and in differentiating variables in graphs, is a powerful display technique, which enhances the role of the spreadsheet as a very effective means of communicating ideas. The use of the spreadsheet as a method of presentation highlights its key potential role in management decision-making.

DATABASE

The database package is the last of the 'big three' general packages for the PC or small business micro. It performs the crucial task of organizing and storing large amounts of data in such a way that information can be retrieved easily in different ways. Most organizations generate huge amounts of data; the computer has, above all else, the vital ability to store information securely and then reclaim selected parts of it rapidly and flexibly. The database package is the software, which enables these functions to be achieved. Some typical database applications are as follows:

- personnel records
- customer mailing lists
- consultant's client records
- club membership records
- plant and machinery records
- equipment maintenance records
- computer dating agency records
- books and journals on loan from a company library.

Before database software became readily available, data storage and retrieval involved writing programs to accept the data onto disk, then choosing disk access methods (see Part Two) and writing more programs which selected and analyzed the information required. Often a file structure would be chosen and programs written, only to find that changing user needs meant more data being added to records in the file or required that data to be retrieved in new ways. This usually meant costly and time-consuming reprogramming in order to accommodate the changes.

The database package significantly reduces the design and programming effort involved in file creation and processing. The package provides a ready-made file structure which is 'empty'; it needs only to be defined in a simple way and then it can be filled with the user's data. Thereafter, the data can be sorted and retrieved in a number of ways using the package's flexible search and selection facilities. When new data has to be added, this can be appended to the end of the file and sorted, or inserted into the correct sequence. If new data must be added to each record then the records can easily be modified to allow this.

In order to achieve this simplicity from the user's point of view, the file structures employed are highly sophisticated and are usually based on relational database techniques.

Most packages are menu-driven and are quite straight-forward to operate; the more sophisticated ones also provide a means of entering commands directly which speeds up work for experienced users. Some packages offer context-sensitive help. The definition of the file structure is achieved in different ways by different packages; usually a record is defined by specifying how many fields are required, the size of each field, the content type of each field (for example, numeric and alphanumeric are handled differently) and then a field label (by which each field can be referred to later). Having defined the file structure, the next step is normally to enter data into it. The package usually displays the empty record structure on screen. This is filled field by field until complete, and then the next empty record is displayed and so on.

Once the data has been entered into the file, it can be listed and processed in various ways. Key features of the database package are the ability to sort data into various sequences and select data for listing or further processing. Data can be initially entered into the file in any sequence, or 'as it come'; it can then be sorted and resorted as the need arises by defining a suitable list of fields for the sorting key. The package can sort the file directly by physically rearranging the file into a new sequence. A different method, which can be more efficient, involves creating an index for the file and then sorting that.

Retrieving data from the file can be handled in several different ways. The entire file can be listed in several different sequences, for example. More usually, it is useful to select records or groups of records for review, or to list them as part of a report. Selecting records is done by choosing fields and conditions, for example:

list for year = 1990

where YEAR is a numeric field in the record. The effect of this command is to list only the records with that year number. More complex criteria can be set up using <and> and also the Boolean operators and, or and not. For example:

list for YEAR > 1857 .AND. AUTHOR_1 = 'Dickens C'

This command selects only those records where the year is greater than 1857 and author name is Dickens. It does not show records with either of the two conditions, this would required an .OR. setting instead of the .AND.

Some numerical work can be done on records. For example, numeric fields can have calculations performed and results entered into a spare field of the record. Also, totals can be made of specified fields for a selection of the file. In this way quite complex calculations and file processing can be carried out. In practice, defining sophisticated calculations may be more difficult to do than on a spreadsheet.

As well as the file structure, sorting and retrieval facilities, some database packages have more advanced features. The first of these is a report writer, which helps to structure the printed or displayed output from the package into well-presented reports. The report formats can be stored in a separate file and reused with the appropriate data file whenever needed. The report writer in dBase 4 is a menu-driven function, which allows the user to build up a report column by column, specifying which fields are to be shown and how they should appear. Report titles and column headings can then be chosen. The report can also be specified with control breaks and subtotals, and elementary arithmetic can be performed on numeric fields.

For more advanced applications that require complicated record retrieval and processing, a command language is used together with an automatic command processor. The command language consists of statements similar to a high-level programming language, which enable complex comparing, and processing steps to be undertaken. A sequence of statements can be prepared and stored, and the command processor executes these automatically. The effect is to offer similar design and programming flexibility to that of a bespoke programmed system. A simple automatic command sequence using dBase 4 is shown in Fig. 10.3.

This command sequence accesses a file called bookfile stored on a floppy disk; the file is listed in its current sequence showing only three fields:author_1,cost and year. The file is then sorted, with the new sorted file being output temporarily to the hard disk under anew filename: bookwork. The sorted file is then listed, but only those records for books published in 1990. Finally the files are disconnected from the system and the temporary sorted work file is deleted.

- a command sequence which lists a file and then lists a
- selection of records in a new sequence
-

```
use a:bookfile
list autor_1,cost,year
sort on cost to c:bookwork
use c:bookwork
list author_1,cost,year for year=1990
use
erase c:bookwork
```

-
- end of command sequence
-

Fig. 10.3. An elementary command sequence in dBase4

There are several database packages on the market; of these, dBase from Ashton Tate holds the dominant market position and represents the industry standard. The first database package to appear was dBase 2; this has been replaced over the years by dBase 3, dBase 3+ and dBase 4, each version being more sophisticated than the last, although each is based on the same basic principles. The dominance of this package is rather surprising as it is not the easiest one to use, and it retains a fixed record length, which makes some applications a little awkward ton design. However, its sophisticated facilities and powerful command language make it the preferred tool of many professional system developers. Other popular database packages include: Database, Reflex, Delta 4, Cardbox Plus and Archive.

Choosing between the main Package Types

The applications which database packages lend them to are very varied, and there may be some degree of overlap with spreadsheet, and even with word-processing packages. Lotus 1-2-3 has its own database routines built in, although these are rudimentary compared to a full-blown database package. It is quite easy to maintain simple lists on a word processor provided that not too much processing is expected. Some word processors, such as WORD have built-in sorting and macro routines, which made data storage quite straightforward. Which package is suitable for your work? Often, it is clear enough that

		Data volumes	
		low	high
Processing complexity	low	word processor	Database
	high	spreadsheet	Specialist/dedicated

Fig. 10.4. Choosing s general package for data storage

A certain type of application is directly suited to a certain package type. Sometimes it is not so obvious because the nature of the work is such that two or three package types may be suitable. A rule of thumb is that where there is a large amount of data with not too much data manipulation involved, then a database may be suitable; where there is a relatively small amount of data with substantial manipulation or calculation involved then a spreadsheet may be the first choice. If there is only a small amount of data, which does not require much manipulation, then a word processor may be best. If the requirement is to process large amounts of data using highly complex selection and processing techniques, then it may be best ton look for a dedicated package or even to create software especially for the application. Figure 10.4 summarizes the choices.

Apart from processing involved, there is the nature of the output to be considered. A straightforward tabular report can be achieved on any of package types. Incorporating substantial text elements and producing awkward or complicated formats is best done on a word processor; spreadsheets are best for producing bar and pie charts and other forms of graphical display. Often the user will want the best of all worlds and would like to pass information from one package to another for further processing. Unfortunately this is not always possible and is rarely a straightforward operation because of the lack of compatibility between packages. This problem has given rise to the integrated package.

Integrated General Packages

Most users have one or more of the three general packages: spreadsheet, word processor and database. Each package is very good at its own particular job but may not be so good at the other functions. If the user wants to take output from one package and use it as input to another, for example, selecting data from the database and inputting it to the spreadsheet for some calculations, then usually severe problems arise from incompatibility between packages. In an attempt to overcome this problem, Lotus 1-2-3 contains a limited database capability in addition to its spreadsheet and graphics components. This might be regarded as the forerunner of the integrated general package, which attempts to combine all the general package facilities in one united set. In addition, some packages also integrate other elements such as electronic diary, communications and e-mail facilities; and there may be a command processor in order to build the complex systems of which these packages are capable.

The idea of the integrated package is that the user selects one and buys only one package for all her needs. The user can then easily transfer data from one facility to another, e.g. form the spreadsheet to the word processor, without the compatibility problems inherent in the separate packages. Thus a totally integrated business application might involve the following stages:

1. selecting data from the database;
2. passing to the spreadsheet to perform what-if calculations
3. graphing the results;
4. building graphed and tabulated results into a report using the word processor; and possibly
5. e-mailing the entire report across the world to a colleague in another division of the organization.

A further potential advantage of the integrated package is that command structure, help facilities and documentation can all be of the same format. This can reduce the user's learning time and help to speed application development. Leaders in the market place for integrated packages are Symphony and Framework; other popular packages include Smart, Open Access, Ability and Gem Collection.

Advanced Financial Modeling Packages

One of the great strengths of the spreadsheet is its conceptual simplicity. The format of the spreadsheet closely follows traditional methods of developing financial plans; the matrix of cells clearly defined by rows and columns and the formula directing each cell supply a direct and powerful means of manipulating data. However, although spreadsheets are ideal for developing all kinds of straightforward application, they have limitations for the serious financial modeler. For example, in the input and manipulation of large and complex data structures there are insufficient advanced features, and some types of evaluation such as sensitivity analysis are not fully provided. In order to expand his or her scope, the serious financial modeler must look to more comprehensive packages. Because of their extensive storage and computer processing demands financial modeling packages have traditionally been based on mainframes rather than micros, but the increasing memory and power of modern PCs has resulted in some of the recent packages being offered in limited versions for the PC. A number of advanced packages are currently on the market, which are aimed at the specialist financial modeler and offer more advanced features. These advanced packages can be grouped into three broad categories: multidimensional spreadsheets, language processing systems and database financial systems.

MULTIDIMENSIONAL SPREADSHEETS

The standard spreadsheet offers a two-dimensional matrix in which to place data. This is adequate for many applications. In financial modeling it is common to develop a two-dimensional model with time along the top axis (columns) and financial variables along the horizontal axis (rows). The model then needs to be developed for several products or divisions. This can be achieved by copying the matrix several times down the spreadsheets, or by having several different data files; but this is not altogether satisfactory because the manipulation of each matrix must be done separately. The solution is a three-dimensional matrix in which the items in the third dimension can be compared to the leaves of a book. The package provides data input and manipulation facilities which cater specifically for this kind of situation and which make model development much easier. Examples of three-dimensional packages include Report Manager and Boeingcalc and the latest versions of Lotus. Packages offering even more dimensions are available; for example VP Planner offers five dimensions.

LANGUAGE PROCESSING SYSTEMS

These packages are based around a similar matrix data structure to the spreadsheet, but the processing logic is not confined to formulate that define individual cells. Instead, a high-level programming language is provided which enables far more complex and sophisticated manipulation to be defined than is possible using a spreadsheet. The user develops a program in the language, which refers to the matrix of data. The program is then run against the data in the matrix.

The programming logic is completely separate from the data, so that several data sets may be run against the same program, and vice versa. These packages usually offer many more financial and modeling functions than usually found in spreadsheets, including perhaps some of the more exotic operations such as sensitivity and targeting analysis, risk analysis and fuzzy logic. In addition to the data manipulation and analysis features the package may also offer advanced graphics and report building. There are many package may also offer advanced graphics and report building. These are many packages in this general category, examples include: Reveal, FCS, Javelin and Mastermodeller. As a corollary to the extra features these packages have to offer, it must be said that learning to use them and using them effectively is altogether a different matter to using a simple spreadsheet; a substantial time is required to learn how to use them and some knowledge of modeling is required. In addition, most packages in this category cost much more, running into tens of thousands of pounds in some cases.

DATABASE FINANCIAL SYSTEMS

These packages are based on a different type of modeling concept. Instead of specifying the precise form of the model to be developed, it is necessary only to outline its main features: the dimensions, the main data elements and the logic, which connects the variables. The logic can usually be specified in a non-procedural manner, i.e. the sequence in which the processing logic is specified is not important. Although the data may appear to be held in multidimensional matrix form, the inherent database structure allows any relations among the data to be explored readily. They tend to require specialist systems experts to develop models and, because of the wide range of facilities provided, they are very expensive. These packages are generally suitable for very large corporate users who have massive and complex data sets for analysis. Examples include System W, Express and FCS-Multi.

To some extent, all computer-based information systems provide some assistance to decision-makers. In some systems, particularly of the transactions processing type, the primary focus is not managing. However, the final part of this chapter considers a family of computer-based systems designed specifically for management use.

11
Information Systems and Society

The Impact of Information Systems

What effects will IS, or its slightly wider counterpart, information technology (IT), have on society in the future? Are we moving towards a post-industrial society where very few people are employed in making things, and most will be involved in the rising industries of information, knowledge, leisure and services generally? What effect will there be on the quality of our lives and our environment? Whatever else we can say about this, we can be reasonably sure that the effects will be dramatic. It is likely that IS will change the way we work, our leisure, the way we commute and travel, and especially the way we communicate with each other. Some of the effects of information systems on our lives are shown below. Not all of these effects will be benign, and some aspects of the new information systems will need to be closely watched.

- National level
  - improved international communication and enhanced visibility of state actions;
  - better governmental data processing systems (e.g. taxation, vehicle licensing, social services);
  - more information, and more integrated information, on individuals (the big brother syndrome).
- Organizational level
  - improved productivity through direct and indirect applications of information technology;

- improved communications, decision-making and data access;
- increased computer crime.

• Personal level
- changed work roles and activities;
- job displacement and occupational changes;
- new leisure activities;
- increasing leisure time.

It is possible that the way nations interact with each other has already been profoundly affected by the shrinking of distances enabled by greatly improved communications. Would the democratic revolutions in Eastern Europe of the early nineties, or the Russian glasnost and perestroika, have happened without the communication systems, which brought the actions of governments and peoples directly to public attention? Nations can no longer isolate themselves from the rest of the world, and this ever-increasing cultural exchange could be a strong influence on the political and cultural development of nations.

The Effect on Work and Jobs

Increases in productivity have consistently reduced the amount of time the average person spends actually working, as a proportion of his or her waking lifetime. In the nineteenth century the proportion was over 40 per cent, in 1985 this has dropped to 18 per cent and by year 2000 this could be about 15 per cent with the trend continuing into the twenty-first century. Information technology still continue to offer substantial productivity improvements, and so increasing leisure time will be something we can all look forward to. This may prove to be a mixed blessing; work offers people important social and psychological rewards as well as economic ones. It may be necessary to replace the work ethic with a leisure ethic, that is, one which recognizes the legitimacy of non-work activity.

The character of employment has also changed. Earlier this century we saw the replacement of agriculture by manufacturing as the major employer; now we are seeing the demise of manufacturing and the growth of service industries. This is not to say that the industries themselves have disappeared; rather that is now takes far fewer people to operate them. Now, more and more people are employed as information workers of one kind or another and the information services industry itself has burgeoned at the expense of other sectors. Over two-thirds of all employees now work in the service sector compared to less than one-third in industry and only 2.5 per cent in agriculture. It is a matter of debate as to whether this trend will continue, or whether service-related industries are dependent upon manufacturing to the extent that they can expand only so far before a balance is struck; naturally, the rise of information does not herald the demise of all that has gone before. The following are examples of growth in the service industries.

- Technological
  - computer services
  - software
  - computer and electronics manufacture
  - telecommunications, local and long distance
- Financial
  - banking and finance
  - insurance
  - accounting services
- Information
  - publishing
  - media industries
  - entertainment
  - education

Many information firms are changing and expanding within the information sector. Reuters, well known as a world-wide news agency until the eighties, has diversified into providing financial information on a world-wide basis; Dunn and Bradstreet, originally sellers of credit information, have diversified into providing computer-based marketing databases.

There is no doubt that automation has dramatically affected all stages of manufacturing and production, including, especially, the factory floor. Computers are now used widely in computer-aided design (CAD) and in computer-aided manufacture (CAM); the robot-manned production line has become almost a cliché of manufacturing technique. Robots can work in areas hostile to humans; they can perform boring and repetitive work for as long as is required, and they can be rapidly reprogrammed to do new tasks. Materials-handling technology has led to fully automated warehoused which can be programmed to select, locate and retrieve items from stock. Putting all these things together gives us a sight of the totally automated factory of the future. The following list shows the variety of occupations that are likely to be changed greatly by information technology.

- Factory and shop-floor
  - materials storage and warehousing
  - manufacturing
  - assembly and repair
  - supervisory and shop-floor management
- Office and clerical
  - financial and banking
  - information and clerical work
  - knowledge work
  - middle and junior management
- Professional and education
  - accounting
  - legal
  - medical
  - higher education.

There are two forces at work. One which removes jobs and replaces them by automated (or alternative) electronic systems, and the other which creates new markets and jobs to exploit the information potential of the new technology. Unemployment as a whole seems to be more closely related to the general economic situation than to structural changes within industry. Work displacement from old jobs to new ones seems to be the main characteristic of the information revolution.

Human Skills in the Workplace

The impact of computers on people's working lives is undoubted; but is the effect generally beneficial or detrimental? There are many cases where the introduction of computers has resulted in the deskilling of traditional jobs. For example, skilled machine tool operators would normally undergo a long period of training and shop-floor apprenticeship, and then be rightly respected and rewarded for their experience and skills. The advent of computer-controlled machine tools has removed the need for these skills in many factories. In clerical work, there are many instances where human information processing skills and judgment have been replaced by automated data processing systems. In the office, the word processor has replaced the secretary's long-practiced and hard-won skills in layout, centering, indenting, tabulating and spelling.

But is the trend inexorably one-way? A counter-argument to the deskilling problem is that factory automation by and large removes dangerous, boring and repetitive work and leaves more time and human capacity for work which really does require human skills. In the office, it could be argued that repetitive and mundane clerical operations are no better for people than their physical work counterparts, and that their replacement by data systems is no real loss. Because the new office systems eliminate repetitive data processing and filing, the work that is left is more varied and interesting and requires more human contact and more real human judgment. It is more likely that the few people operating the new system will be responsible for the whole of the system rather than just one small part, and therefore this will improve job satisfaction.

It used to be the case that processing a skill or gaining a job in a profession was considered enough to last the working lifetime; now this may no longer be true and far greater employment flexibility will be required. The information society makes much stronger demands on individuals in terms of educational requirements; many more people are now required to understand the technology of information systems. People may have to train and retrain several times over during their working lives, perhaps in order to work in completely different disciplines.

Are any jobs safe? Surprisingly, it may be that unskilled and semi-skilled jobs such as cleaning and manual labouring, and service tasks such as restaurant waiting and hairdressing may be with us for the foreseeable future. Creative and imaginative jobs will also be hard to replace; artists, musicians, writers, designers, thinkers and performers will always be needed. The previous section on artificial intelligence came to the conclusion that we are a very long way off from reproducing real human skills in computers.

Do Computers for Everybody?

When computers first became consistently reliable in the sixties, it was thought that information, on an organizational and national scale, would be concentrated in the hands of a few people, aided and abetted by the few technocrats who were trained in the mysteries of computer science. George Orwell's vision of the future in 1984, in which Big Brother would control everybody's thoughts and actions, was thought to be a distinct possibility. Instead we have had the home computer, and now we have the PC: computers are for everyone. The rise of end-user computing and the general trend to decentralization of organizational computing power have both acted so as to diversify control of the technology out of the hands of the few and into the hands of the many within organizations. The increasing visibility of government activity in the modern state seems to act as a protection against the autocrat and the madman.

What of computers for individual's own use at home? Surprisingly, perhaps, the home computer has not yet had a very great impact. It was thought that there would be great demand for systems which could offer home banking and finance, personal tax analysis, share portfolio analysis, tele-shopping (i.e. shopping interactively using television and telephone), and data and electronic mail services such as those offered by Prestel. Indeed, at first, British sales of home computers outstripped the rest of Europe. But those people who bought home computers did so out of curiosity, for the games, or for their children. Many parents recognized that both they and their offspring would benefit from exposure to information technology and bought home computers for their educational value. The home banking and other facilities have not become widespread; some people use a computer at home in preference to a typewriter, but this is still not a common use. Perhaps the last surge of home computer marketing was aimed more at the hobbyist and would-be programmer, and for its games and educational benefits, and when suitable software becomes available which really does cater for people's needs home use will become more widespread.

An exception to the general rule that home computing is not popular has occurred in France. Here, the electronic telephone directory system Minitel has become for some and electronic addiction. The most popular services on Minitel are the messageries, direct-dialogue electronic mail networks. Protected by a pseudonym, the caller sends messages to another; unknown recipient and a dialogue may then ensue. Conversations can be polite, flirtatious or outrageous, and many different human needs are offered and received. Some communicators swap telephone numbers and meet in person, but for many the main goal is purely emotional: risk-free communication with another human being.

The Electronic Cottage

Advances in electronic office products, and especially in communications technology, have given rise to the forecast that soon few people will need to travel to work, rather they will stay at home and communicate through their PCs to central computers. There may well be strong economic arguments (and environmental ones, too) against everybody physically commuting to the workplace when electronic links can be forged to their homes. This has not happened so far, except perhaps for some people involved in writing and editing, and indeed a switch to the electronic cottage may never happen for most. Social interactions at work are subtle, and are not limited to transmissions of data between individuals. As well as the work-base necessity for social and political communication, there are the human needs for personal interaction which are an important part of working life. Research shows that telecommuters tend to suffer from a range of psychological problems including feelings of isolation and loneliness,, stresses and strains within the family, a lack of motivation and self-discipline, and an inability to organize their working lives effectively.

MIS Audit

There has been an unparalleled growth in the development of information systems due to the improved techniques of data processing, which made it possible to obtain large quantities of information at high speed in the form desired. With the growth of an increasing reliance upon the information system, it hardly needs any emphasis to point out the importance of providing managers with sufficient information at the right time to enable them to perform their job. Thus, there is a clear need for the audit of an information system to ensure the efficient functioning of an organization. The other important reason, which necessitates such an audit are elucidated below.

(*a*) The cost involved in system development, installation and implementation and substantial.

(*b*) The development of an integrated information system requires coordination of several departments and activities, which involve lot of interdependence. The review by an auditor helps in ascertaining the extent to which important areas are covered and to identify overlapping of information requirement in these areas.

The auditor reviews the information system in the light of its objectives and evaluates its usefulness to management in conducting the affairs of the company. Normally, the following steps are taken to conduct such audit.

(*i*) To begin with, the auditor reviews the past information generated in the company to determine whether there are indications that managers are performing their duties with a lack of relevant information.

(*ii*) Next step for an auditor is to evaluate whether the characteristics of systems, degree of sophistication and cost involved are in accordance with the management decision-making process. It is also important to review that the work of specialists is closely coordinated especially in case of integrated information system involving large and complex computers.

(*iii*) Finally, the auditor tests the procedures for originating, storing, retrieving and transforming data, which are part of the information system. He reviews the manner in which available sources of data are utilized to facilitate the preparation of needed information. He also tests the storage of retrieval system to assure that data are readily available.

Information Systems Security

Computer information systems pose numerous security and ethical problems for managers. They must assess risks that information systems represent and apply controls that are appropriate to those risks. The controls used may be physical, electronic, software controlled or a set of management policies and procedures. The threats posed to the information systems may be in the form of natural disasters, employee errors, crime, fraud and abuse are increasing and include industrial espionage, hacking, toll fraud, theft, viruses, software piracy, and invasions of privacy.

Managers should consider security measures for a wide range of information system components, including information systems facilities, the communication systems, database systems, and application development process. Many ethical problems involved with computer information systems have been the subject of legislation and court action. Nowadays Information Act was enacted and severe punishments will be for cyber crimes.

Security of Data on Internet

There are a few methods for securing transactions on net. They are given hereunder.

Secured Hypertext Transaction Protocol (S-HTTP) – It has the features of authentication of user, encryption of information, digital signature as a proof for establishing data.

Secure Sockets Layer (SSL) – This is applied below the level of actual web server for authentication, encryption and data verification.

Private Communication Technology (PCT) – Microsoft's PCT uses SSL has improved authentication.

Fortezza – Using password the users can have security of data.

Encryption – Using encryption software, i.e., used before the messages move out of the sender's computer. At the receiver's end, message is decrypted before use.

Firewall – These are hardware and software solutions that restrict the traffic from unsecured network.

E-cash – It eliminates the credit card number. E-cash and e-wallet systems are linked with banks for maintaining the record of cash.

Virtual checking – Chekfree and Net Chex are the companies offering these services along with a few other on Internet.

The above are some of the security methods and measures to have control over cyber crimes and abuse. Anyhow the information systems and society should be secured for the better use of modern technologies for development.

PART–II

MIS APPLICATIONS IN COOPERATIVES

12

Cooperative Information System

Cooperatives: Cooperatives are voluntary associations wherein persons join together for a common purpose to meet their economic, social, cultural and aspirations through jointly owned and democratically controlled enterprise.

Information: Information is required by all at various levels in cooperative enterprise in order to take and make timely and proper business decisions.

System: System is a process which receives input (data), processes it and gives output (information).

Cooperative Information System: Cooperative Information System is a process to gather data regarding the cooperative business environment to analyze and assess the same so as to get the information to feed it to the cooperative information center and cooperative decision centers to have better decisions. The following figure presents the process of cooperative information system.

The financial, human resource, marketing, production, materials and legal data from the external and internal environment will be gathered by the cooperative information system. The data collected / gathered from various sources will be analyzed and assessed by using various techniques and methods. After assessing the data the cooperative enterprise will have the information in different functions and areas. The information as output will be fed with the cooperative decision centers so as to take and make timely and proper useful decisions for the success and sustainability of cooperative business. This is the continuous process of cooperative information system.

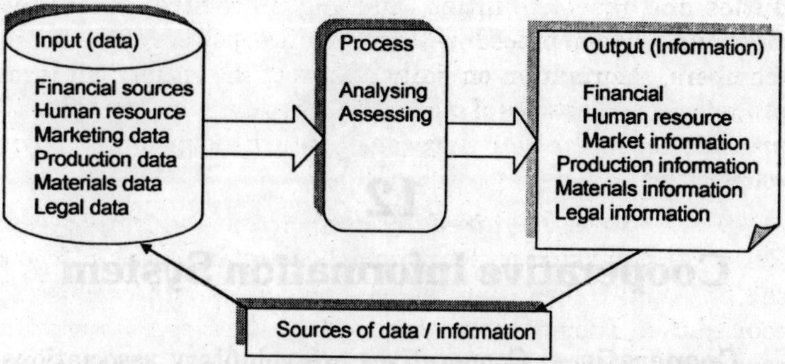

Fig. 12.1. Cooperative Information System

Information sources: Internally the accounting information, reports, books and registers maintained by the cooperative enterprise, byelaws, general assembly meeting minutes, board meeting minutes, cooperative organization manuals and such other documents; externally government policies and procedures, directives and circulars, cooperative proclamation, other related / allied laws and acts, information from other competitors, etc.

To whom information: various persons involved at different levels of cooperatives and supporting and controlling agencies require Information. The persons / agencies need cooperative information are: members, management committee, chief executives and employees, policy makers, public, federal cooperative organizations, NGOs and the government.

Information required by members: Members are the owners of cooperative enterprises and they should know all required information regarding cooperative basics, principles, values, their qualification, rights, share holdings, powers and duties of general assembly, their duties and responsibilities, legal information starting from registration upto the winding up of the cooperative society, and all necessary information about their cooperative enterprise.

Information required by management committee: The management committee members should know the information on cooperative basics, principles, values, their qualification, duties and responsibilities, meeting procedure, contesting elections, election procedure, term of office, powers of the board members, information on daily affairs of the society, all legal procedures and articles of cooperative proclamation and byelaws provisions, and other necessary information about their cooperative.

Information required by executives and employees: Being the managing professionals the executives should know the basics of cooperation, values, principles and practice of cooperation. Then only they can manage the cooperatives with cooperative knowledge. The employees should know their conditions in respect to their job and other procedures to be followed at work.

Information required by policy makers: Policy-makers are involved in framing the policy for cooperatives. There are policy makers within and outside the cooperative enterprise. They should know all about the cooperatives i.e., all information regarding cooperatives right form idea formulation to start a cooperative up to winding up of the society. The environmental factors and their influence on the cooperative business, the government policy and procedure for cooperative development, the policy makers should also know level playing of other agencies. Then only they can frame a conducive and effective workable policy for the promotion of cooperatives.

Information required by Public: Cooperatives are the growth centres for the overall development of the community where they exist. The general public can be converted into members of cooperatives. Cooperative education and extension programs effectively among the general public can do this. The public needs cooperative information on benefits of cooperation, cooperative principles, values and such other basics on cooperation.

Information required by Federal cooperative organizations: The federal cooperative organizations support cooperatives at the grass root level. The federations and federal cooperative organizations for the development and promotion of cooperative enterprise undertake all measures. The federal organizations require periodical reports regarding the funds utilization by the cooperatives, progress of cooperatives, services rendered by them, problems faced, and measure to be taken. Since they offer financial, technical assistances and cooperative support services they require such information from the cooperatives.

Information required by NGOs: Some NGOs support the cooperatives, even they organize cooperatives of various types based on the requirements of the people in a particular community. They help cooperatives financially, technically and in all respects. They need information about the finance utilization, beneficiaries and benefits through such cooperatives and other necessary information.

Information required by the government: The government is the sponsor, initiator, promoter and supporter for the cooperative movement in most of the developing and least developed countries. The government needs all about the cooperative movement as a whole in the country in order to formulate development policies, fund allocation through budgets, administrative support through departments.

Areas of Cooperative Information: The important areas of cooperative information system are: Human resource information, financial information, marketing information, production information, materials information, cooperative environmental information, and cooperative legal information. These information systems are dealt with in various sessions of this training program.

Cooperative Information Dissemination: The cooperative information can be disseminated through the following: Notice boards, circulars, reports, news papers, journals, books, research reports, seminar, conference, workshop proceedings, online (internet) systems, radio and TV, film shows, exhibitions, etc.

MIS IN COOPERATIVES

Growth of cooperative organizations in various dimensions and swelling of their business volumes with wider geographical coverage have necessitated the adoption of management information system for their successful operation, enabling them to achieve the objectives of stability, growth, continuity and congenial interaction. The installation of Management Information System (MIS) in cooperatives will facilitate them in accomplishing objectives of transforming socio-economic conditions of general masses specially the weaker sections of the society. Because of new technique, it is desirable to develop an understanding about MIS in right perspective, including its various elements and allied implications.

The MIS is a system using formalized procedures to provide management at all levels in all functions with appropriate information, based on data from both internal and external sources, to enable them to make timely and effective decisions for planning, directing and controlling the activities for which they are responsible.

As a matrix, in cooperatives, the relationship between information and decision areas like, planning and programming, and monitoring and evaluation MIS can be understood.

The framework of MIS in the context of cooperatives is seen as a architecture encompassing aspects like nature of the enterprise and its information needs, sources of information, users profile and their needs, degree of centralization, scope and range of information needs of various users, degree of computerization required, compatibility of the MIS with other external MIS, monitoring and evaluation and updating / upgrading of the system.

Thus, the framework should include three major aspects:

1. MIS – its meaning, scope and relevance, and basic characteristics of MIS;
2. Type of information needs, users needs, system for collection, processing, storage and dissemination, formats to be used, its operations, and organizational positioning; and
3. Relevance of MIS to the members, leaders and managers of cooperatives.

It is possible to design a MIS which is partly operated at the primary level and partly at the federal / apex level. It is possible to develop MIS which cover, on the one hand all relevant information needs of all types of cooperatives, while on the other it has the possibility of incorporating the specific needs of a particular type of cooperatives. Similarly, it is possible to have centralized-decentralised computer aided or manual information system within a cooperative / cooperative structure. The size of the cooperative and its information needs, degree of integration that exists between the primary and federal structure, maturity and quality of leadership and management are some of the aspects that finally determine the framework of MIS in a cooperative.

A typical framework of MIS in cooperatives is presented in Fig. 12.2.

Identification of MIS in Cooperatives

The MIS in cooperatives can be identified through the understanding of the basic characteristics of MIS. They are:

- Output should be of value to managers at various levels of the cooperative.
- Minimum demand for new data
- Data collected must be of use
- MIS must be simple, but should have the capacity to address most of the issues / problems
- MIS must provide the opportunity to aggregate or consolidate information at higher levels and vice versa.

The MIS in cooperatives can be made understood by the following facts:

- Business performance over a period
- Financial status of the cooperatives
- Scope of expansion of the cooperative business
- Decision-making process
- Planning process
- Reporting process
- Data base management system of the cooperatives.

The MIS in cooperatives helps in collecting, storage, processing and analyzing data / information from various sources, and provides and feeds processed data (information) to the

decision centers so that the top level executives can make timely and quality decisions for the achievement of end results.

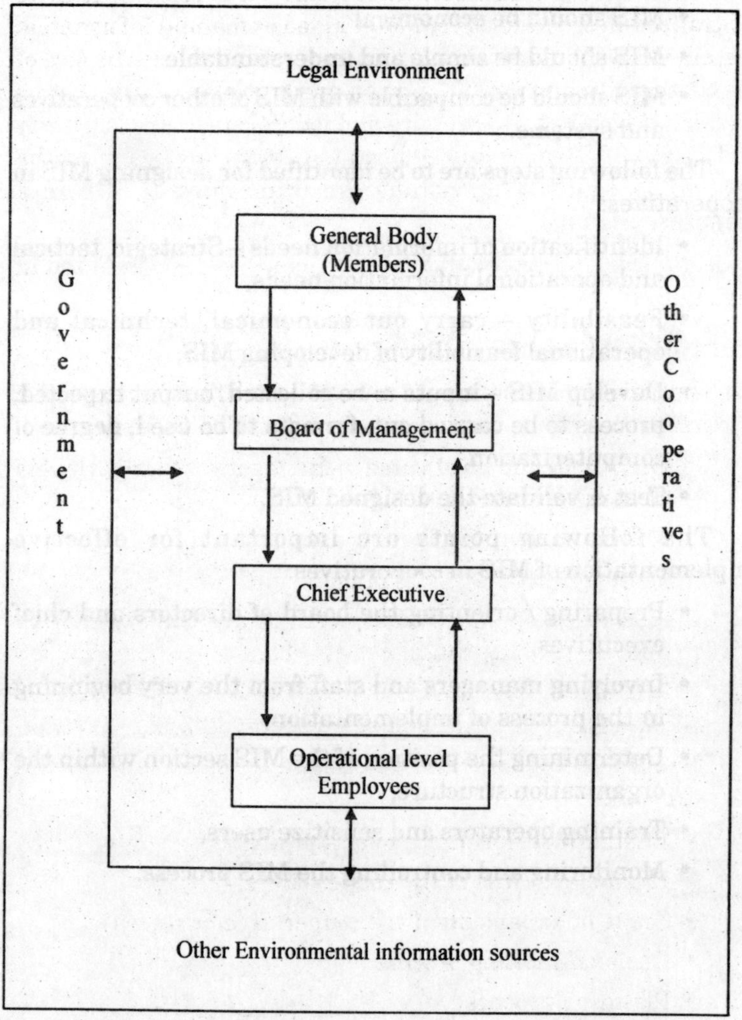

Fig. 12.2. Typical framework of MIS in Cooperatives

Designing and Operating MIS in Cooperatives

While designing MIS in cooperatives the following overriding considerations ought to be kept in view:

- MIS designing should be a participatory exercise
- MIS designing should be entirely needs-based
- MIS should be economical
- MIS should be simple and understandable
- MIS should be compatible with MIS of other cooperatives and systems.

The following steps are to be identified for designing MIS in cooperatives:

- Identification of information needs – Strategic, tactical and operational information needs,
- Feasibility – carry out economical, technical and operational feasibility of developing MIS,
- Develop MIS – inputs to be collected, output expected, process to be carried out, formats to be used, degree of computerization,
- Test & validate the designed MIS.

The following points are important for effective implementation of MIS in cooperatives:

- Preparing / orienting the board of directors and chief executives,
- Involving managers and staff from the very beginning in the process of implementation,
- Determining the position of the MIS section within the organization structure,
- Training operators and sensitize users,
- Monitoring and controlling the MIS process.

13

MIS and Cooperative Management Pyramid

Management Levels in Cooperatives

The first term is management. Management can be defined as the dynamic process of planning, organizing, coordinating, directing and controlling of available resources to achieve desired objectives of an organization effectively and efficiently and managers are responsible to discharge these functions in the organization. Cooperative management Pyramid presented in Figure 13.1 pinpoints the distinction between different levels of management members within the organization performing various functions.

Top Management: The organizational chart clearly defines three layers of management: top, middle, and operating management. In a cooperative, the general body, the board of directors, the chairman and the chief executive constitute top management. They determine the short and long-range objectives of the organization, the physical, and monetary and personnel resources to realize these objectives and the policies and strategies that best utilize the resources. This activity is called strategic planning and formulation of policies. The general body in its general meeting gives final decisions over objectives, planning, policies and budget of the organization.

Middle Management: The managers of various departments reporting to the chief executive may be considered as middle management. Although elements of planning, organizing, coordinating, directing and control exist at all levels of management, control is the predominant element in the middle manager's job. Whatever the overall goals and objectives of the middle managers to acquire and control the necessary resources in order to implement these objectives and policies.

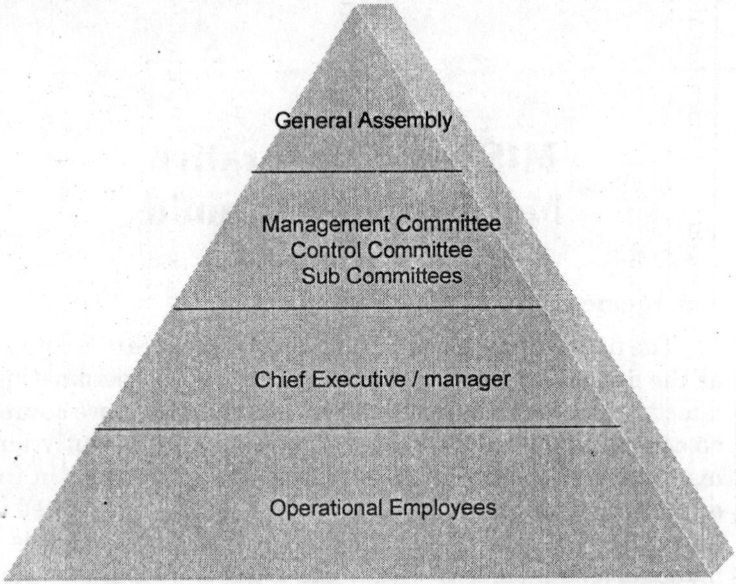

Fig. 13.1 Cooperative Management Pyramid

Operating or Bottom Management: the supervisors or various sections in charge reporting to the middle management constitute the operating level of management. At this level, there is less planning in with the overall aggregate of functions and activities, then operating management is concerned with more finite and specific activities. These specific tasks are to be performed within the prescribed rules, processes and procedures.

Interaction among Management Levels

These three management levels interact among themselves leading organizational performance upward or downward depending on its nature. Top management establishes the objective, polices, plans and a general budgets framework within which the various departments operate. These factors are promulgated any passed down to middle management for their implementation.

Job content of Management Levels and their Characteristic

S. No.	*Particulars of Job*	*Top Management*	*Middle Management*	*Operative Management*
1.	Planning	Heavy concentration	Moderate concentration	Lowest
2.	Organizing	-do-	-do-	-do-
3.	Coordination	Organization a whole	Department as whole	Section as a whole
4.	Direction	Minimum responsibility	Highly responsibility	High responsibility
5.	Control	-do-	-do-	-do-
6.	Time dimension	One to five years or more	One to two years	Day to day
7.	Scope of activities	All pervasive	Entire functional area	Single substask specific activity
8.	Nature of activities	Instructed	Structured	Highly structured
9.	Level of complexity	Highly complex multiple factors	Moderately well defined factors	Very clear
10.	Job measurement	Difficult to measure	Comparatively easy to measure	Easy to measure
11.	Result of action	Establishment of objective, policies, strategies and budget	Implementation of programs schedules, performance, standard and actuation	Production of goods and services

S. No.	*Particulars of Job*	*Top Management*	*Middle Management*	*Operative Management*
12.	Nature and type of information	More external and less internal	Less external and more internal with more accuracy	Completely internal with high accuracy
13.	Mental qualities	Creative, imaginative, innovative and progressive	Executive, persuasive, supportive and responsible	Efficient and effective
14.	Involvement of persons	Few in the board and all members in the general body meeting	Moderate number	Many
15.	Organizational interaction	Interdivision covering the entire organization	Interdepartments	Within departments

Distinction between management levels

After drawing the levels of management in a cooperative organization – three layers for our analysis purpose – it is desirable to compare and contrast the job content of the three levels of management.

Before devising MIS in the cooperative, it is essential to understand and install the management process first because it is prerequisite to MIS. Every management job is the representative of the total organization.

Information needs at Various Levels of a Cooperative Organization

At the General Assembly (members)

- Performance indicators of the cooperative enterprise
- Planning and control
- Cost of service rendered to members
- Comparative achievements of the cooperative vis-à-vis other cooperatives
- Board of directors – duties and responsibilities
- Members' satisfaction
- Cooperative value orientation
- Cooperative Policy and Organization's policy
- Indicators of review and control
- Human Resource Development
- Financial information
- Physical environment
- Environmental factors

At the Board level

- Procedures, programmes
- Budget and control
- Information on organization structure
- Communication flow
- Managers profile
- Office administration

At the Chief executive level

- Quality indicators
- Service level and customer satisfaction
- Productivity indicators
- Execution
- Factors for effectiveness of MIS.

At the Operational level

- Operations
- Maintenance
- Routine affairs
- Reporting system.

14
Functional MIS in Cooperatives

FUNCTIONAL MIS IN COOPERATIVES

Cooperatives are engaged in all kinds of business activities to uplift the community. Like other business organizations they have functional areas of management: marketing, finance, human resources, production and accounting. MIS can be applied in all these functional areas. In this chapter the applications of MIS in cooperative business functions are discussed elaborately.

MARKETING INFORMATION SYSTEM FOR COOPERATIVE BANKS

Market information system – an overview

Every enterprise must organize an effective flow of market information to its marketing managers. Companies are studying their managers information needs and designing market information system (MIS) to meet these needs. The information a company needs is usually available by socially acceptable means, if the firm will just establish a market information system.

A MIS consists of people, equipment and procedures to gather, sort, analyze, evaluate, and distribute needed, timely, and accurate information to marketing decision makers.

There may be certain situation where the decisions cry out for information, which is not available at any price. The availability of additional information will improve the odds of making a good decision. The collected information has no value unless the manager tends to change or modify ties decision. Generally, information is most useful in cases, where one is not sure of what is to be done, and where extreme values, huge profits or losses, are involved. Marketing information required for marketing excellence. Marketing excellence is the net outcome of correct market decisions.

Information Needs of Marketing Function in Co-op. Bank

Co-operative banking is information intensive sector. Information needs of co-operative banks can be identified under functional areas of management. However, at the very outset it is essential to point out that the present market realties suggest that the force of all business should be the customer of any business. For attaining aims and goals a co-operative bank manager needs information, serves and networks that would enable him to focus on customers.

Marketing, though being and essential part of business, gets the least attention from the designers of the information systems. The productivity of the marketing function depends, in part on the dynamics of market forces and the market information system.

The information needs of marketing function in a co-operative bank would include 6 p's such as, product, price, place. promotion, people and procedure information. A marketing information system of a co-operative bank may encompass the above stated six marketing mix or 6-p information. Effective banking marketing service can be enrich through proper combination of these six in gradients in the background of business environment and organizational objective.

MARKETING MIX IN CO-OPERATIVE BANK

Product Information

A product is anything which is handed over by the bank to its customers to satisfy their needs and wants. Like all other banks and financial institutions. Cooperative banks are also offering three kinds of products namely, deposits scheme, credit scheme and ancillary services.

Product differentiation is becoming the key element in the marketing strategies of modern banking. The market research, sales analysis and other related information can be used to understand the characteristic feature of the product that would be more appealing to the potential customers of co-operative banks. In the competitive banking business environment co-operative banks must develop new products with the availability of new technology and differentiate the product from others competing banking products. At present, It infrastructure offers information regarding the risk profile, cost structure, revenue estimates, product life cycle etc., of proposed products. This enables the manager of co-operative banks to make an informed choice regarding the product development, differentiation and launching of new schemes in the market.

Price Information

Price denotes service charges and interest rates on deposit, loans and advances. Co-operative banks act in dual capacity of buyer while accepting deposit and seller while issuing loans and advances simultaneously.

Pricing is one of the most crucial decisions to attract customers taken by a Bank Manager. This decision is influences by many internal and external environmental factors and thus, requires information regarding costs, competitors pricing policy etc. The whole gamut of information can be gathered, analysed and exchanged with the help of IT infrastructure. Co-operative banks already offer attractive interest rates on loan. The Manager of co-operative bank must know the role of IT infrastructure in the process of taking price decisions of their products.

Place Information

Place refers to the location of a co-operative bank where it offers its services. Manager of a co-operative bank should gather information regarding competitors' place/location and he has to decide to have the bank in a place which should ideally be near and suitable for the target customers to render services at their door steps.

Promotion Information

Promotion is a major tool for informing educating and communicating with the customers regarding the products of a

Co-operative bank. The co-operative banks should focus on high degree of customer satisfaction which may insure serve as a tool of promotion.

The role of IT is significant to establish and maintain contact with the potential customers and it can be done by the Co-operative banks through establishing electric kiosks (Multimedia machine designed to be user friendly and interactive in the process of delivery of information to the customers) at selected sites often insisted by the potential customers and web sites on Internet. Industrial Development Bank of India (IDBI) sent more than 50,000 mailers, spending Rs. 6 lakh to solicit response for its Rs. 1,000 crore bond issue. The response was negligible. Instead, the website for the issue, costing Rs. 50,000 generated 10,000 to 15,000 hits every week. Co-operative banks can also use the same method to raise their business transaction.

People

Banking is essentially person to person business. Whatever is handed over to the customer is intangible. So, Whatever is handed may be important but the way in which it is handed over. It is often found that customers prefer to do business with the bank whose staff members are well mannered and well informed.

The co-operative banks must plan to have a specific type of computer co-operative for meeting the training needs of their staff. It is notable point that the Mehsena Urban Co-operative Bank Ltd. (MUCOB) boasts of Rs. 2 crore business per employee per year (199596).

Customer is a main source from whom the performance of the co-operative bank can be appraised through pooling of information from the users of the bank.

Procedures

Bank business comprises of various process and procedures to be followed. The customer demands faster service and less cumbersome procedure. So the bank which takes less time in delivering service to the customers commands a competitive edge over others. Keep this point, the co-operative bank must deliver services in time. The (Head Quarters) main branch bank has to plan to connect all branches through NET (Network) and apply E-Banking concept to provide faster service to customers centralized administration and decision making system. It will certainly speedup in delivering services of various branches. The co-operative banks may embark on a system which would provide faster service in issuing DD. clearance of cheque, and issuing certificate.

The co-operative banks may start integrated marketing in banking business by decoding a right kind of marketing mix. They should adopt proper marketing mix depending upon the external and internal environment to realize the benefits of bank marketing.

Co-operative Bank Manager's Role in MIS

Managers are decision makers. They have to play a vital role in MIS planning, execution and control of information of Co-operative Banks.

Cooperative Bank Marketing Information System

Marketing Information System of a co-operative bank stands between the market environment and market decision makers. Marketing data related to 6Ps flows from environment to the marketing information system and it is processed and converted into marketing information flow which goes to the marketers for decision-making and communication flows back to the environment.

A Bank Marketing Information system continuously retrieves data i.e. facts and figures from the internal or external sources, stored out, classified analysed and stored for future reference. The restored information can be recalled or restored immediately for reference in a manner required for decision-making by the manager of a bank.

The Marketing Information System performs six functions such as assembling of marketing data, processing i.e. editing, tabulating and summarizing the data, analyzing the data, storage and retrieval, evaluation regarding accuracy & reliability of data, and dissemination or distribution of relevant wanted information to decision making managers.

Model bank looks assembling and processing of data. Analysical bank is in charge of analysis of evaluation. Data Bank is interested in storage, retrieval and dissemination of market information.

A well-defined Co-operative Bank Marketing Information System (CBMIS) begins and ends with they customer – members who decides the growth and development of cooperative banks.

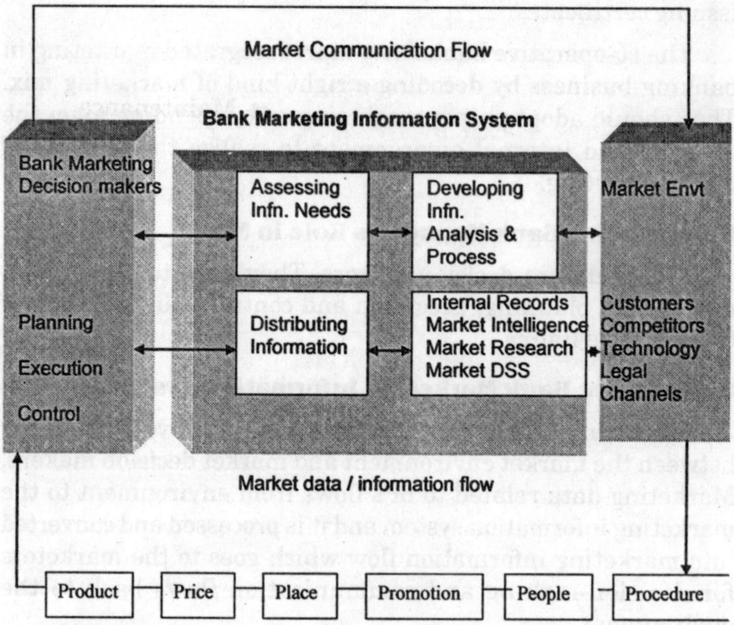

Fig. 14.1. Bank marketing Information System

A CBMIS has its own sub-systems. The first assesses information needs by interviewing bank managers (marketing) and surveying their decision environment to determine what information is desired, needed and feasible to offer.

The second develops information and helps bank's marketing managers to use it more effectively. It consists of four areas viz., internal records, marketing intelligence, market research and market decision support analysis.

Internal records provide information on sale of bank's products, costs cash flow and accounts receivable and payable.

Here, the cooperative banks may develop advanced computer-based internal records system to allow for speedier and more comprehensive information.

Market intelligence supplies marketing personnel of co-operative banks with every minute information about developments in the external marketing environment. Intelligence can be collected from bank employees, customers and from other external factors, or by monitoring published reports conferences, advertisements. competitor actions and through network advertisements in the environment.

Marketing research involves collected information relevant to a specific marketing problem facing the bank. Bank market research involves a five-step process. The steps are.

- defining the problem and research objectives,
- developing the research plan,
- collecting the information,
- analyzing the information and
- interpreting and reporting the findings.

The marketing decision support analysis consists statistical techniques and decision mode is to assist marketing manager of cooperative banks in making better decision.

Finally, the bank marketing information system distributes information gathered from the system of Developing Information to the right personnel (Bank Manager Marketing) at the right time for making right decision which is to be executed and controlled by them For this purpose cooperative banks must decentralize their information systems through networks that allow managers to have direct access of information from all sources.

FINANCIAL INFORMATION SYSTEM IN COOPERATIVES

Finance is the lifeline system of every business. The role of finance manager has undergone a sea change over the last two decades. Now-a-days the finance manage is dealt with the total amount of capital raised from various sources and employed with the enterprise, allocation of funds to various activities and measurement of the outcome of these activities in the enterprise.

Moreover. Financial Management has a profound impact on the business efficiency of any enterprise.

In a Cooperative enterprise, sound financial planning and management of fiancé is the most, vital requirement for successful management. Finance has far reaching impact on cooperative business organization though ideologically it does not assign much importance to it.

But the role of finance is broadening and becoming more vital to the over all development of cooperatives. Because it has now crossed the rudimentary stage and has entered into large scale ventures. Although many cooperative societies of large scale, the responsibilities of their finance functions are still confined mainly to processing funds, keeping accurate financial records, preparing reports, managing the cash position and maintaining the means for the payment of bills of liquidity. The financial management of cooperatives are not the same as other type of enterprises. The following are the distinctive characteristics of financial management in cooperatives;

- They depend on their membership for business.
- People of lower group can subscribe share.
- Distribute major portion of their surplus to members.
- They believe in self-help and place a ceiling on the maximum borrowing power.

FINANCIAL INFORMATION SYSTEM IN COOPERATIVE ENTERPRISES

Finance Function Mix

The Financial Management in a cooperative comprised of finance function mix viz., funds mobilization and funds utilization.

Procurement of funds and their employment in different channels of investments are nothing but the two sides of the same coin and as much diligence, prudence and care should be exercised in the method of investment as in raising resources.

Funds Mobilization in Cooperatives

Cooperative societies can raise funds through various sources which can broadly be kept in two categories-owned funds and borrowed funds. Further, from fixed cost and charge point of view it can be grouped into two heads-funds carrying fixed cost and charge and funds with any cost or charge. The problem of raising resources is not a critical factor as long as cooperatives are small and fulfilling the limited needs of members. But in recent years, they have drawn in all respects whose capital requirements are substantial and they must raise capital. For example a cooperative bank may raise its finance through

- Equity Capital (Sale of shares of stock and collection of members capital contribution)
- Accumulation of reserves and
- Loan capital – deposits, borrowings, sale of bonds and debentures and donations, grants & gifts.

Procurement of funds refers to the task of providing funds needed by the cooperative venture on terms that are most favourable in the light of its objectives. For raising it is essential that finance manager must know the instruments, institutions and practices through which funds are obtained. He must know legal and accounting relationships between a cooperative society and its sources of funds. Under this function, his main concern is to keep the business supplied with enough funds and related information to accomplish it objectives by observing legal and other implications.

Funds Utilization

This is the most important finance function mix because effective use of capital in the business generated additional benefits compensating for the cost and risk involved in raising funds. This function entails a decision making after analyzing the alternative uses and sources of funds. It covers financial planning, forecasting of cash receipts and disbursements, the raising of funds, use and allocation of funds and financial control. Following budget and other devices of financial control, the finance manager attempts to bring performance closer to the targets economically.

According to V.S. Alenne,

> "The chief problem in cooperative finance is to use capital both membership capital and loan capital in a manner that most economically secure the objects for which the cooperative association has been established".

The cooperative, in the light of the supreme objective of maximization of service to their members, employ their precious resources in a judicious and prudent manner according to the nature of their functions and objectives. There are four points to be observed in the application of cooperative's finance in order to ensure optimum utilization of available resources. They are – there should not beunnecessary stock of merchandise; there should not be excessive accounts receivable; there should not be unnecessary large bank balance; and there should not be too much investment in establishments, buildings, fitting & furniture etc.

Need and Justification

Financial organization of cooperative societies specially at lower structural levels is not scientific because they do not have clearcut and rigid organization structure.

However, broad management framework of a cooperative enterprise is provided by General body; Board of Directors; Chairman: Managing Directors or General Manager or Executive Officer. These Management bodies influence the finance functions according to the power and functions entrusted to them by the provisions of the bye laws of the cooperative enterprise. Many big cooperatives have created finance department with finance manager as head of the department who enjoys implementation and control authority over finance functions delegated by the board of directors. Finance manager is assisted by subordinate officers who are responsible for routine fiancé functions. The cooperative enterprise has to go a long way in organizing its finance functions on sound and scientific forecasting.

Financial decision is concerned with the size of the enterprise and it determines the best financing mix or capital structure for the firm. Financial decision is taken in relation to the overall valuation of the cooperative enterprise. The finance manager is required to decide the proportion of ordinary share capital (owner's capital) and borrowed capital Further, he is to examine the various methods by which he goes to the market for the short, medium or longterm debt. In short, it is the ability; of the finance manager to adopt advances and alternative methods of financing which are evaluated in relation to costs and the best fiancé mix is selected for successful running of the cooperative enterprise.

Sound financial decision making need the support of information system called the financial information system. Cooperatives must have such financial information system so as to find sources of information and to extend supporting hands for the effective utilization procured funds in a right sense. It will enable cooperatives to achieve managerial efficiency and effectiveness.

Information needs on Financial Management in Cooperatives and Information Technology

Financial Information System involves investment decision, financing, dividend decision, portfolio, financing, dividend decision, portfolio management, asset management etc. At this juncture the finance manager performs functions leading to liquidity, profitability and viability that leads to proper management of assets with the help of information Technology infrastructure.

The information required by the finance manage, sources of information like principles and practice, the cooperative legal system, publications etc., and IT infrastructure (application) with respect of areas stated above are discussed and the functions of a finance manager, thus, fall into following major domains:

General Ledger Information

The first application of IT in finance departments began and still begins with automation of general ledger accounting procedures. Modern financial accounting software packages now offer reports on financial ration analysis, budgetary control, credit management, ageing analysis of debtors, etc., in addition to the vanilla type general ledger reports, such as statement of accounts receivable, expense reports, budget deviations reports, statement of assets acquisition and disposal, etc., so that exact business position can be assessed.

Financial Planning and Budgeting

Allocation of funs to various activities in the business is one of the major functions of a finance manager. Budgets as financial plans involve prediction of outcome which are made on assumptions regarding the future. The outcomes of the activities need to be interactively investigated so that a corrective action could follow without loss of time. Use of IT infrastructure has made it possible to develop real time flexible budgets and investigate the outcome of activities to enable the fiancé manager take quicker and informed decisions.

Assets and Liability Management

Profitability is determined by the utilization of resource of an enterprise. The asset management is thus one of the key responsibilities of a finance manager. IT infrastructure can provide information to a finance manager for management of assets and monitoring their utilization on a regular basis. IT infrastructure can be used for identifying assets with low utilization factors and generating necessary information for evaluating proposals for hiring of assets as and when needed, or exploring possibilities for sub-contracting. Similarly, the finance manager can effectively manger liabilities of the cooperative enterprise if the needed information is available from various sources regularly.

Profitability Analysis

Profitability analysis is an important activity in the finance department. This profitability analysis not only forms the basis of the plan for allocation of funds for various activities (income on assets over the expenditure on liability and increase in non-interest income and reduction in operating cost decide the profitability) but also guides the finance manager in taking decisions like continue or quit and pricing. IT helps the finance manger to keep a track of the product life cycle and taking decisions regarding product mix. Modern IT infrastructure provides a finance manager with the information required for profitability analysis of such information. Cooperatives of diversified wings with large number of branches or sales offices find IT infrastructure very useful in profitability analysis.

Cash and Funds Flow Management

Management of cash and funds flow has always been the concern of finance mangers. For an effective cash and funds management, it is essential to have information regarding the demand and likely availability of liquid resource from operations, investment decisions and financing decisions. A large amount of information regarding activities in operating cycle is required for decision making in respect of cash and fund flow management. Advanced techniques for modeling of cash management need to be used to ensure that there are funds just enough to meet the requirements. IT infrastructure can help a lot not only in extracting such information from the databases but also in estimating the demand and availability of funds from various other sources. IT infrastructure can help in generating information required for such decisions using more complex models of estimating and forecasting.

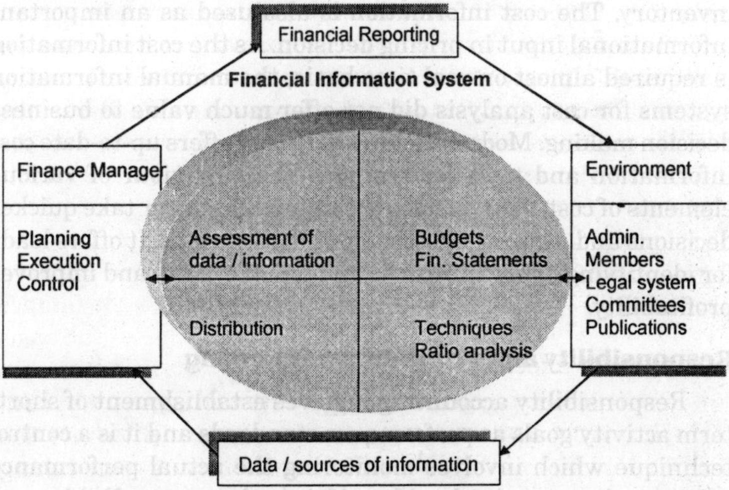

Fig. 14.2. Financial Information System

Evaluation of Funds and Investments

Investment decision refers to the selection of assets in which funds should be invested. Cost of funds or capital is the basic element of the selection criteria. The information required for evaluation of proposals is becoming more and more probabilistic and the estimation is becoming more and more complex as we enter new pastures and unbeaten tracks in business. IT infrastructure can help in using more sophisticated models for estimating costs and cash flow, and measurement of risk-return ratios for different projects. Use of different profitability models is feasible with the help of suitable IT infrastructure. To evaluate each investment proposal with speed and accuracy almost automatically, this encourage implementation of zero-based budgeting, a technique that has the potential of avoiding wasteful expenditure on redundant activities. In fact, zero-based budgeting became a popular technique only after IT infrastructure became available for regular evaluation of each investment proposal, in a short period of time.

Cost Analysis

Cost analysis is an important activity that a finance manager undertakes regularly in order to control the cost and value of inventory. The cost information is also used as an important informational input in pricing decision. As the cost information is required almost on real time basis, the manual information systems for cost analysis did not offer much value to business decision making. Modern IT infrastructure offers up-to-date cost information and tools for studying the behaviour of various elements of cost. This enables the finance manager take quicker decisions and exercise effective control over costs. It offers leads for identifying opportunities for reduction of costs and improves profitability.

Responsibility and Profitability Reporting

Responsibility accounting involves establishment of short-term activity goals as performance standards and it is a control technique which involves monitoring the actual performance against the standards, identifying the controllable and uncontrollable costs and revenue factors, and measurement of performance in view of the information so generated. It has gained much of its popularity after the availability of IT infrastructure for maintaining detailed information for its purpose and analysis of variances to establish reasons for variances from plans needed for exercising proper control. IT infrastructure can provide a platform for effective responsibility accounting and reporting of profitability of each of the organizational units separately. The reporting framework has changed from periodic statements in predefined formats to interactive reports in the desired format. The financial information is up-to-date and its availability is automatic. The reporting approach is proactive in the sense that the predefined information needs are met without periodic requests from the user. Use of IT in financial management should also help to ensure consistency in data at different levels in the organization so that the aggregation of values for various financial factors of all the departments match with the value given by the division, and vice versa.

Financial Reporting of Cooperatives – A Source of Information for Management

Financial reporting is the total communication system of any business enterprise to its different users. The objective of the financial reporting is to communicate economic measurements of and information about the resources and performance of reporting entity, useful to have reasonable right to take decisions. It also plays an important role in building confidence among the users of financial information.

The financial reporting of cooperative is a distinct form of reporting from other corporate organizations due to the distinct features of cooperative form of organization. It is set up with a group of people for attaining a common economic development needs.

The call for financial reporting of cooperatives are very much necessary for the management to discharge their responsibility to its members.

The conceptual framework of cooperative financial reporting should be based upon timeliness of communication, reliability of information communicated, materiality of the information, relevance of the information to the users and form of presentation. These reporting framework satisfy the objective of cooperative accountability through accounts and audit to its members and strengthen the internal reporting more efficiently and effectively.

Financial Information System Audit (FISA)

Audit is an appraisal activity carried out by people who are not actively involved in performing the affairs under appraisal. It aims at prevention and detection of abuse of the corporate resources. Financial information system audit (FISA) is carried out by professionals, the link between software development team and the management of finance, who are not only well versed with complex information system issues but also know how to relate them to the financial function of a cooperative. It is conducted to evaluate the FIS and suggest measures to improve their value to the business of a cooperative enterprise. The FIS auditor evaluates the review of every project on behalf of the management. The process of FISA involves four steps – identification vulnerability of FIS; identification of source of threat; identification of high-risk points; and check for compute abuse. To sum up, cooperatives have to adopt available IT infrastructure for the implementation of financial information system for their betterment thereby they can achieve managerial efficiency.

HUMAN RESOURCE INFORMATION MANAGEMENT SYSTEM

Human Resource Management

Human Resource Management (HRM) is an integral part of modern management which plays a key role in the success of any business enterprise. It assists management to run the cooperative in such a way that both the organization and its employees can benefit. The relevance of this function is increasing due to the increasing knowledge intensity of jobs in business enterprise. There is no dearth of people locking for jobs in the market, but the shortage of right type of manpower has been as serious handicap in the path to successful business.

Human Resource Management System (HRMS) as opposed to traditional view of personnel function should be considered a total system that interacts with the other major systems making, production, finance and the external forecasting and planning the personnel needs, maintaining an adequate and satisfactory work force and controlling the personnel policies and programmes are the major responsibilities of HRM System in a cooperative enterprise.

Human Resource Information System

Human Resource Information System (HRIS)is the information system that supports human resource management sub-systems such as man power planning,, recruitment and selection, training and development compensation and incentive plan, and performance appraisal. It deals with the flow of information about people working in the organization as well as about future personnel needs and the system is concerned primarily with the aforestated five basic subsystems.

MIS in this area provides related and adequate information to help personnel and other management in the subsystems of HRM. In addition, information must be provided for the development and implementation of policies on welfare, health and safety, work environment, and industrial relations, computers play a crucial role we can say that IT application in HRIS is more important. It can be named as Computerised HRIS.

The change from deciding what to charge for ordering seeds, or when to place these orders, to determining what to do next is a difficult one. The transition will be much easier if the directors understand that devising policies as the information for the chief executive to follow is much more important for the success of the cooperative venture that what they were doing before. For which a HRM information system must be designed and developed.

Management Hierarchy and HRM information

Information warding human resources can be identified at all management levels.

Strategic management level required information for evaluating alternative strategic for recruiting, salary, training, builds and training personnel or human resource.

Management control level requires information about employees hired, cost of recanting composition of skills inventory, use of training, salary paid, distribution forage rates etc.

Operation a control level requires information regarding decision procedures for at such as hiring, training, job description, job specification, termination, changing pay rates and issuing benefits to work force.

HRM Subsystem and Information Needs

With flowing size of cooperative enterprises and the increased mobility manpower and legislation regarding protection of rights of employees, tax is a problem of shortage human resourcs. In spite of this, HRIS he is the authorities of cooperatives, to hide, retrieval, store and supply of relevant information regarding human resources.

The subsystems of HRM that would determine the information needs are discussed hereunder.

Information and Manpower Planning

The data bank with regard to the existing manpower (human resources), their strengths and limitations has become an important information input for decisions regarding the manpower planning. Careful planning of manpower requirements and sensible recruitment of applicants are not limited to young, small or isolated cooperatives. They represent, on the contrary, essential and crucial activities in the life of all cooperatives Two initial rules can be laid down in this respect.

- It is necessary to appoint the best general manger available, even if this means going outside the district.
- It is important not to appoint too many of the friends and relatives of leading directors. In some communities this is a real danger.

Such kind of information can be had only through well designed and developed HRIS.

Information – Selection and Recruitment

There are secondary cooperatives which provide a selection and recruitment service for all their affiliated societies. Alternatively, a cooperative consultant or government department for cooperatives could possibly give information in the form of advice on the choice, probably also supplying a list of candidates. There is a shortage of technicians, and the cooperative may have difficulty in getting well qualified and equipped personnel for different cadres.

Recruitment policy should concern itself with a number of factors which provide information regarding recruitment and selection. Does the candidate fit the job description with respect to education, age and experience? Is he or she medically fit? Should he candidate be disqualified as close relative, of a director or the manager? Would he or she be prepared to serve a probationary period and / or take further training? Answers for the above questions can be had from HRIS of a cooperative enterprise. If such information system is in existence and it is easy to gather information with regard to the recruitment and selection process.

It is essential to have date base or information in the form of procedure for the recruitment and selection process for the introduction of the new employee-to the job, to the rest of the staff, to policies that affect him or her, and particularly to the cooperative itself. It all these procedures are informed, they will undoubtedly improve the chances of making the best choice possible and of smoothing the entry of newly recruited members of staff.

Information – Training and Development

IT can help a cooperative enterprise to keep a track of the right people in and outside the organization. Career and succession planning systems help managers to identify the training needs of people in the light of succession plan. A more recent application of IT infrastructure in human resources management is the development activity. With the help of multimedia and simulation techniques, it is now possible for an enterprise to train their employees for different jobs. Introduction of intelligent agents in software solutions make people understand the business processes easily by analyzing the information available in the database of the enterprise. The expert systems formalize, store and make available the knowledge base of the enterprise, empowering new entrants with the wealth of knowledge acquired by experience and experimentation by the earlier performers.

Subsequent follow-up of objectives, revisions of training curricula, identification of improved training methods and materials, and the elaboration of programmes for the training and upgrading of trainer in national training systems can be possible only through a proper and well designed HRM information system and that would lead to development in all respects.

Information – Compensation and Incentive Plan

Keeping detailed information regarding the compensation to manpower is one of the most common activities that offer tangible benefits to justify investment in IT infrastructure. The basic advantage of IT in this regard arises from the analysis of the compensation packages to different class of employees and estimating the potential impact of any decision of the overall profitability of the enterprise. Such information is not only useful in collective bargaining but also in rationalizing the compensation packages, so as to minimize human resources costs while maintaining the motivational level of each employee at a high level. It helps in retaining and maintaining the suitable people in the organization.

As regard promotion to really senior posts, there is much to be said in favour of the principle that cooperative should "promote from within", if only because it offers an attractive "ladder' to the best type of junior. Decisions taken in this, regarding transfers, suspensions, dismissals or redundancies should, however, respect due process information like cooperative principles, and the relevant procedures should be conducted in accordance with existing legal provisions and collective agreement clauses. To well advised to take as a guide for those aspects of personnel management concerning job security the principles contained in the Termination of Employment Convention, 1982 (No. 158).

Cooperative in some countries have had comprehensive policies on conditions of work and staff benefits for many years. Secondary societies usually give leadership in drafting such policies and subsequently encourage primaries to modify these in the light of local conditions and adopt them for their own societies. The distribution to all employees of copies of texts concerning existing terms and conditions of employment removes uncertainties and promotes better relations within the society, especially if the policies are fair. If they are uniform throughout a system a affiliated cooperatives, they make possible opportunities for promotion without loss of accumulated benefits, and thus improve employee motivation.

Money is not only the incentive, which makes employees work and work well, but it is even necessarily the most powerful. Encouragement and praise can be very precious and can change the workers' attitude more quickly 'than blame.

In cooperatives it is a matter of board policy that employees may belong to a union of their choice, but that only a single union will be recognized the cooperative for purposes of collective bargaining. Modern personnel management pays particular attention to the handing of grievances. Suitable procedures are provided for in collective agreements or in basic statements of personnel policies for the quick and impartial settlement of individual and collective complaints. Such provisions seek to avoid the appearance of an atmosphere of conflict and the decrease in productivity that usually follows the accumulation of unsettled grievances.

Information and Performance Appraisal

Performance appraisal is now more detailed and based on the entire set of responsibilities than just on the basis of select, easily quantifiable factors. IT has made the performance appraisal more regular, systematic and comprehensive. Modern tools of performance appraisal that ground place only in management literature are increasingly gaining population among the managers in many organizations. This has been possible mainly due to timely, availability of detailed information regarding performance of each employee and each unit of the enterprise.

"Human Resource (HR) and Information System (IS) will be the key toe the future of an accelerated organization. At the same time the HR and the IS is departments as we know them, will be dead and buried. How can both statements be true? Because to offer the services required of them, the HR and IS functions will have to change beyond recognition".

PRODUCTION INFORMATION SYSTEM IN COOPERATIVES

Production in simple sense means to produce or to create something which is non-existent in a form suitable for human use. In technical terms, production can be defined as transformation of raw materials from a given state to desired form through a sequence of operations.

The management of production aspect of an enterprise occupies a predominant position constituting an integral part of overall management of the enterprise. This is widely referred to as production or operations management. Production management is a process of managing the manufacturing resources and their efficient utilization for catering to the needs of the customers.

Production management deals with the application of management functions in the field of production. Roscol defines "production management as the direction, coordination and control of material, labour and capital brought together for industrial production". In cooperatives, the scope of production manager apart from productivity and profitability, extends to such non-profit objectives as the services provided by the organization to its member producers, employment and income generation and other intangible benefits extended to the members.

Production Management System

Resources, systems design & control, transformation & value added activities and managerial policy are key elements or sub-systems to the understanding of production management system.

Resources

An organization employs resources to acquire material and non-material assets to achieve predetermined objectives. Resource inputs to the production system includes materials,. Machines, equipments, capital and human resources. Material and equipment cover physical energies namely electrical, mechanical etc., used in production operations. The human inputs includes physical labour and intellectual exercise. The closer integration of human and physical systems are important in this respect because by using the intellectual capabilities of people, labour inputs are magnified many times, resulting in increased productivity. Capital is essential to establish and regulate the amount of material and human inputs. Effective and efficient use of funds increases the profitability of a firm.

System Design and Control

System design covers building and plant layout, installation of machines, processes and procedures of treatment etc. Production system design varies with the nature of production like continuous and intermittent. System control consists of all actions necessary to ensure that activities conform to preconceived plans. Control involves measurement, feedback, comparison of actual with standards and corrective action.

Transformation and Value-added Activities

The controlled production system, reflecting the technology of the transformation process and the methodology of managing the process, transforms the resources following sequence of treatments or operations into goods or services.

Managerial Policy

By using functional, behavioural and system approaches manager can lay down concrete objective, suitable managerial policies and accurate programmes leading to effective organizational performance.

Need for Production Information System in Cooperatives

The cooperative movement has made a dent in the field of industrial production ranging from small and cottage industrial cooperatives to large scale industrial cooperatives. To run industrial ventures on cooperatives basis require the knowledge in the field of product ion management. Big industries under cooperative sector are facing basic problems, which have been identified in respect of production management. They are organizational problems, like location disadvantages, absence of technical know-how, lack of proper inter-cooperative relationships, lack of consistent Governmental efforts and functional problems like non-availability of raw materials, lack of financial stability, lack of marketing approach, lack of quality consciousness and lack of managerial competence.

Designing and developing an information system named as Production Information System can entail these problems. It helps the production manager and other personnel involve in the production function in assessing information needs and gathering information related to the production function of cooperatives. Hence, it is pertinent to evolve a Production Information System in large-scale industrial cooperatives. Industrial activities are complex and they cannot be handled with simple business approach and traditional attitude. Since we are living in the age of large-scale production system, this has to be with cooperative framework in respect of production system equipped with a well-designed information system.

Production Information System (PIS) in Cooperatives

The production planning focuses on scheduling of production so that the movement of all resources needed for production can take place as per the plan. The production control focuses on the product design, manufacturing process control and quality assurance. The emerging market environment is posing multiplicity of challenges before the production managers. On the one hand, there is a pressure to reduce costs by reduction in inventory levels, substitution of raw materials, increasing productivity of man and machine. On the other hand, there is a pressure to improve performance in terms of quality of product, customization by offering greater variety in the product, shorten delivery time, etc. Information technology can play an important role in meeting the challenge of these pressures. Computer Aided Designing (CAD) and Process Control System helps the production manager in the production process, while the production information systems help him take decisions regarding production scheduling and plan procurement and movement of different production resources. With the application of artificial intelligence in manufacturing, some of the major elements of the challenge can be successfully met.

The basic advantages that IT has to offer to the production management are flexibility, control and customization. These advantages occur due to free flow of information to and from the production process to all other organizational units assisting the production planning and manufacturing process. The quicker flow of information not only helps in reducing the wastage, common cause for high costs, but also adds flexibility to the production activity. These together help the organization cater to the specific needs of the customer and target niche markets that may not be tapped by other market rivals. With help of proper IT infrastructure, it becomes feasible to take a broader view of production management and create a more interactive environment for production management. The MRP-II software solution offers links between sales orders and work orders, advises on issues such as when to place orders for purchases and how much to order in the light of the orders received, order cancelled, inventory of materials in different stages of production, purchase orders awaiting deliveries, etc., for each type of material required. The work orders are tracked and production schedules are revised accordingly, in case and discrepancy is noticed in the planned and actual implementation of work orders. Such information system integrates production scheduling, procurement, inventory management, process control and other such activities with financial and marketing plans of the enterprise.

PIS Development Process

The functional goals of the production management are fuller utilization of the manufacturing capacity, minimal rejections, maximum uptime of plant and equipment and meeting the delivery promise. The function assumes key importance, when business strength is in technology and manufacturing and the market for product and services exists. The function is pegged with the responsibility of managing high investment in plant, equipment and machinery. It also has to control the large labour force at its disposal PIS development process encompasses six steps to be performed by a production manager who is in charge of production information department of a cooperative enterprise.

Input Transaction Documents

The production management is conducted through innumerable transactions. They relate to planning, issuing and controlling the various tasks – from production schedule to customer order – involved in the course of production.

The input data in each transaction would very from according to the nature of the cooperative and the production methodology adopted. The system and procedures used by the organization in performing the production function also vary respectively.

Applications

The production management is performed through production planning and control, bill of material processing, drawings and process planning, scheduling and monitoring systems as support systems.

Production management accounts for a number of entities like quantity, labour hours, machinery utilization, breakdowns etc., in a systematic manner to fulfill the needs of production management functions in various tasks and activities.

Accounting of the entities is essential a build up the information base to develop norms and standards for use in planning. It also provides day to day or period by period update on the events. Activities and tasks that the production management is expected to perform.

Queries

The queries in the production management are related in seeking of status of job or information on fixed entities such as machine or worker or process data.

Decision Analysis

The production management function is expected to make a number of decisions both for long-term and short-term period which needs information in the field of production. The typical decisions are: make or buy, make or subcontract, use of alternative material, use of alternative process, evolving optimum product mix/job mix, rescheduling and loading of jobs, planning and scheduling of jobs, selection of production facilities and selection of alternative maintenance policies.

These decision analysis applications, based on the production information, help to make policy decisions on techno-economic basis. The decision implications are on cost, productivity, efficiency, proper utilization of the manufacturing facility and usage of material and physical resources.

Control

Applications are developed to control production programme, production capacity and quality of production. The other issues with which the production management has to deal, are utilization of the production capacity and labour force. It has to ensure that plant, machines and equipment, having high investment are fully utilized. There are always some jobs, which have to be pushed through the production programme by way of scheduling and loading the jobs on the machines. These are the areas where control of the production management is essential.

The exceptions which need to be highlighted are:

- Excessive product rejection on account of material and/ or process.
- Hold up of key jobs beyond a certain limit.
- Excessive work in process inventory.
- Continued breakdown of the manufacturing facility beyond a certain period.
- Utilization of key facilities below a limit.
- Continuous significant deviation from standards or norms of production rate.
- Backlog of a large number of orders and failure to meet promised delivery date.

Production Reports

Production reports can be had from the above process, which will give a clear information on production activity of a cooperative enterprise do their base for production planning and control.

Toe sum up, cooperatives which engaged in production activity should design, develop and install production information system to ensure production planning and control efficiently in line with the goals and objectives to be achieved.

COOPERATIVE ACCOUNTING INFORMATION SYSTEM

Accounting is the mirror replicating the business activities of a firm. Cooperatives have adopted the traditional system of account keeping. A cooperative enterprise had to maintain a daybook as the only book of prime entry with columns for receipts and payments. Transactions were recorded in the book in a serial order. There were hardly any credit transactions. It was therefore simple and easy to close the cash balance.

In cooperative account-keeping system transactions involve either receipt of money or payment of money. Even credit transactions involve in effect though not actually, receipt of money and payment of money. Thus, it involves one receipt and another corresponding payment. These receipt and payment aspects of transactions form the basis for the traditional system of account keeping. Cooperative account keeping systems (see figure 14.1) may better be described as 'receipts and Payment System for Account-keeping'.

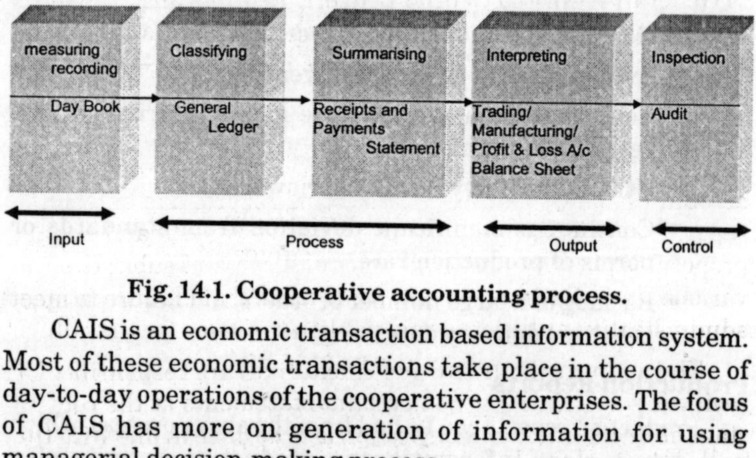

Fig. 14.1. Cooperative accounting process.

CAIS is an economic transaction based information system. Most of these economic transactions take place in the course of day-to-day operations of the cooperative enterprises. The focus of CAIS has more on generation of information for using managerial decision-making process.

CAIS is designed to achieve the objective (i) to meet the statutory reporting needs of the cooperatives: and (ii) to provide reliable information on accounts to top, middle and operation level of management.

CAIS deals with transactions which are of financial nature and can be expressed in terms of money. It caters to the information needs of both internal and external users. This quite simple and well-structured information system. The information contained in the accounting record is recognised by the cooperative law and as such these records are treated as evidence in the Court of Law, in case of dispute. The source of data is mainly internal to the cooperative and thus, data base is well-defined, integrated and controlled. CAIS, as any other system, encompasses four sub-systems viz., input, process, output and control.

At the input state, the cooperative accountants collect various accounting information needed for recording based on the principles of cooperative accounting system. They record transaction based on the principle of treating a transaction as either receipt of payment of money in Day books the book of original entry.

At the second stage: processing of accounting information recorded the transactions recorded in the Day books are posted to General legers and Special Ledgers. Receipts and Payments Statement, a summary of transactions made, is also prepared on the basis of totals of the balances arrived in General and Special Ledgers.

The third stage is the output stage where the final account statements (trading/manufacturing account and profit & loss account), balance sheet and accounting reports like enterprise reports account documents, investigative reports and budget proposal report are prepared for the purpose of submitting to various levels of management, the financing bank, federations, administrative authorities and publish the same for the public.

The auditors (both internal & external) are responsible for reviewing and checking the account statements at the control stage of CAIS. Audit and inspection is to be done in line with the cooperative law principles and values. After the verification they issue Audit information reports.

To Whom Accounting Information

Accounting information is needed by two categories of people, who use accounting information to measure a cooperative's performance against established standards and goals-internal external.

Internal users are those who are associated with management of the cooperative enterprise for which information is sought to be retrieved and processed. The management team consists of General Body. Board of Directors and employees. General body and Board of Directors require accounting information in the form of accounting statements in judge a cooperative enterprise's management by reference to these statements. The employees of the cooperative enterprise are interested in the accounting information because both, their present and future are tied up with the enterprise's fortunes.

Accounting information is needed by external users, financing banks, federations, administrative authorities and the public, for measuring whether the cooperative has economically and properly utilised the finance or not. Financing banks and federations need to know how their financial assistance is being utilised. Accounting information helps them to decide about (1) assisting financially (2) quantum of finance; and (3) making investment more on deposits /share capital and holding on to the deposits / share capital they already own.

Administrative authorities (government officials of cooperative administration) need accounting information to locate misutilisation and mismanagement of finance and to have a control over the cooperatives. The public is to be fed with accounting information which leads to create confidence with the cooperative enterprise.

Computerised CAIS (CCAIS)

The rendering of management services by accountants has transformed the accounting function into one dealing with the measurement and communication of economic data and the elements in the accounting function i.e., accounting information would have to do with the observing, measuring, recording, classifying summarizing, interpreting and inspection of economic data. Thus, the management has to carve out a place in tits organisation chart for a responsibility which has to do with the entire process of quantitative information gathering, inclusive of accounting function but definitely not limited to it. The purpose is to organise the entire figure gathering process into a ophisticated management information system which would supply of all levels of management with the information they need to run the business.

CCAIS (see Fig. 14.2) is, the computerised information system with the flow of accounting information through the system, management may be appraised on a timely and effective basis of the need for decisions.

Cooperative Accounting System can be said to have been computerised only when most of the more important accounting operations. i.e., recording, posting, tabulating etc., are completed through mechanical devices, that mechanization may be said to have been introduced in accounting system of the cooperative enterprises.

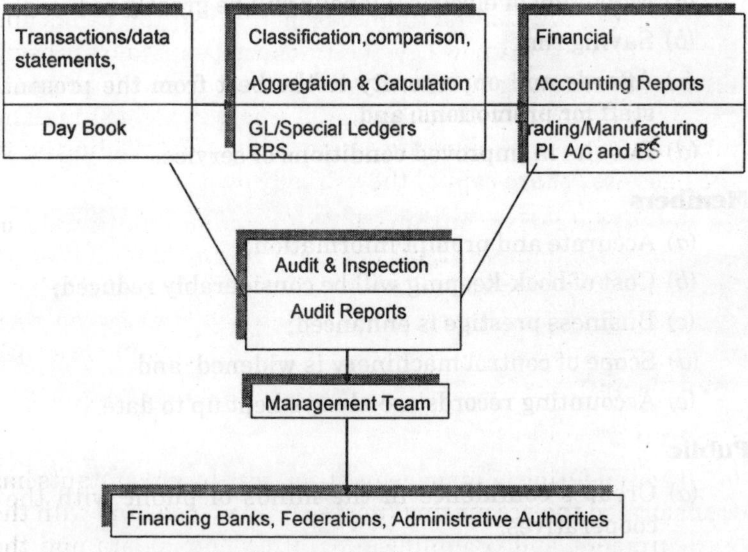

Fig. 14.2. Cooperative Accounting Information System.

The principal factors responsible for the growth of mechanized computerized accounting in cooperatives are:

(*i*) increase in the size of cooperative units leading to an enormous in crease in the accounting data to be collected and recorded in a limited time:

(*ii*) the need of the modern management to have a detailed analysis of accounting and statistical data promptly in order to run the cooperative business efficiently; and

(*iii*) a number of accounting statements and returns etc., have to be submitted to financing banks, federations, administrative authorities and various levels of management. It requires speedy collection and preparation of statements of accounting data.

Advantages of CCAIS

CCAIS is advantageous to the Accountants, members and the public.

Staff of the Accounting Department

(*a*) Monotony of electrical labour will be greatly reduced;

(*b*) Saving time;

(*c*) Affords and opportunity to the best from the present staff for promotions; and

(*d*) Results in improved conditions of service.

Members

(*a*) Accurate and prompt information;

(*b*) Cost of book-keeping will be considerably reduced;

(*c*) Business prestige is enhanced;

(*d*) Scope of control machinery is widened; and

(*e*) Accounting records are always kept up to date.

Public

(*a*) Creates confidence in the minds of public with the cooperatives.

There may be chance for retrenchment of accounting staff, errors in pickingup and wrong keying, and data loss. It is thus, obvious that there should be proper planning of the equipment to be installed staff should be trained.

Development of CCAIS

Development of CCAIS consists of six steps.

1. Cooperative Enterprise Module
   - identifying entities

- activity analysis
- grouping activities is sub-systems

2. Database Module
   - traditional
   - database approach
3. Interface Module
   - input screens
   - report screens
   - dialogue screens
   - CASE tool
4. Applications Module
   - Data Flow Diagram (DFD)
5. Implementation Module
   - testing
   - installation
6. Post Implementation Review
   - review of accounting system installed.

To sum up all forms of Cooperatives should have an accounting information system. The exact way in which accounts are kept and present will depend on the nature of the society's business. Many National Cooperative Federations publish book-keeping manuals and model account books for the use of member cooperatives carrying on different form of business Accounting information system would help the cooperatives to keep accounts systematically and submit same as accounting reports to federations, financing banks administrative authorities and different levels of management so that the performance can be appraised.

15

Cooperative Business Environment and Information System

COOPERATIVE BUSINESS INFORMATION SYSTEM

The managerial job has to take into account the several kinds of environment obtaining within their departments and within the organization itself as a whole and at the same time be constantly responsive to and interact with the complex environment, which surround cooperatives externally.

Every cooperative society, while undertaking an activity or introducing a service, must take into account the information needs and desires of its members and potential members as well as the information on material and human resources, technology and other requirements in the external environment. Sometimes the forces of external environment favourable help the working of an organization while sometimes they constrain it. Hence, managers must identify information needs, evaluate and react to the forces to the cooperative institutions that have a bearing their operations.

The environmental information system of a cooperative business can be classified into economic, socio-cultural, political and legal, technological and ethical information sub-systems. Cooperative business has to watch on the information in prevalence from the above mentioned environmental information sub-systems.

Environmental Information Needs of Cooperative Business

Economic Environmental Information

Every organization receives data/information from the economic environment and provides output by way of goods and services to it. Finance is one of the most important ingredients of the economic environment required by any organization-business or non-business. Cooperatives raise their finance through share capital, deposits, borrowings and self-generated funds. The information on identification of proper source of finance and its wise utilization and the cost of its acquisition can be gathered from economic environment. Information on workforce, its availability, quality and price has to be taken into account by the cooperatives from the economic environment. price is the most peculiar aspect of the economic environment. The change in prices has a clear effect on the input and output aspects of a cooperative enterprise. Therefore, a constant watch on information regarding price trends is necessary for good cooperative business. Prices are particularly relevant to cooperatives because they are supposed to render goods and services to their members at less than market prices under the service motto. Price information must be taken into consideration while fixing prices for goods produced and marketed by the cooperatives. Clients, the customer, is basic to the existence and survival of the organization. Cooperatives have their members and potential members for whom they produce goods or render services. Naturally they must know the tastes, desires and purchasing capacity of their customers to keep their products or services always in high demand. The information on changes in customers' habits, tastes, attitudes and expectations must be retrieved and cooperatives have to satisfy the needs of its members and customers.

Socio-cultural Environmental Information

The socio-cultural environment is composed of variety of complex forces and factors that surround people. it includes attitudes, desires, aspirations, education, beliefs, customs, levels of intelligence, values and culture of people in a given group or society. Since people respond to their environment it is important that a manager would try to design such a socio-cultural environment in the organization, which is conducive to effective performance and satisfaction.

The identification and knowledge of the socio-cultural environment is essential for co-operatives because they are constituted of people representing various socio-cultural environments among whom a balance or rapprochement has to be established. Hence, cooperators have to keep a close watch and gather information on these socio-cultural forces.

Political and Legal Environmental Information

The political environment is primarily that complex of laws, regulations and government agencies whose actions affect every organization in varying degrees. Laws are ordinarily passed as a result of social pressures and problems.

Managers are expected to know the legal restrictions and requirements applicable to their actions. They are supposed to carry out their functions under the legal framework. Side-tracking legal considerations creates legal complications. Cooperatives have to establish an information system named as cooperative legal information system to retrieve, process and function in line with the legal environment.

Ethical Environmental Information

The ethical environment includes sets of generally accepted and practiced standards of personal conducts. These standards may or may not be codified by law, but for any group to which they are meant to apply, sometimes, have virtually the force of law.

Cooperative organizations have many ethical elements in their principles and practice. They also work to elevate people's moral and ethical base through socio-economic transformation. But it is confined purely to business and membership and is limited to a few aspects. A code of conduct covering information on vital areas should be prepared for members, business employees and customers. The will minimize the problems of misdemeanor in the cooperative organization.

Technological Environmental Information

Technology is an all-pervasive term designed to cover the knowledge, which is concerned with the ways of doing things, covering, tools, techniques, inventions etc. The survival of an organization in the modern, dynamic world necessitates adoption of new technological innovations suitable to its products and services. The technological emphasis is laid on modernization, technology for their survival and success.

To sum up, the success of cooperative business depends on the environmental information on economic, socio-cultural, political and legal, technological and ethical sub-systems of the external environment. The establishment of such environmental information system, which includes retrieval, analyzing, process and distribution of environmental information is essential to make valuable decision of environmental factors influencing the cooperative business. It will lead to the total success of a cooperative business positively.

COOPERATIVE ENVIRONMENTAL INFORMATION MANAGEMENT SYSTEM (COOPENVIMS) FOR ENVIRONMENT PROTECTION AND CONSERVATION

Cooperatives cover all aspects of human life. They are particularly strong in agricultural, consumer, housing, credit, workers, transport, and fisheries, and in many other areas in the countries of Asia-Pacific region. Agricultural cooperatives in Japan, sugar and dairy cooperatives of India have created a large variety of services for members besides giving them generous economic returns.

A Cooperative enterprise is a form of organization created to meet the needs of the community, in a given situation, without exploitation, as a value-based institution, committed to build a social order characterized by equity, equality and distributive justice. Cooperative enterprises provide the organizational means whereby a significant proportion of humanity is able to take its own hands the tasks of creating productive employment, overcoming poverty and achieving social integration. Being a socio-economic institution, cooperatives try to look after both the economic satisfaction and satisfaction of social needs of the members and the community as a whole. More the use of services of the cooperatives, higher is the outflow of social services leading to a stronger social integration in the community.

The qualities such as self-confidence, human dignity, security and a sense of belonging are central to social order, democracy and peace. Cooperatives are the vital component of a civil society with strong ties to local communities. As stated earlier, cooperatives are both economic and social in character – they are business enterprises with a deep sense of social and environmental responsibility.

The cooperatives could strengthen our democratic fibre and are the most effective instruments of socio-economic, cultural transformation and environmental protection *(Sharma M.L 1998)*. "Save Democracy" is the etiquette of cooperatives which also stress about "save nature", "save trees to save man" to protect the environment *(Editorial, TNJC 1991)*. With their tremendous wide range of activities in the field of production, processing, distribution and all other areas, cooperatives have a significant role to play in the protection and conservation of environment. The reason is that the programme of environmental conservation and protection cannot be expected without the mass support of the people. Cooperatives in India cover almost every village in the country and more than 95 percent of the rural population. They also exist in almost every important sector of the economy in urban areas. Thus, they have a direct access to a large population and it is easy to muster the public support for the implementation of environmental conservation and protection programme to a grand success.

"Concern for Community" is one of the cooperative principles. It is, therefore, natural to expect that they should encourage proactive stance on the environment protection and take interest in its conservation and protection for the larger interest of the community. However, since cooperatives are user-member driven enterprise, they may take up those issues which are common to both the members as well as the community such as environment, health, youth and women welfare, care for the aged and children, etc. Realising that the cooperatives "existing for the benefit of their members" the ICA in its statement on Cooperative Identity has emphasized that the cooperatives "have a special responsibility to ensure that the development of their communities – economically, socially and culturally – is sustained". Broadening the scope of cooperatives' work the statement adds that they "have a responsibility to work steadily for the environment protection of those communities".

It is noteworthy to state that cooperatives in various countries are engaged in the protection of environment directly or indirectly. The forest cooperatives in Canada, forestry and wood cooperatives in the Americas and other European countries, and Kobe earth-quake resistance services / disaster management cooperative in Japan are appealing in the activities related to the environmental issues. As for India, sugar cooperatives in Maharashtra took the lead in providing various community and environmental services in their area of operation. They have established schools, colleges, hospitals, gymnasia, etc., benefiting not only their members but also the public at large. They have constructed roads for making transportation easier for the farmers *(Sharma, M.L., 1996)*. The Bajpur and Nadehi sugar cooperatives have also contributed towards the same social developmental activities and they have installed equipment to check environmental pollution *(Veera Nabar 2000)*. Hospitals and medical college are the remarkable contributions made in Kerala alongside the action plan given for the community health through cooperatives by Smita Nair *(1994)*. In Tamilnadu housing cooperatives are running colleges, polytechnics, ITIs, and rendering environmental services for better being of the community. Gradually other cooperatives like IFFCO entered the field and are rendering laudable service to the environmental development programmes of their communities. IFFCO has covered over 1150 villages where it is providing service like family welfare, adult education, child care, medical and veterinary check ups, tree planting, sanitation campaigns, etc. Further, to contribute to environment protection, IFFCO has afforesting more than 4000 hectares of wasteland and social forestry *(Sharma, M.L. 1997)* and in Tamilnadu it is advocated to start forestry cooperatives and social forestry schemes in order to control pollution and environment *(Ramanujam K.N. 2000)*. KRIBHCO has diversified into bio-fertilizer since 1995 and also in the area of seed multiplication programme. Bio-diversity conservation through ground level cooperatives and Bio-diversity Cooperative Commonwealth is propounded for joint pricing as well as sharing of the bio-diversity wealth *(Khushalani. A.V and K. Kavita 1999)*.

The Cooperative land development banks are doing wonderful environmental services by means of advancing loans for minor irrigation projects (sinking of wells and energizing water-lifting devices) and major irrigation projects (soil reclamation, land leveling, bunding, field channels, etc.). These banks can render a lot of constructive services to the water management *(Chandra Mohan, 1999)*. The banks have also made a beginning in financing forestry as part of afforestation and development of wastelands. Financing to farmers for utilization of scarce ground water resources and management has been done by the Mulukanoor cooperative in Andhra Pradesh *(Veera Nabar, 2000)*. The increasing awareness on environment and rehabilitation of large dams, of Project Affected Persons (PAPs) has led to a rediscovery of a useful base and purpose for cooperatives – organizing PAPs into cooperatives to demand, manage and exploit the reservoirs for fishing, tourism and entertainment *(Sunil and Smita, 1996)* as also the community dugwells in Orissa *(Mallik, 1996)*, a lift based canal irrigation system in Andhra Pradesh *(Shah, 1996)*, and fisheries with eco-friendly technology for pollution control and income generation through the Mudiali Fisherman Cooperative Society in Kolkatta *(Datta 1996)*. Evidences are there about cities for all by housing cooperatives in developing countries to curtail social and environmental problems so as to have safe environment *(Khurana M.L., 1999)*. This shows that cooperatives have helped in the overall development of rural and urban areas, alongside have helped ameliorate the welfare of the community and protect the environment.

Cooperative Environmental Information Management System (COOPENVIMS)

Cooperatives may adopt the policy of three R's viz., Reduce, Reuse and Recycle to encourage environment upkeep and protection through sustainable consumption pattern. Their objective should be to encourage production and consumption patterns, which would reduce environmental stress. They need to educate individual consumers and organizational consumers to make purchase decisions of environment friendly. Although cooperative movement has a large scope to contribute efforts towards protection of environment, the vast size of the cooperative movement in India cannot be taken too seriously because it is rather a weak movement barring sectors like milk, sugar and fertilizer, which are its strong segments. The absence of proactive management in most cooperatives has been responsible for their callous attitude towards this important concern of extreme social significance. This would need an information system and advertising campaigns, descriptive labeling beamed at various consumer segments called Cooperative Environment Information Management System (COOPENVIMS).

The Cooperative Environmental Information Management System (COOPENVIMS), which integrates descriptive information (metadata) and data, is a system to capture, store, manage, and distribute information about environmental resources collected, developed, and used by cooperatives and its state and regional partners. COOPENVIMS may be established as a part of cooperative movement and a separate wing of National Cooperative Union of India to have integrated approach to the management of metadata about scientific resources produced or used by the cooperatives.

COOPENVIMS may be developed in response to the increasingly complex nature of environmental assessments. Today's assessments require the integration of human and ecological data and utilize data collected at multiple spatial and temporal scales. The assessments typically involve multiple information management systems and numerous researchers located in geographically dispersed work sites. Successfully completing environmental assessments requires the development of shared inventories of information that support finding and evaluating the information resources for secondary use.

Environment Management Capacity Building Technical Assistant Project as in ENVIS of the Government of India may be launched for the purpose of providing with information on various aspects of the environment besides giving details about the state of environment, the rich biodiversity of the nation and other environmental activities undertaken in our country through a web based information system.

Objectives of COOPENVIMS

The objectives of COOPENVIMS are:

- To Create web Based databases on the state of environment and its conditions of all regions.
- To establish Cooperative Environment Queries Clearing House to answer environmental queries
- To establish linkages with environmentalist, researchers, experts and public, and other related national and international organisations at large through Knowledge Centres for Environment Protection (KCEP).
- To identify environmental Information/data gaps and design action plan needed to fill these gaps to have stress-free environment.
- To make arrangements for dissemination of Environmental Information to be reached to the public.
- To present 'Environment Report' periodically to provide a benchmark for future environmental reporting and also serve as the database for policy making and preparation of environmental management plans.
- Formulation of suitable management measures through Environmental Management Pan (EMP) for amelioration of adverse impacts.

Green Cooperatives

In order to achieve the objectives of the COOPENVIMS, Green Cooperatives may be organized specially for offering / rendering the environmental services to the community. The Green Cooperatives may render services in the following environmental conservation and protection activities / areas:

Agricultural - Animal Production - Crop Production - Forestry

Building - Private Office Building - Public Office Building - Warehouse - Historic/Monument - Museum

Defense Site - Air Force Base - Coast Guard Station - National Guard Base - Defense Site

Development - Subdivison - Trailer Park - Apartments/ Townhouses - Office Development - Industrial Development -

Medical Facility - Commercial Development - Educational Facilities

Industrial - Degreasing Facility - Coal Gas Facility - Chemical Plant - Power Plant - Wood Treatment Facility - Other Industrial Plant

Miscellaneous - Construction - Church/Synagogue/Temple/ Mosque - Undeveloped Property - Unclassified - Other

Park/Golf - State Park - Private Park - Private Open Space - Public Open Space - County Park - Local Park - Nature Preserve - Golf Course

Recycling - Tire Pile - Salvage Yard - Other Recycling Residential - Single Family

Residential - Multiple Family Residential Retail - Dry Cleaner - Garage/Auto Body Shop - Gasoline Station - Other

Transportation - Railroad - Port/Marina - Airport - Highway

Waste - Dredge Spoil Disposal - Debris Disposal Area - Landfill-Municipal/Industrial - Contaminated Marsh - Spill Site - Contaminated Backfill - Dump-Unathorized - Drum Storage/ Disposal Area - Waste Transfer Station

Waste Water - Sewage Treatment Plant - Spray Irrigation Treatment - Combined Sewer Overflows

Water Production - Agricultural Water Production - Drinking Water Production

Wildlife Area - National Wildlife Area - Artifical Reefs - State Wildlife Area - Private Wildlife Area.

Environmental protection programmes aimed to create environmental awareness and a change in the attitudes in the society with the main objective of making the people to understand environmental awareness and education bring them into direct contact with the environmental problems facing the society that they live and make them think of solutions. The role of cooperative movement in this field of environment protection can be as follows *(Neb D.P., 1997)*:

- Cooperatives are engaged in production, processing, fertilizers and so on, and it is their sense of duty not to harm or disturb the environment;

- through the network of cooperative education and training facilities they should sensitize their members, directors, leaders, employees and the public about the environment related issues with the hope for transformation of man and society through cooperative way of doing things *(Jha.D and S.K.Jha 1998)*;
- environment protection fund may be allocated from the net profit of cooperatives so as to enable them to advocate in favour of environmental protection and conservation; and
- they may frame and adopt appropriate policies for encouraging eco-friendly business and services.

In order to trim cooperatives and make them fit for fighting the challenges calls for imperatives in the fields of improving productivity through proper utilization of resources such as raw material, manpower, capital, equipment, etc., to bring about reduction in wastes (rejections in inventories) and costs (overheads) so as to have competitive price and quality *(Chellappan, K. 1998)*. To create environmental awareness among the school and college students, "Cooperative Eco-Clubs" may be formed with the objectives (1) to educate the children about their immediate environment and causes for its deterioration; (2) to impart knowledge on the concepts of eco systems through field visits and demonstrations; (3) to mobilise students towards scientific enquiry into environmental problems; (4) to involve them in efforts to preserve environment.

In addition to above all, the Ministry of Environment and Forests, while refining the National Environment Policy, may consider cooperatives to play a major role in the protection and conservation of environment and due weightage may be given to implement environmental awareness programmes and other related activities as cooperatives are being the prime and effective instruments of the Government.

To sum up, with the mass support the cooperatives should engage themselves in the environmental protection and conservation process by establishing a COOPENVIMS is the need of the hour. COOPENVIMS is a set up responsible primarily for imparting knowledge and educating the members, leaders and officials of various cooperatives throughout the nation on the need and importance to conserve and save environment. Similarly, employees also need to be sensitized to environmental issues and their role with reference to their job in the enterprise so that they are able to answer questions on environmental aspects of goods and machinery produced, handled or sold by them. This will enable the entire cooperative effort takers, through COOPENVIMS, to make the people to have a clean and green environment of their own towards cent percent eco-friendly business and service system.

COOPERATIVE LEGAL INFORATION SYSTEM

It is generally accepted fact that the executives in an organization spend their major time of their office work through passing information. Cooperative enterprise is no exception to this. Information channel is a means by which cooperative ideologies; principles, objectives and practices are disseminated. People's mind is molded to come under cooperative fold, behavior is modified, information is made productive, resources are unified, human activities are directed and ultimately objectives of a cooperative enterprise are accomplished. From cradle to grave information channel is needed at every stage and without transfer o information any cooperative effort is impossible.

Cooperative Legal Information System

Cooperative Legal information system (CLIS) can be defined as a system which encompasses legal aspects or provisions of the cooperative societies Act, Rules and byelaws and other related/relevant circulars or materials for the development of the cooperative sector. Data regarding to legal aspects of cooperatives may be gathered from various sources of both internal and external environment by assessing the legal information needs, analysis and processing of such information and distributing of such information and distributing legal information cab be called as cooperative Legal information can be called as cooperative Legal Information System.

A couple of postulated of CLIS will provide perspective:

CLIS feeds upon input:

- **Some of that input comes from the outside environment**

- Some of that inputs comes from the output of the internal environment itself.

CLIS produce out put

- Some of that output is delivered to the outside environment.
- Some of that output is fed back to the input end of the CLIS that produced it.

At this juncture, cooperatives should establish an information system for retrieving, storing, processing and distributing the legal information to members, employees, policy-makers and external worlds for enabling them to act upon the defied legal provisions of cooperatives (see Fig. 15.1).

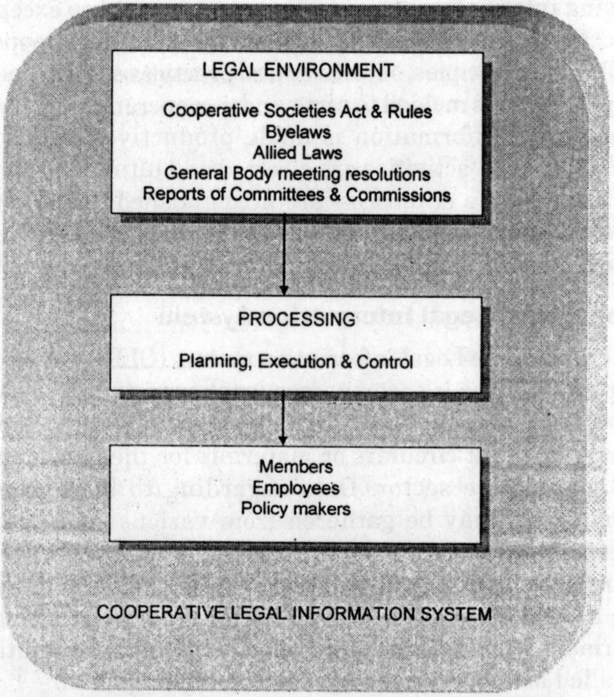

Fig. 15.1. Cooperative Legel Information System.

Sources of Legal Information in Cooperatives

A number of information sources are available for informing

legal aspects in a cooperative enterprise. They are mostly formal in nature and few informal one.

Cooperative societies Act and Rules

This is the legal status sanctioned by the state Government in respect of cooperative enterprises. A cooperative enterprise before assuming its function requires registration under the Act. The act and rules, play as legal information tools, lay down various provisions relating to registration, organization, re-organization amendment audit, inspection and liquidation. Hence knowledge of this information tool is essential for the management team of a cooperative enterprise.

Byelaws

Every cooperative enterprise must have its byelaws on the basis of its registration. It carries with it legal, administrative and financial sanction/ information of the registrar of cooperative societies. It deals legal information with all aspects of the organization.

Other Related acts and Rules

Cooperative business has entered into various fields like agriculture, production distribution, marketing, industry and on-trading activities. The government has enacted various acts such as Indian Contract Act, Indian Limitation Act, Indian Arbitration Act, Bonus Act, Wages Act Consumers Protection Act and such other acts which are related to cooperative business rules and regulations framed to direct and control those activities. Hence every types of cooperative must know these legal framework and business rules of external legal environment within which it has to work.

Resolutions passed in the General Body and Board Meetings

Cooperative enterprise's policy decisions and other important business decisions are being taken in various meeting convinced for the purpose. These processed information must be passed as legal decisions to the workers who are responsible for their implementation. The resolutions adopted in the meeting must be disseminated to the persons directly or indirectly concerned with these legal information.

Circulars, Orders of Instructions

Various circulars orders and instructions are issued by various sources guiding or directing various business activities of every cooperative enterprise. This information's of legal provisions are to be informed to the concerned workers.

Reports of Committees and Commissions

Legal information can be had from various reports of committees and commissions appointed by the government for the development of the cooperative system. These in formations must be taken into and circulated among various field of the cooperative sector.

TO WHOM LEGAL INFORMATION

Legal Information to Members

The members are the owners of the cooperative enterprise. Hence, they must get information about the principles and philosophy of cooperative objectives and benefits of cooperation and legal provisions on membership qualifications general body, participation in general body meetings, powers duties and responsibilities of members, etc. Dissemination of these information makes people know about the cooperative enterprises. This transmission of legal information does not end here These members in the owners capacity have to participate in the general body meeting review and approve past performance, to set future plans and policies and to decide various other issues based on such legal information for the successful operation of the cooperative enterprise.

Legal Information to Policy Makers

Board of directors are the elected management authorities by the members from among them. Legal information regarding the qualification and disqualifications of board members, functions of the board, term of office of the board, procedures for holding board meetings, cooption of the board, nomination, limit on the period of service, relationship between the board and executive, relationship between the board and members shall be informed and the board members should know such legal information as to act accordingly.

Legal Information to Employees

Employees are in constant need of information, instructions, opinions and counseling from recruitment followed by placement, organization operation, development and appraisal to final separation from the enterprise. The prevailing staff regulation and business rules, processes and procedures of work, division of power and functions, compensation and availability of various facilities in written form and their understanding are important areas of legal information communication with the employees. For which every cooperative enterprise must have special byelaws regarding the conditions of employees.

To conclude, the legal information my be canalized through conducting periodical review meetings, panel discussions and refresher programmers on legal aspects especially to the policy makers employees refresher programmers on legal aspects especially to the policy makers employees and members of a cooperative. Members meetings shall be convened once in three months so as to have broader discussions and deliberations on cooperative legal system and its provisions which have been revised of amended can be informed with. Panel discussions and refresher programmers shall be organized for the purpose of supplying information to the policy makers and employees on the recent amendments made which enables them to know and rely on the rules and regulations of cooperatives Seminars conferences and workshops are the useful media to exchange the views and expressions of experts with regard to legal aspects. Hence, through the above sources an effective legal information system for cooperatives can be established and it serves as an effective tool to maintain the follow of legal information.

15.4 COOPERATIVE COMMUNICTION SYSTEMS

This section attempts to relate communication, its sources and problems as they pertain to cooperatives and to dovetail the need for developing an information system, as a communication imperative in co-operatives. Both are considered as the two sides of the coin of organization and management of cooperatives.

Communication is a concept that has been in vogue in cooperative organizations ever since their inception, but perhaps not as effectively as the originators though it would be. In practice, it seems to have met with mixed functioning and mortality among o cooperative societies can be the lack of purposeful and efficient communication system in them. Major bottlenecks like resource constraints, the proliferation of cooperatives with inadequate understanding of the 'system' character of their organization and management and the measurement of their impact and development in India have all appeared to have conspired against better communication and information system in cooperative organizations. Lack of properly defined and developed communication system reflects is effective management and control of various types of cooperative activities. As rightly observed an efficient communication system in cooperatives "enables us to organize our resources, abilities and efforts in common Endeavour". Further more no organized activity and cooperative effort is possible without better communication among those engaged in it and between them and their environments.

Communication occurs only when the receives the same intellectual and emotive message which the sender sends; which means effective communication implies that the communicator, but also accept and comply with it. This has certain pre-conditions to it and can be applied to any communication structure in an organization, including the cooperatives. So for effective communication in co-operatives, the message needs carries:

(*i*) Clarity,

(*ii*) Brevity,

(*iii*) Precision,

(*iv*) Timeliness,

(*v*) Compass,

(*vi*) Integrity (etc.).

Cooperatives to-day have to pay continued attention to improving communication within the organization and with the out side world. Smooth flow of information to the management and the employer, and the members and feedback from them has assumed particular significance especially for management process. Continuously, innovative and imaginative Programmers having diverse dimensions have to be executed in response to the changing needs of the members who are influenced by constantly changing economic and social conditions. The recent development such as strong competitive forces etc, necessitate formulation of appropriate communication policies with a view to improving the percentage of active member participation in management, finance and business of cooperatives.

Advantage of Effective Communication in Co-operatives

An organized two-way functioning communication process has many advantages. It provides complete and specific data and guidance to management team. Policymaking is facilitated. Top management normally does not have in its absence, close touch with details of activities conducted in the field.

Reliable, important information fed through communication on a systematic basis can help in correct decision making and in its implement ensuring cooperation and support of all concerned employees, members etc.

Clarity, accuracy and relevance are the qualities that are required for successful communication process. Chances of communicating both ways are better when then process is taking place in a climate of belief (credibility). Communication programme must have relevance to the environment and provide for participation and play back. Content o communication also must be compatible with value system of the receivers. Clarity makes for unanimity in voice. Sense of responsibility for the system is another precondition for an effective communication system. This brings us to the need to develop information system in cooperatives.

The need for Communication and Information System in Cooperatives

Information system in cooperatives has of late around cont storable interest to cooperatives and cooperative management experts. The essential of better communication and information system in cooperative lies in both the demand side. Cooperatives do generate data while other in the role of department officials, planners and programme for cooperative development confront the problem of securing relevant and processed and complete information at the right time in the right place.

Cooperative organizations of different types are exposed every day to decision-making. Such a progress depends on accurate information. There is severe competing demand for financial and human resources in cooperatives and so the cooperative departments and organizations will do well to staff an information system equal to its decision-making need and requirements fro cooperative management and the effective functioning of the existing cooperative institutions in the State.

We may look at this problem of developing information wisely in support of the cooperative development efforts from three angles:

1. It must promote: Identification of the information required for most important decisions in the cooperative organizations, specifying the kind of information that deserves highest priority.
2. Utilization of the methods for collection, processing and analyzing data that are accurate, timely and adequate while at the same time minimization of the involved financial and human coasts.
3. Setting up of an institutional structure which helps to bring users and suppliers of information for a continuous dialog and which could adopt itself to economic changes and changing demands of information and new methods of generating it.

In any cooperative organization/ institutions the information system is a subsidiary set of the social system since the cooperative is part of the society and is organized to meet social/ economic and since it processes information relating to the social system for decision-making at the various levels of cooperative organizations. This process must accurately reflect the reality in finding useful information for decision-making. This depends on the degree to which measurement and data on the one hand, are complete with specification and testing of the analytical frame work on the other; which means that the suppliers (sources) of data must be in effective communication continuously with the users of information. Both political (policy oriented) and objective process must validate the information for any effective useful decision-making. Information is valuable and expensive. Cost of poor decision and subsequent lack of relevant information can be enormous. Returns to effective decision, both socially and economically can be large. So of information to these who effectively make decisions in cooperative is therefore the foundation of effective information management and strengthens the communication system in cooperatives.

Suppliers of Cooperative Information through Communication Systems

At the National level the information sources include the RBI, the NCUI, ICA, National level cooperative Federations, the ministry of cooperation and Vaikunthlal Mehta national Institute of cooperative management, at the state level statistical gathering units cooperative departments cooperative unions, state level cooperative Banks and federations colleges and universities may have their own information gathering sections to gather benchmark data and can supply processed information for top level policy makers at the National and state level such as planning commission, Government/key personnel.

Now-a-days the personnel of the Department of Cooperation and officials as well non-officials (both present and potential beneficiaries) are informed about cooperatives through newspapers, journals, booklets, pamphlets and other printed forms, notice board, circulars, personal letters, oral communication and radio broad-casting.

Problems in Communication in Cooperatives

Most of the misunderstanding, critical problems, and noticeable lass in cooperative are the results of lack of effective communication and poor appreciation of requirements of communication and in

1. *Perceptual differences:* Most of the misunderstandings and conflicts occur due to procedural differences. What seems to be sol vivid and clear to A,B, does not see at all. For eg. In consumer declining sales differently from the procurement manager. The salesman may view the problem from consumers view point.
2. *We hear what we expect to hear:* We generally hear what we expect to hear, and see what we expect to see. We

tend to block out the new information if it conflicts with our existing knowledge. for instance, in cooperative splinting mill, if employees perceive management as unfair, they interpret all management communication in that light, therefore when management emphasizes the need to cut costs in order to enable the institution to more management attempt to introduce one or the other efficiency device or to retime the job.

3. *Different management:* Words have different meanings to different people. Words like ('profit' surplus, efficiency mean different things to members and the society. When the marketing cooperative society announces that it will give 'high' prices to the produce on the basis of quality only, it means to farmer members to bring qualitative produces and to trader merchants it means an attempt to control the market price and so on. This difficulty in communication is compounded by the fact that most words have a variety of meanings.
4. *Motivation and interest:* It is difficult to get across a message to a person is not interested in it. In order to receive a communication the receiver should have interest in it. For instance, in Dairy cooperatives payment of milk price according its fat content has not yet brought the desired increased in the quality of milk of member-producers. It is just bewildered why milk producers do not try to make extra money, which they need. Milk producers on the other hand, do not respond to it because they are more interested in quantity than in the quality of milk.
5. *Source credibility:* When another person gives us any information or message, we tend to evaluate his credibility. If we conclude that the communicator is unreliable and his massage cannot be trusted, we tend to reject his communication. Our trust in the communicator depends on our past experience with him. For instance, special officers are appointed by replacing the elected board of directors for managing state and district/ big cooperative organizations in Tamilnadu in may of successful cooperatives now became doomed and

are in their death-bed and employees and members have lost their faith and trust with official/ special officers.

6. *Hidden agenda:* In may of the cooperatives, it was noticed that there was no cordial relation between the board (elected members) and the executive (paid officials) paid executives who are experts in knowledge and skill reveal some intrinsic point for decision-making in hidden words, This 'hidden agenda' in communication hampers the sharing of understanding between the sender and the receiver.

7. *Context:* Words have meaning only in context. Thus when the price of on item is a bit high in consumer cooperative society it has different meaning to consumers. Those who are having quality consciousness will construed the price in correct view and others may not.

8. *Hoarding:* Especially the persons who are in the helm-of-affairs of cooperatives derive a sense of power and prestige by helping information,. Some mangers have on instinctive morale and efficiency of the personnel.

9. *Information overload:* This screening and sifting of information materials coursed omissions and discretions. For instance, failure to communicate about declining milk collection in dairy cooperative union has aggravated the over cost.

10. *Pressure of time:* Executives, particularly those at higher levels, work under great pressure of time. They cannot afford to interest and communicate frequently with heir subordinates and members. This caused communication get between the higher and lower echelons and the members.

11. *Hierarchical differentiations:* Cooperative organization is usually structured as a pyramid with status and position differentiations among employees located at various levels. Organization structure also prescribes channel of communication along the liner of authority, which tends to structure and control the flow of communication. Explicit status differences such as

superiors and subordinator, high middle and lower level of management, operatives and managers etc, inhibitions in communication due to status differences tend to weaken communications. It flows more freely and is lass distorted if the superior-subordinate relations are characterized by mutual trust and confidence and the suppler is not statue conscious.

Strategies for Improving Communication Effectiveness

These barriers to effective communication exist in all organization in a greater or lesser extent. Distortions, delays and incomplete information adversely affect the speed effectiveness. Hence, major strategies for improving communication effectiveness area:

1. Creating of an environment of trust and confidence.
2. Be clean about the objective of communication.
3. Utilization of feedback.

Communication system is the base for information system and the messages that run through it constitute the life-giving stimulus to cooperative organization and management; ineffectiveness is any one of them will only point to the collapse of the total apparatus that makes for better trade-off decisions to optimize cooperative performance. It is recommended to have an effective communication system in cooperatives for designing and having a well-equipped information system for smooth flow of information.

COOPERATIVES PUBLIC RELATIONS SYSTEMS

We all need to do exercise in respect of our role function in media relations. First of we all have to assess our present and future activities. We must study our product. What are we broadly doing? What is our future plans? What are new products we are trying to develop? Everyone is in search of new things today. It is not that people want only new soaps and detergents. They as well want innovations in credit, new services, refinements in credit, new services, refinements in present practices. We must therefore jot down activates vis-a-vis a message we want to communicate which will sustain human interest.

1. **Where are we in the minds of target audience?** We need to have an insight into how much the target audience is aware of our presence in the market, Hence perception mapping of the target audience is the first priority before taking up any step. They may know us only vaguely. Our functions and activities and how we work remains largely unknown.
2. **Where are we in the environment?** What are our financial base and an established clientele, and government provided authority Competition. Today may be slowly penetrating, but one but one day we may finally find it challenging. The current level of awareness about our presence in the market is extremely low.
3. **Why are we there?** Media as a matter of fact is quite passive to the sector in which we are working. Naturally, we get a very moderate media coverage. Hardly do we occur on the front page. The scene in the electronic media is even far gloomy.
4. **Where do we go from here?** We have been already reaching a huge target audience through our work, what is lacking is to make it known, that it is we who had been engaged in the development process. We need to behave like a more corporate organization, be more business like. The sector today intends to diversity its activates and broad-base its services, but these efforts can be more fruitful if we have a high visibility in the economy. The desired mindset of the target audience would be that we are commonly and specially widely known as the trendsetter and leader. For people who know you well tend to think well about you.
5. **How do we get there?** The desired goal being high visibility we need to identify such channels and media options which are of relevance to us.

AVAILABLE OPTIONS FOR MEDIA STRATEGY

The Press

The Press enables us to reach out to various categories of external public. Ranging from financial dailies, to general and regional dailies-the press covers a huge audience. Though we have been dealing with them, it is mostly an occasional reference. What is required is a more human interest based, orientation to our newsworthy material. An effective packaging of our items is required which give them some news value.

Some of the steps that can be taken in this regard are:

Success stories with local and mass appeal which influence the general readership and evoke general interest can be brought to the attention of the media. Till now we have maintained a shy character, and would keep our dfficials from coming into the limelight. This requires a definite shift, and we need to give up our conservative attitude. For, when we are doing good work, we need to shout about it and make it known to the people.

Another good way to keep ourselves news, is to bring out various research findings we intend to implement, to the attention of the media. Generally people take a lot of interest in reading items that are substantiated research.

The Electronic Media

The same applies to the electronic media, which today has become a powerful medium, with so many channels booming up.

We have to initiate panel discussions on desired topics and also participate in channel discussions regularly without fear. A programme like magazine on agriculture for DD can be conceived. Such a regular TV programme at a prime time will go a long way in boosting the image.

Radio

Radio is still popular in certain areas. We must make use of this avenue.

The Internet

The last couple of years has seen the emergence of websites by corporates. Because of its interactive character, the medium has great public relations potential to build corporate image and attract the best talent. We can have user friendly website with precise information, which catches the attention of the visitor. It need to give an all comprehensive information about the organisation, what work it is doing the way media is covering it, the way people can participate in the rural development activity. Further adequate publicity needs to be given to the website.

Film/Video/Mobile Vans

Videotapes can be use for communication with a variety of publics like employees, members, specially invited audiences or the general public during exhibitions. The latter medium has become a potent platform to attract effective media and public attention. An attractive stall with large screens or video film attracts lot of attention. We can also attempt to use mobile vans for the purpose. These vans can come about as an effective medium to reach out directly to the rural people with the kind of programmes they will be interested in.

Direct Mall

Direct mall in some circumstances is very powerful and most cost effective. It uses the postal service to deliver the messages to a selected target audience. In fact, it is one of the best selective marketing techniques. The banks can consider to start a small journal to reach the targetted audience regularly.

Press Conference

Regular press conferences by the chairmen /Chief Executives can help better press relations.

Press Tours/Facility Visits

In Press tours or facility visits, much of the exercise is similar to organising a press conference. Such tours facilitate an in-depth study of the projects and the issue gets better coverage by the media.

Special Events

Special events are the visible component of a community relation's programme. Special event can range from participating in a community related activity related activity to sponsoring a local event. The India Tobacco Company (ITC) for instance organizes a music concert every year known as ITC Sangeet

Sammelan. The banks also can consider organizing such annual events at district places.

Seminars and Symposium/ Meets

The rural farm audience whom we are catering to should be informed of the various programmes that exist for them street theatre with a local appeal can ply a useful role in conveying the message directly to the people. We can take the help of some local agency or NGO for spreading information among the masses. The same can be effective medium in urban areas if planned properly with involvement of the media. This needs to be done through local celebrities.

Information Desk and Kiosks

Another tool to reach out to the people is establishing into desks in rural and semi-urban areas. Many people want to know about various schemes of the banks, but they do not have the means to go about it.

Cooperative Public relations Systems must be established at all levels to publicize and propagate the cooperative basics, principles, values and philosophy among stakeholders of cooperatives. The information systems play a vital role in dissemination of cooperative principles and values among all stakeholders of cooperatives. Proper public relations system should be evolved for creating awareness among stakeholders about cooperatives, building cooperative image and maintenance of the same.

16

MIS Applications in Cooperatives

COMPUTER APPLICATIONS IN MANAGEMENT AND ADMINSISRATION OF COOPERATIVES

At present, cooperatives have emerged as an important segment of the Indian economy. Today this movement consists of 3.65 lakh cooperatives of various types at different levels consisting of about 200 million members and its working capital amounting to Rs. 700 thousand million. Emphatically Indian cooperative system is doing very useful and remarkable services to the entire population of India.

The gist of this paper is an attempt made to explicitly employ and inculcate the culture of computers in Indian cooperative system. In the modern age of computers and advanced technology the application of computers in cooperative sector is to some extent negligible and as such modern sophistication has no even entered into the premises of our cooperatives, more especially at lower level and medium level of the cooperative structure.

The then president of NCUI Thiru. B.S. Viswanathan in his article "Challenges of cooperatives in next decades has mentioned cooperatives to become relevant should modernize by introducing computers in their offices". This must be taken in the right spirit and right direction to make cooperatives get strengthened from and face head-on the competition of other organizations. In the year 1989 NCUI had introduced the National Cooperative Data Bank and which can be utilized by all cooperative institutions. NCDC is yet another apex institution which is providing financial assistance for computerization and it must be utilized by our cooperatives.

There is a vast scope for the application of software in the management and administration of cooperatives. In the modern competitive banking business system as a result of globalization/ privatization for the survival of the cooperative banks at district and urban level is highly imperative, therefore, the use of computers is widely felt. Computerization has to receive the due focus in cooperative to compete effectively with other organizations. Following these, need based phenomenon, state level marketing federation and consumer federation, housing societies, marketing cooperatives, Engineering cooperatives. Weaving societies and dairy cooperatives have enlisted the used of computers in their day to day affairs.

In Indian scenario the entire computer industry is dependent upon the private companies for the supply of computer and software. In this situation, it is paramount that the state Government must take necessary and action-oriented steps to launch one special type of computer cooperative, which may encompasses the specific objective of (*i*) offering computer education and training to the employees of cooperatives; (*ii*) Undertaking DTP and offset work to print books and forms for cooperatives; (*iii*) Information services through network; (*iv*) supplying computer software technology for various types of cooperatives; and (*v*) selling computers and peripherals to them at reasonable/ affordable cost and maintain those computers in due course.

This will eventually lead to the development of cooperatives at all levels and therefore make the movement as sound enough in the country.

WHO-WHAT OF COMPUTER CO-OPERATIVE SET-UP

Cooperatives have to fall in line and take full advantage of technical development for their efficient working and they should fine-tune themselves to face the new technological changes and challenges. In connection with the adoption of new software technology, cooperatives should think of the following bricks, to be strengthened, for building cooperative system as effectives:

(*i*) Professionals available with the system; (*ii*) Software availability; (*iii*) Network for information services; (*iv*) Dealers to supply computers and peripherals and maintenance of such devices.

It is essential to have sufficient number of professionals with computer knowledge and efficiency while cooperatives are being computerized. Application of essential approaches such as in service training programmer, practical training programmer may be conducted by the proposed special types of cooperative to the following target groups:

- Board of Directors,
- Executives,
- Delegates and Branch Officials,
- Mangers Secretaries,
- Accountant,
- Internal Auditors, and
- Stores Clerks.

Special courses like seminars, workshop, management games etc., are to be organized with the main objective of providing exposure to the personnel of various types of cooperatives emphasizing on the latest software technology and computer technology.

Cooperatives must be capable of developing their own soft wares in different fields and activities. Based on the nature and scope of activities, soft wares are to be drafted. It is worthwhile to note that already designed software are amply available in the market for various fields like banking housing, engineering, consumers etc. However, serious and competent cooperative institutions should avail and modify those software's such that it can be operated easily by the personnel already in the cooperative movement.

COOPERATIVE BANKING

All the District Central cooperative Bank branches can be connected with the registered office. Such a network facilities are also available nowadays in modern computers. This will help the cooperative banks to offer useful and speedy services to the customers. Moreover, the administrative authorities would be able to know the deposit position, advances position and over dues status if any, and daily operations of the various branches can be easily known in a fraction of seconds.

The table below shows the computer facilities utilized by the existing co-operative banks in India.

Computer Facilities Utilised in the Co-operative Banking Sector

Banks	*Number*	*No. of Offices*
Centra Co-operative Banks	361	11787
State co-operative Banks	28	742
State co-operative Agricultural and Rural Development Banks	19	1048
Primary Co-operative Agricultural Rural Development Banks	-	732
Primary Co-operative Banks Including Urban Bank	-	1715

Sources: Indian co-operative movement a profile-by NCUI 1994-95.

Followed by the DCCB, state Cooperative land development banks, primary agricultural cooperative banks and urban cooperative banks can also utilize software in the long run. Now the number has been increased to an expected level.

The move to computerize the cooperative operation would also help to check ever growing frauds, irregularities, mismanagement and malmiministration at the same time to stamp-out corruption in the cooperative banking sector or otherwise.

Unless cooperative banks adopt the latest available software technology in banking operations they cannot stand the competition by other sections of Banking Industry. Cooperative Banking should move alongside other commercial Banks During Karnataka Urban Cooperative bank's workshop pertaining on MICR (Magnetic Ink Character Recognition) Technology of cheques clearing system, Mr. Narasimhan Rajagopal both of the MICR Technology which helps sorting at the rate of 1700 to 2000 cheques per minute as against the time consuming manual handling hitherto in vogue. The average volume of instruments processed per day is around 2 lakh in Chennal and Calcutta, 3 lakh in delhi and around 5 to 6 lakhs in Mumbai, according to the RBI. From these, we can accrue the most desirable services of compute Technology, therefore enhance the Efficiency, Effectiveness, Performances of cooperative banking system in India.

The areas which may be taken into consideration while developing soft wares for cooperative banking sector are as follows:

Savings Banks and Current A/C

- Cash Credit and Over Draft A/c
- Clearing
- Bills
- Other loan
- Jewel loan
- Agricultural loans
- Draft A/c
- Establishment and
- Other modules like, Share A/c, Furniture, stationery, locker, MIS and other Banks A/c
- Non-performing Asset position Statement (weekly/ monthly)
- Monthly statement for Apex institutions.

CONSUMER STORES AND MERCHANDISING

Suppose, if a cooperative super market in a city is fully computerized it will be very easy for them to know the cash credit utilization present stock available on various items funds position and cash flow also precisely ascertained. In certain super markets "walkout by customers" due to non availability of certain items will be avoided by using computers. The daily sales, sales of fast-moving items, non-moving items are also known to the authorities in a fraction of second. This will improve the performance of the super market by taking proper, correct, short-term and long-term decision-making.

HOUSING COOPERATIVES

Software like AutoCAD visual solid state are already available in the market and that can be utilized in housing cooperatives to draft site plan building plan and allied activities related to the same. These will boost the overall performance of the housing cooperative institutions.

ENGINEERING COOPERATIVES

AutoCAD' is very much useful in drafting designs for various type of machinery and tools used by cooperatives.

MARKETING COOPERATIVES

Essentially in today's highly competitive and sophisticated marketing world marketing orientation and functions posses a challenging scenario especially in the Administration and Management in terms shouldering heavy positional managerial responsibilities. In the case of private enterprises and undertaking, thy are mainly concerned, urged to maximize profits continuously as a driving force. But in the case of cooperative, the situation is extremely different. Having this backdrop in mind, it is essential for the computer cooperative to tailor their operations keeping the basic tenets of cooperative principles and management, hence stimulate demand and supply of marketing services to their clients. Information regarding demand and supply of agricultural produce can be crated, retrieved and supplied by marketing cooperatives to its member farmers through cooperative network. Nafed is having its own website for agriculture for supplying information in the field of agriculture and allied activities to the state, district and grassroots level cooperatives.

Business sector is basically an information intensive sector. The main source for a business success is "accurate and reliable information". It has a systematic process of collecting sources for information input and processing of data and getting output levels of management.

For this purpose an information service provider may be started. The role of such wing may be as follows:

(*i*) Collect source of information from different environment,

(*ii*) Processing of such data; and

(*iii*) Supplying of information to the needy cooperatives

The Taminadu Hon'ble Chief Minister had announced launching of 100 community Internet centres all over TamiNadu. Out of which a number of centers may be allotted to the cooperative in each district, therefore strict follow-up to this effect is highly desirable. Cooperative Network system will result in rendering the services like cooperative education and extension to the rural people about the cooperative, business operations, information regarding all fields of cooperative system, employment position and opportunities, marketing strategies and up to date statistics related to cooperative enterprise. The proposed computer cooperative can supply computers to the cooperatives at a reasonable price and sustainable rates. Hardware and software engineers are to be recruited for the purpose of maintaining the computers of cooperatives and developing soft wares respectively. Outlet for computer peripherals may be started in order to satisfy the needs of cooperative system and enterprises.

To sum up, suitable software for each and every type of cooperatives will be developed with the assistance of computer professionals of the proposed computer cooperative. Now-days the cost of computers are relatively cheap and all the cooperative institutions can afford to pay for this new device. If it is so cooperative should be in a position to computer with other organizations and therefore more service will be rendered at the possible earliest time to their members especially to the peoples of rural India who are the immediate members of rural-oriented cooperative institutions. This technology is no only to develop cooperative but to potentially educate the rural people through cooperative computer Network. For the purpose of organizing a special type of cooperative dealing with computer technology a comprehensive feasibility study for software cooperative system must be conducted and this shall pave the path for the emerging cooperative and place it in a sound footing in the future once for all.

IT AS A TOOL FOR SUSTAINABLE DEVELOPMENT OF COOPERATIVE SECTOR

This millennium heralds the emergence of new paradigms that will keep pace with a world rapidly changing under the impact of development in info-tech. IT's millennium bunch comprises the entrepreneurs, the innovators and the visionaries on the side of the both industry and government. The entrepreneurial environment has changed rapidly as we are entered the millennium. What does this change means for cooperative entrepreneur? What strategies would enable them to cope with emerging challenges? How can cooperative entrepreneurs recreate and remodel themselves to benefit from new opportunities and retain relevance of cooperatives.

Cooperative Sector and IT

Cooperative sector continues to occupy an important place in India's economy. In the fast growing and changing economic scenario in the context of economic reforms, liberalization and globalization, the cooperative sector can no longer afford to be indifferent to the cost effectiveness and commercial orientation in recent days. Against the aforesaid backdrop, if the cooperative sector is to equip itself to operate energetically in the face of the competitive pressure of an open market, it will have to rise to the occasion to convert the challenges on the fronts of IT into opportunities to its advantage. Application of IT in business in developed countries is rapid and dynamic, but in developing countries like India is relatively slow due to number of inter-related socio-economic and cultural factors.

The IT is now a buzzword in business organization. It has significant contribution towards profitability and providing value added services to customers. Rapid technological developments both in terms of computer hardware and software have made their use simple, user-friendly and cost-effective. That is why the negative attitude of not using computers (resistance) in the work places is being absorbed into business organisation more and more gradually.

IT for Sustainable Development of Cooperatives

Cooperative movement is one of the important segments of economic growth. In cooperatives, entrepreneur is one who has the initiative, skill for innovation and who looks for high achievements. Cooperative entrepreneur should always search for change, respond to it, and exploit it as opportunities. The challenges facing cooperative entrepreneur is to increase the effectiveness of IT in order to achieve superior business performance. As successful organizations have taken a process-oriented view of their business, they will have to re-evaluate the role of IT in terms of alignment with corporate goals.

Cooperative entrepreneurs must come to term to with shorter product technology life cycles. Rapid changes to product and process pose a huge challenge. Can the cooperatives afford to the high cost of development and keep pace with technology? How should cooperative entrepreneurs respond? Finally as customers/members expectations and life cycles change, quality (or reliance) as a measure of product quality will become a given. The ability to innovate and product designs and to create and satisfy emerging needs will distinguish the winners from the losers. While all these factors represent challenges to cooperative entrepreneurs, they also represent opportunities that will arise. In such a competitive environment, IT helps the cooperatives to meet the challenges and exploit the opportunities. For which, the cooperatives should modernize their operations adopting modern IT techniques. If cooperatives adopt new technologies of IT they can face the challenges and make them opportunities to exploit. The following strategies can be made through IT adoption by the cooperatives:

- Customers / members focus and mass customization
- Differential supply, core competencies and shared services
- Measurement of member service quality through new standards
- Improvement and quality and productivity
- Generation of data for control and MIS
- Proper planning, monitoring and control of business
- Reduction in operating cost in long run, etc.

To conclude, IT can be used as a tool for sustainable development of cooperative business and provide them with more information to generate new opportunities to exploit.

Executive and innovative use of IT to create the right kind of information from its knowledge base that is associated with technology can create value that can provide the competitive edge. Advance It releases a potent set of possibilities for cooperative business improvement with implications for the psychological experience of work, the nature of skills, social integration and the strategic framework for commercial and managerial policies. Cooperatives should go for new models that allow cooperative business to do things quite differently. Mass customization is a technique that allows customers/members to visit a manufacturer's website and specify the exact requirements. Dealers / distributors (branches) of goods and services can use the Internet to interact with officials whom they do business. In this line, IT as a tool can play for the sustainable development of cooperatives.

16.3 MIS IN FEDERAL COOPERATIVES

A federal or federated cooperative is a cooperative owned by other cooperatives. Control and flow of information and benefits between the federated cooperative and its member cooperatives corresponds to that between members and their local. Local cooperatives elect (through their board or elected delegates) the board of the federated cooperative and receive benefits in proportion to their patronage with the federated cooperative.

Directors may represent geographic districts or they may represent a combination of members and managers. The number of voting delegates may be one per cooperative, or it may be based on membership size or business volume with the federation. Federated cooperatives are organized and controlled from the bottom up. The passing of information to the member cooperatives depends to a large degree on the effectiveness of member communications through information systems. The information flow within a federal cooperative is based on the framework of MIS in cooperatives. The structure of the federal cooperative may vary from one type of cooperative form to another. Based on the nature and type of the federal cooperative the departments and sections may vary and the MIS framework can be designed and developed. Having the MIS in a federal cooperative can pass the information to other external systems. The MIS model that can be followed in a federal cooperative is presented in hereunder.

MIS Model for a federal Cooperative

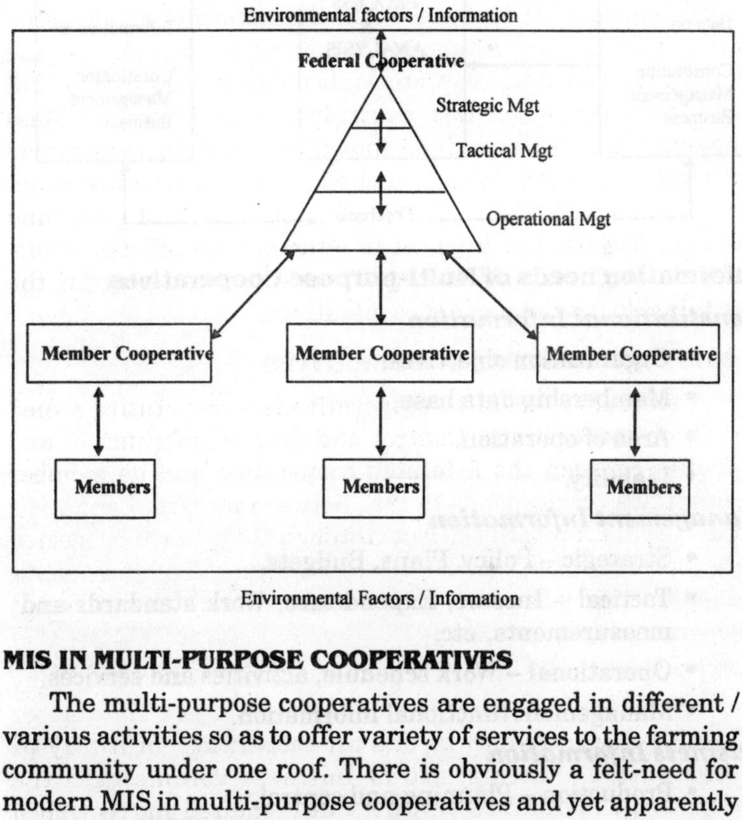

MIS IN MULTI-PURPOSE COOPERATIVES

The multi-purpose cooperatives are engaged in different / various activities so as to offer variety of services to the farming community under one roof. There is obviously a felt-need for modern MIS in multi-purpose cooperatives and yet apparently no effective MIS at the cooperative level is in operation. The various reasons identified for this are:

- No genuine interest in MIS,
- Little knowledge of MIS,
- Difficulties in collection of data.
- Cost of installation and maintenance is not affordable.

The recommended application of MIS in multi-purpose cooperatives is given in the following chart.

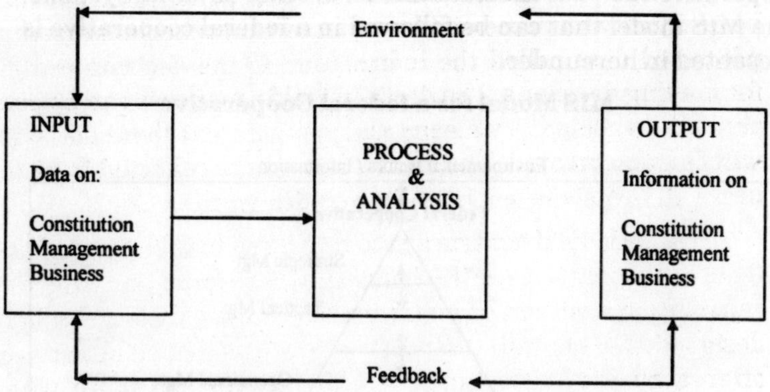

Information needs of Multi-purpose Cooperatives

Constitutional Information

- Organization objectives,
- Membership data base,
- Area of operation,
- Liability.

Management Information

- Strategic – Policy, Plans, Budgets,
- Tactical – Income, Expenditure, Work standards and measurements, etc.
- Operational – Work schedule, activities and services,
- Management functional information.

Business Information

- Production – Planning and control,
- Market – Product, Price, Physical distribution, Promotion, Power & Public relations,
- Service mix – Purchasing / pooling of agricultural produces, distribution of fertilizers & other inputs / seeds, PDS, credit facilities, supply of improved implements, marketing of produces and other related activities.

From both the internal and external sources the data can be collected by the multi-purpose cooperatives with regard to constitution, management and business. The collected data can be analyzed and processed based on certain criteria for feeding processed data called the information to the decision centers for making decisions. The decision making process can be done through participatory means and methods and those decisions will be implemented. The feedback has to be collected from the users at various levels in order to redesign the MIS.

The periodical reports are to be passed to the regional and federal cooperatives. MIS helps in this regard and effective reporting system can be maintained by having installed a well-designed MIS in multi-purpose cooperatives. Since the services offered by the multi-purpose cooperatives are more when compare to other types of cooperatives, it is a felt-need to have an efficient and effective MIS. As part of information system the multi-purpose cooperatives may have the information kiosks (multimedia machines), which supply agriculture information (crop production details, seasonal details, crop protection measures, pest control system, rainfall, price information, market information, etc.) to the farmers.

MIS APPLICATIONS IN COOPERATIVE BANKS

Need for MIS in Cooperative Banks

As the banking industry is information intensive, the most important resources the banks deal in apart from cash is "information". As such information is the key result area in banks. Hence, monitoring the information resources has become an important task before the banks. Also, as the cooperative banks have distinctive features compare to other banks, the information resource need to be handled through a well-designed MIS.

The following conditions warrant a scientific MIS for cooperative banks:

- Information is required at all levels of the organization structure.
- Database regarding the banking activities and potentials for the future business.
- Membership database.

- To device innovative and competitive marketing strategies a perfect information system is needed.
- The cooperative banks have to submit reports periodically to the regional cooperative promotion bureau, the federal cooperative agency, the government and other external agencies. This warrants MIS.

A well designed MIS can facilitate a cooperative bank to accomplish the objectives by means of,

- Improving the managerial skill of personnel
- Developing network among cooperatives.
- Creating effective monitoring and control system.
- Office automation – speed, accuracy, volume of work, etc.
- Streamlining the system – finance, accounting, audit, etc.
- Strengthening the reporting system.
- Maintaining database in all respects.
- Making effective decisions.

Structure and Operating MIS in Cooperative Banks

While designing and operating the MIS for any service industry, the people, process and technology to be used should be identified and an information support on these factors should be provided to the management to make decisions to design service strategy. The following table shows where the focus area is in the MIS for these key factors.

Key factors and MIS focus

Factors	*MIS focus*
People	Understanding the expectations and the perceptions of the customers
Process	Evaluating and controlling the process output standards of the service operations
Technology	Evaluating the efficiency and the effectiveness to make technological decisions.

The following points should be taken care of while designing and operating MIS in a cooperative bank:

- *Customer / Member database* – The service expectations and perceptions revolve around: members and public, class of customers.
- *Banking services* – Main services like deposit mobilization, disbursement of loans, etc and ancillary services like remittance of electricity bill, insurance premium, etc.
- *Reports* – Reports on the non-operating accounts, accounts having more balance and down below minimum balance, the routine payments, routine credits, defaulters list, delay on crediting cheques and other related service reports.
- *Index monitoring system* – MIS to monitor the variety of indices ratios, and norms within the acceptance limits, Decision support system to handle the problem of not meeting the standards.
- *Human resource upgrade* – Upgrade the skills and knowledge of the bank employees in recent trend and technology.
- *MIS maintenance* – Operating MIS effectively and effectively needs good maintenance of MIS.

The cooperative banks should adopt and apply the MIS in banking operations so as to withstand in the competitive banking business industry.

Information Reporting System in Cooperative Banks

As for information reporting system, the cooperative banks are submitting reports to the government, federal cooperative agency, regional cooperative promotion bureau, NGOs and other promoting agencies, other cooperatives, which have transactions with the cooperative banks, and to the member customers and the public. To the government, federal cooperative agency, regional cooperative promotion bureau, NGOs and other promoting agencies the cooperative banks have to submit periodical reports on the financial position and business activities. The cooperative banks send reports regularly to other cooperatives and members about the transactions i.e., credit availed, repayments made, balance to be paid, defaults, etc., with the bank.

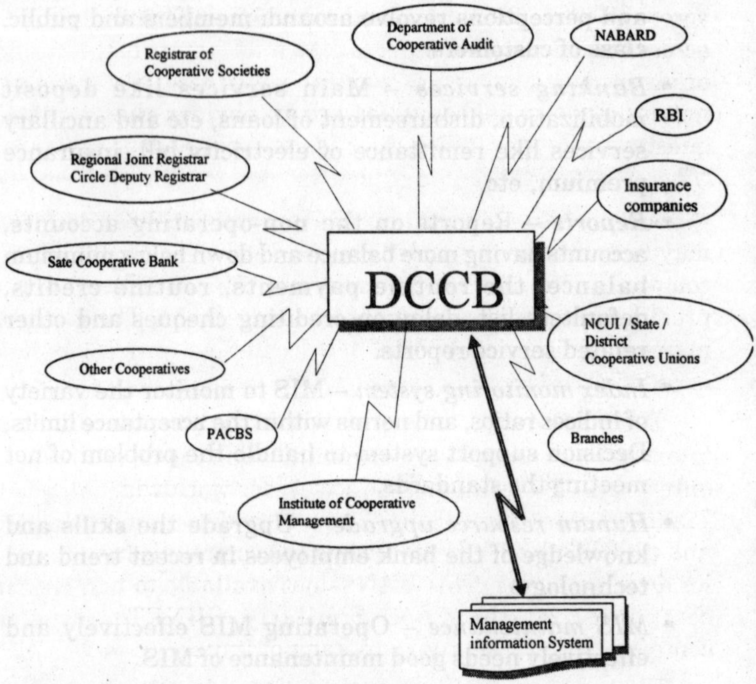

Chart 16.1. Information Reporting System in CCB

INFORMATION PRECESSING AND TRANSFER OF TECHNOLOGY

The operations of a modern, multi product business enterprise are scattered over a wider geographical area. As result, one of the main concerns of today's manager is to integrate scattered business functions in order to improve productivity. This will require effective communication links among the scattered organizational units. Earlier the networks were content specific. A paradigms shift from content specific communication network to integrated networks is taking place1. The information highways are using wire-lines and wire-less networks to carry voice, data and video using common computer platforms. Thus the modern networks are content natural and ensure the vertical and ensure the vertical and horizontal integration of information.

Computer network enables managers to share information across the enterprise, across the departments and plants, and across the industries in order to get a total picture of the business environment instead of partial view. The advantages of networking the IT resources are so obvious that the basic, question today is not "whether to network them or rot" rather, "how to network them to exploit the potential fully"

A computer network may be localized to given premises or may be spread over a wider geographical area. The network of computer systems that are located within an office or factory premises is called Local Area Network (LAN). The computer network threat connects remotely located network components is called wider Area Network (WAN).

The WAN may be owned by individual business enterprise to exclusively cater to the communication needs of the owner enterprises. For example, the society for worldwide inter-bank Finance Transactions (SWIFT), a non-profit organization, owns and maintains a WAN that meets the communication needs of its member banks. This WAN is not available to non-banking companies for their use. Similarly, SBNET serves the communication needs of state Bank of India.

Electronic cash: a mole futuristic solution to payment problem on the internet is electronic cash that eliminates the credit card number, the most sensitive part of information in internet transaction, from the transaction. The electronic cash or electronic wallet systems are generally linked to banks for maintaining the record of cash and debits and credits.

Virtual checking: In this method, the customer authorizes the seller to draw a cheque for the amount of purchase on his banker who is approached by the seller, later, for collection. Checkfree and Net Chex are the companies offering these services along with a few others on Internet.

Banking is a potential application is where the networks are put to use extensively. The branch banking operations are the LAN applications. The networks help to establish service centers at locations where the customer arrives. The focus has shifted from the account center data processing model to the customer service model. The banking operations are handled by switching over the client server model implemented on the network platform. The loan application processing, the credit card operations and round the clock banking service are feasible because of the network based client server applications called as IPTT model.

Amul is one example of cooperatives using E-commerce route, similarly the cooperative Banks in the competitive environment could undertake their transactions on the Net, which involves less cost compared with branch transactions mostly in the urban and metro cities. And, Internet banking also helps banks in reducing branch loans ingeneration of statements, who are techno savvy people. Better funds management and greater convenience could be the advantages from customer point of view. As how the computerization of cooperative banking operations being undertaken the online banking transaction holds a high potential for E-com and E-Banking.

We are in an information age. Information is a critical resource for any organization and management for planning, reviewing and decision-making, needs accurate and timely information. As the cooperative Banking industry is an information intensive industry, the most important task before the cooperative banks. Cooperative Banks occupy an important place in the cooperative Banking structure. The new liberalized are posed critical challenges before the cooperative banks, viz.

- Competing meaningfully with comparable institutions in the rural market
- Revitalizing organization structure
- Effective technology management
- Effective human resource management
- Rethinking on the classical modes on delivery of banking services, and
- Bringing new standards of customer service, quality and technology to the mass.

The vertical and horizontal growth of theses banks is struggling to answer and take decisions on these problems. Here comes the role of effective information processing and transfer technology model.

Information Channels

The information flow between two devices through which data are transmitted is called the information channel.

The media includes wires, coaxial cables, microwares, fiber optics and digital networks. Among these satellite communication system using VSAT technology is very popular in the banking and financial services sectors. The VSAT nodes are networked together using a tenna fixed to the geo-stationery satellite. Communication satellite is a microware relay station positioned in stationary orbits approximately 35784 km. above the equator. It operates a number of frequency bands called transponders. A typical transponder has a bandwidth of 38=6 to 76 MH2. It may provide point to point link or bread cast link to receivers.

There are two options for setting up a VSAT network

Private Network: In India, only a handful of big companies have the license to setup their private network. (Eg NSC (National Stock exchange and BANKNET).

Shared Hub Services: A Number of communications companies are offering services for sharing the hub with others.

Information Processing and Transfer

Information processing and Transfer technology is a combination of hardware and software tools that allows transactions on accounts of a branch. This model helps the customer to operate his Account from any of the branches irrespective of his Account at any branch. This system provides withdrawal and deposit facility to the customers from any of the branches and thus saves a lot of time and efforts.

The customers of the bank get following facilities-namely.

- Customer can check the balance amount in his account.
- Customer can withdraw/Deposit the amount from to his account.
- Customer can update his passbook.
- Customer can purchase demand draft (DD).

The customers are allotted with Account number and first four digits indicated the branch code. With entry of this code, customer gets all the details as per his instructions. But transactions relating to the closing of accounts bill of purchase etc, need to be done at the Home branch.

The banking software enforces discipline of account number. The first four digits indicated the branch to which the account belongs. This means the counter staff-need not do anything special when they enter the account number on terminal at Branch. Banking software recognizes it as information processing and transfer transaction by inspecting the account number. It looks up its own telephone directory and dials the home branch number and establishes connection, and carries out transaction as if the terminal is connected directly to the computer at the home Branch.

The data of all branched is stored on the computer at the branch itself. If customer of Branch-1 goes to Branch-2 for a cash withdrawal, the software passes on the transaction details on telephone line to computer of Branch-1. The branch A computer performs usual checks, such as whether the customer has enough balance and sends the response to the terminal of Branch-2 counter indicating success or failure of the transaction. Accordingly Branch banking software recognizes it as information processing and transfer transaction by inspecting the account number. It looks up its own telephone directory and dials the home branch number and establishes connection, and carries out transaction as if the terminal is connected directly to the computer in home Branch.

The data of all branches stored on the computer at the branch itself. If customer of Branch-1 goes to branch-2 for a cash withdrawal, the software passes on the transaction details on telephone line to computer of Branch-1. The counter staff at Branch-1 informs the customer reasons for not honoring the transaction (such as "insufficient balance").

The information in Branch-1 computer is instantaneously updated to reflect new balance after the transaction for the customer. This "On Line Real Time" transaction data up data "Feature" is a unique feature, which prevents misuse and fraud.

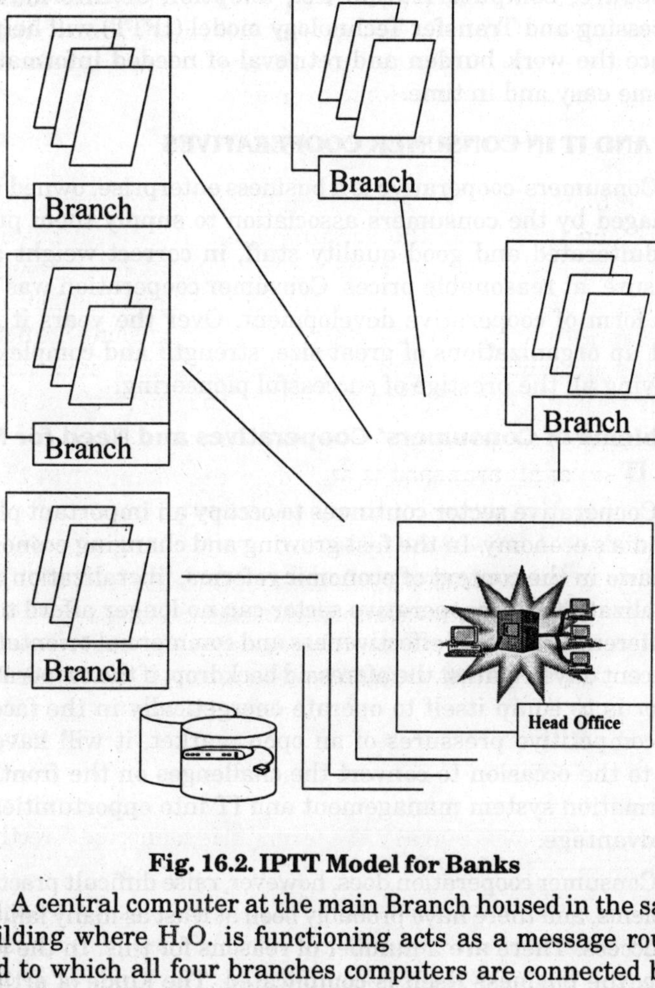

Fig. 16.2. IPTT Model for Banks

A central computer at the main Branch housed in the same building where H.O. is functioning acts as a message router and to which all four branches computers are connected by a leased line. A device called multiplexer allows several terminals, printers in branches to share a single leased line for the purpose of connecting to cluster computer. The functioning of cooperative banks are governed by the state cooperative societies Act and rules and Banking Regulations Act. Hence periodically they have to submit returns and reports as per the requirements of these Acts to RBI, NABARD, the Regulations of cooperative societies and such other apex bodies. Since this has been a routine procedure, computerization i.e., adoption of Information Processing and Transfer Technology model (IPTT) will help to reduce the work burden and retrieval of needed information become easy and in time.

MIS AND IT IN CONSUMER COOPERATIVES

Consumers' cooperative is a business enterprise, owned and managed by the consumers association to supply them pure, unadulterated and good quality stuff, in correct weight and measure, at reasonable prices. Consumer cooperation was the first form of cooperative development. Over the years it has built up organizations of great size, strength and complexity, enjoying all the prestige of successful pioneering.

Problems of Consumers' Cooperatives and Need for MIS and IT

Cooperative sector continues to occupy an important place in India's economy. In the fast growing and changing economic scenario in the context of economic reforms, liberalization and globalization, the cooperative sector can no longer afford to be indifferent to the cost effectiveness and commercial orientation in recent days. Against the aforesaid backdrop, if the cooperative sector is to equip itself to operate energetically in the face of the competitive pressures of an open market, it will have to rise to the occasion to convert the challenges on the fronts of information system management and IT into opportunities to its advantage.

Consumer cooperation does, however, raise difficult practical problems, and there have probably been at least as many failures as success. There are a number of reasons for this. In the first place, the business itself is complicated. The kinds of articles sold by the consumer cooperatives may run into thousands. All these must be chosen with an eye to local tastes. They must, moreover, be purchased in the right quantities with best quality so that they can be sold within a reasonable time, and at least before they begin to deteriorate. All goods have to be paid for, which means a considerable capital outlay. They have to be sold and payments received and recorded. Stocks have to be replenished before they run out. A quite complicated system of accounting has to be adopted and kept up to date. Another difficulty is that consumer cooperatives face intense competition from other traders.

The route for achieving success is become clear if the MIS and IT are designed and adopted, through such system only the different business problems of consumers' cooperatives can be examined, analysed and right business decision can be taken.

The following information can be had from a well designed MIS and application of Information Technology for the successful functioning of consumers' cooperatives:

(*i*) membership and capital,
(*ii*) right choice of site,
(*iii*) choice of stocks,
(*iv*) layout of shops,
(*v*) competition between cooperatives,
(*vi*) competition from other traders,
(*vii*) price and quality,
(*viii*) bookkeeping and stock control,
(*ix*) purchasing and sources of supply,
(*x*) management of consumer cooperatives,
(*xi*) relations between consumer cooperatives (whole sale & retail coops),
(*xii*) relations between consumer cooperatives and other cooperatives.

Areas and the Application of MIS and IT

The MIS and IT are now two buzzwords in business organization. They have significant contribution towards profitability and providing value-added services to customers. Rapid technological developments both in terms of computer hardware and software have made their use simple, user-friendly and cost-effective. That is why, the negative attitude of not using computers in the work places is thrown away by people and computerized MIS and IT is being absorbed into business organization more and more gradually. Information system is the analysis of demand and the Information technology is the analysis of supply and both are adopted for the collection, analysis and process of data and dissemination information to the management team for taking right business decision.

A consumers' cooperative should not be an exception to this pervasive phenomenon. Adoption of computerized MIS and the application of IT in a consumers' cooperative enables faster service to consumers/customers and better business activities. It solves the need of a lot of paper work, more staff time and mental stress.

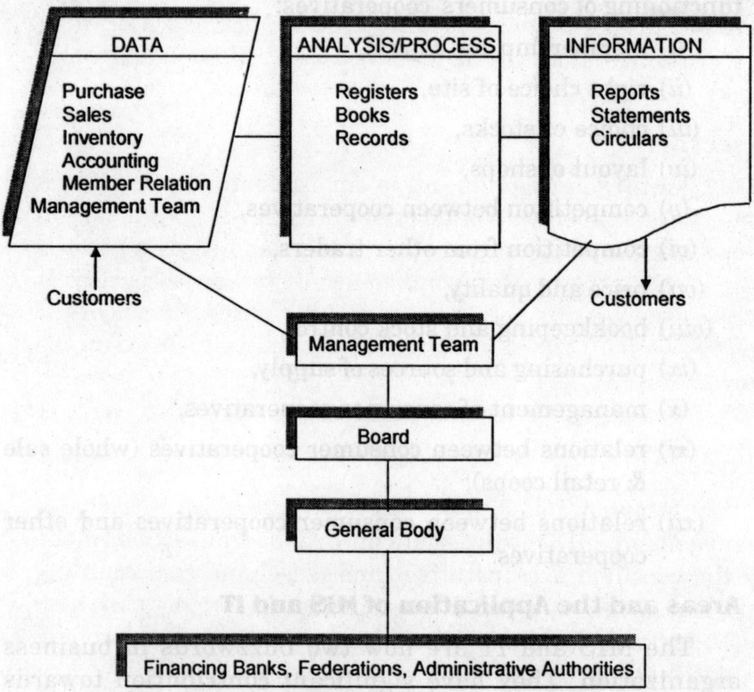

Fig. 16.3. MIS in consumers' cooperative enterprise

The main activity of a consumers' cooperative is to purchase goods and sell it to consumers at reasonable prices with good quality and of correct measurement. The adoption of MIS with IT should be in the main areas of purchase, sales, inventory, accounting, member-relation and management structure.

Purchase

Purchasing of goods involve a lot of time consuming work and well designed MIS helps in this process through reducing the clerical chores drastically by automatic order tracking, invoice receipts and payments, supplier selection, quality goods and competitive price.

Sales

Computerization leads to easy and speedy billing system and it is just required to stroke the item code and quantity. Fast, slow and non-moving items can easily be identified which pave way to take better business decision and demand forecasting of a particular item can be made based on the ongoing sales trend.

Inventory

Inventory management is an important area for a consumers' cooperative enterprise. MIS plays a vital role in keeping track of the status of each item and signs when the item reaches the reorder point to avoid stockout situation. It helps in calculating cost of inventory for better management and facilitates inter-cooperative transfer of items based on the movement rate of a particular item in different consumers' cooperative branches and retail stores.

Accounting

Financial statements provide information on better cash management. MIS receives data on various transactions made by the consumers' cooperatives and disseminates accounting information in preparing different periodic statements like cash book, day book, ledgers, trial balance, trading account, profit & loss account, balance sheet etc., for monitoring cash flow.

Member Relation

Member relation is to be considered in a consumers' cooperative to enhance the growth of membership and cooperative movement in long run. Because, consumers' cooperative is a member-based organization where customers may be different from members. MIS is very much helpful in keeping up-to-date information on members and their shares facilitate better member relation and payment of dividends based on the participation through transaction in the business of consumers' cooperatives.

Management Structure

Management of a consumers' cooperative is complex since it deals with a variety of items to be sold. Keep in mind that managers have been catapulted into an era of professionalism and they must be trained on modern managerial methods. Adoption of MIS and application IT could make the managers and other personnel in the management structure be informed about their duties and responsibilities, job description and specification. The relationship between management team and board (reports to the board to which it is accountable), the relationship between board and members(reports to the members to whom it is accountable) can be strengthened through proper information flow on all aspects by the adoption of well designed MIS with an advanced information technology application.

Benefits of MIS and IT in Consumers' Cooperative

Consumers' cooperative adopted with well-designed MIS will enjoy the following benefits:

- Faster service to customers;
- Easy access to information in all respects at any time;
- Proper purchase procedure and system;
- Increase efficiency in managing inventory and sales;
- Proper planning, monitoring and control of business;
- Utilization of cash credit;
- Information on funds position and cash flow;
- Reduction in operating cost in long run;
- Improved performance efficiency and productivity;
- Better member relation and customer satisfaction;
- Strengthened management-board-member relations; and
- Right business decision for success of consumers' cooperative.

In the face of increasing competitive business environment the consumers' cooperative cannot afford to remain lukewarm to the forward march of IT in other business enterprises and yet hope to grow. It is a choice, for not only to consumers' cooperatives but also to the cooperatives as a whole, between survival and extinction. The amazing speed and accuracy with which computers are able to process, store, transfer and reproduce data, have made them highly instrumental in augmenting the efficiency of an organisation, which can be done through adoption of well designed MIS and proper application of Information Technology.

MIS FOR DAIRY COOPERATIVES

The purpose of any organization is to achieve certain objectives by using the resources available to it. Planning is a process of pre-determining the objectives within the constraints of the resources available to an organization. Planning could include both, short term planning as well as long term planning. Having pre-determined the objectives would not automatically lead the organization to attainment of those objectives. It would be necessary to periodically measure the actual achievements from time to time, to compare these with the planned targets and take the required corrective action to overcome the shortfall in performance.

To facilitate these processes, it becomes necessary to provide relevant managerial information to those who may be in a position to take such corrective action. The entire gamut of planning, controlling by way of provision of information and consequent corrective action is termed as "Management Planning and Information System" (MPIS).

Essentially, MPIS consists of the following sub-systems:

(*a*) Budgeting system;

(*b*) Management Information System (MIS); and

(*c*) Performance Review and Follow-up System

This note discusses each of the above sub-systems with a focus on the dairy industry.

There are several agencies involved in the accomplishment of the tasks relating to the dairy Industry in the cooperative sector. These are the village Dairy cooperative societies (VDCS) at the village level, the cooperative Milk produces' Union (usually) at the district level and the cooperative milk producers' federation. Each of these is an independent organization with district tasks and responsibilities in the contact of the dairy industry. Apart from these, at the apex level, the entire dairy development programme in the cooperative scoter is guided and monitored by National Dairy development Board (NDDB). The finances fro the various projects are provided by the Indian Dairy corporation (IDC). In this note MPIS will be discussed with reference to each of the above agencies.

Management Structure in the Cooperative Dairy System

When we look at a management structure, we are essentially looking at how the total organizational task is divided into tasks (or group of tasks) or groups of specialized activities which are controlled by specific mangers. These specific managers have the responsibility for accomplishing the objectives of such task groups or organizational sub-units are also referred to as "Responsibility Centres" as a specific manger is responsible and accountable for the performance of the sub-unit.

A responsibility center should have the following features:

(*a*) It should be headed by a manager, who is accountable for its performance, and would take corrective actions when plans are not achieved;

(*b*) It should have distinct and measurable inputs as well as outputs;

(*c*) It should be distinguishable, in terms of its distinct technology or method of operation, from another responsibility centre;

(*d*) It should serve clearly identified markets or other responsibility centers within the organization.

As mentioned earlier, there are several autonomous agencies involved in the accomplishment of the tasks concerning the dairy industry. Broadly, there are four tiers with the VDC being at the lowest level.

It is useful to understand very briefly what the several agencies involved do. A VDC is formed by the residents of a village who would like to supply their milk to the Village Dairy Cooperative and in turn receive not only the price for the milk, but also certain services like animal health care, artificial insemination, supply of cattle feed at subsidized prices supply of fodder seed at subsidized prices guidance about increasing the milk output etc. A VDC is managed by a Secretary and has elected Managing committees.

A union is a body formed by the different VDCs in the district, which become its members. Through the formation of a union VDCs are in a position to jointly own a processing plant for the milk, so that the milk of required combination and quality could be supplied to the consuming centers and/ or milk product like butter ghee, powders, chocolates cheese, etc, can be produced. As a VDC is not in a position to render the animal husbandry and the related services on its own because of its small size and low capital base, these facilities are also centralized with the Union. The union has a responsibility for marketing its products with the district in which it operates. However, to provide for better coordination in marketing outsides the district some of the unions jointly form a Federation. The Federation undertakes the responsibility for coordination the marketing efforts of about seven to sight unions particularly in relation to the sales outside the district in which the Unions are operating. The federation may also have centralize facilities for production of frozen semen and diagnostic laboratory. The Production progrmme for each Union is determined on a monthly basis by the programming committee of the federation the Managing director of each Union is a member of the programming committee. The Federation also has the responsibility for monitoring implementation of the dairy projects on behalf of the NDDB/ IDC. It would be evident from the above that the Union is one of the most important organizations in the cooperative dairy system. It would be useful to discuss MPIS with reference to the union. It would also be useful to understand the various activities in the in the responsibility centers in a union.

A specific manager heads each of the responsibility centers. Each responsibility centre has a distinct task to perform. For instance, the manger-procurement has the responsibility for procuring the milk from the various VDCs as also from the other sources, if it becomes necessary. He must ensure that the milk procured is of required quality in terms of fat % and SNF %. He has the responsibility for supplying the milk either to the chilling centers if the supply sources are located far away from the processing plant or directly to the processing plant of the Union. The chilling centre in turn supplies most of its milk to Manager-production, though, the milk may be supplied to a 'customer' which may be a city dairy directly from a chilling centre if the chilling centre is located close to it.

The Manager-Production has the responsibility for processing the milk, separating the fat, processing white butter, converting white butter into table butter or ghee, processing milk powder, etc. He also has the responsibility for packaging the products, wherever applicable. The Manager-production transfers the milk products to Manager- marketing/ dispatch. The Manager- marketing Dispatch has the responsibility for ensuring that the milk is sold or disposed of within the district, milk products like ghee are made available to the VDCs. He would also have the responsibility for ensuring that processed milk or milk products is supplied outside the district to the consuming centers as per instructions of the federation.

The Correlation of Budgeting and Information System to Organization Structure

It was evident from the above that each manger has a set of distinct tasks to perform and distinct targets in relation to his tasks. The allocation of the targets for the responsibility centers is determined by a budgeting for (or target setting) system. The MIS would accomplish the periodical monitoring of the actual achievements of the responsibility centre or of the total organization. It is perhaps not necessary to over emphasis that a manger would be able to budget only for such activities, which fall within the specified understanding of his role and responsibilities. Likewise, a manger would only find such information useful as is relevant to his own needs for managing the operations controlled by him. This again is determined by his assigned role and the related responsibilities. Both, the budgeting system as well as the MIS would need to be linked to the management structure for greater effectiveness.

Budgeting System in a Union

As mentioned earlier, the production programme of a union is determined by an allocation made by the programming committee of the Federation. This is done each month. The Managing Director of a Union is a member of this programming committee. The targets are allocated to a Union in consultation with the concerned Managing director. Targets are allocated keeping in view the common interests of all the members of the federation. Once a union has accepted the targets of production, the targets for procurement for the month get automatically determined. So do the targets for efficiency of operation and capacity utilization of plants get determined on this basis?

The union is also expected to meet the annual targets which were originally formulated in consultation with NDDB /IDC in terms of milk procurement, development of societies, development of membership, number of artificial inseminations, increase in milch herd etc. farmers' organization and animal Husbandry would need to be determined over a longer timeframe. The programming committee does not determine these. However, the Federation and NDDB/IDC would certainly have a say in formulation of the annual targets for these activities.

Need of Reporting Financial & Non-financial Information

Any reporting system, which restricts the reporting to only financial information, will be inadequate in managerial terms. It is necessary to provide information an non-financials /physical indicators of performance along with the financial information. A physical (or quantitative) indicator of performance reflects the performance in physical terms e.g. quantity to production, conversion efficiency index, capacity utilization % etc. in relation to each responsibility centre it is important to report information in relation to non-financial performance, Examples of non-financial information are:

- Average daily procurement,

- Fat % SNF % and Sour %
- Conception rate for AI,
- Availability of trained manpower,
- Cattle feed consumption per liter of milk procured, etc.

The financial information to be reported in a format should consider all costs or revenues, which are readily identifiable with the department. In relation to a union, the revenue would be identifiable largely with the marketing department. Examples of costs identifiable with department are:-

(*i*) salaries of personal employed for a department;

(*ii*) transport cost for milk procurement identifiable with the procurement department;

(*iii*) Cost of medicines identifiable with animal husbandry department;

(*iv*) Stores consumption or cost of repairs and maintenance identifiable with the production department.

It is necessary that while reporting the information on costs, common costs which are incurred for more than one responsibility centre should not be allocated to the various responsibility centers on any basis, e.g., the administrative expenses incurred at the union level like salaries of personnel in accounting department, should not be allocated to the production, sales or purchase departments. The allocation to a responsibility centre of costs not identifiable with it would vitiate the process of cost control and performance evaluation.

Highlighting Critical Indicators

The information, which is being reported to a manager, should be generated in a concise form so that information overload is avoided and the manger's in attention is drawn to critical indicators of performance. It is necessary for the performance report to highlight the critical indicators of performance. A critical indicator of performance can be a financial performance indicator or non-financial/ physical performance indicator. What can be classified, as a critical indicator would be based on circumstances of each case. For instance, what may be classified as a critical indicator once may cease to be critical beyond a certain time. A critical indicator of performance is such an indicator that a continued failure shown by that indicator would substantially affect the overall objectives or goal of the responsibility centre. Example of critical indicators of performance is:

(*a*) For procurement Department:

(*i*) Average daily procurement

(*ii*) Fat %, SNF %, sour % in milk procured

(*b*) For Animal Husbandry:

(*i*) % societies not covered by mobile clinics

(*ii*) Conception rate for AI

(*iii*) Cattle feed consumed per liter of milk procured

(*c*) For farmers' Organization :

(*i*) Growth rate in number of VBCs

(*ii*) Growth rate in number of members

(*d*) For production department:

Conversion efficiency index

(*e*) For cattle feed Operations:

Raw material cost per tonne of cattle feed

(*f*) Actual performance should be reported against budgets or standards:

The design of formats should be such that the information on actual performance is reported against budgeted/standard performance and the variauons between the two are highlighted. Such a design feature readily draws the user's attention to the areas, which need to be watched. It follows from this that it is necessary to set standards of performance so that controls become meaningful. It is particularly useful to set standards of performance in the following areas:

(*i*) Consumption of utilities

(*ii*) Consumption of stores

(*iii*) Conversion efficiency index

(*iv*) Quality performance, etc.

Aggregation of Financial Information

The reporting system should be so designed that the financial information can be successively aggregated at each higher level to ultimately give the profit for the entire organization. Such a design feature would facilitate tracking of variations from desired financial results to their sources of occurrence; e.g., if there is a variation in the financial performance as is evidenced in the consolidated performance report for the union, it should be possible to trace the variations to the specific departments where it has arisen.

This concept of MIS design where by the results for higher level are obtained by aggregating the reports of immediately lower level is also known as 'modularity'. Once this feature has been incorporated in the systems designed, it is not necessary to provide to each manger all the reports from which his own report has been prepared. It would be adequate if a manger is provided with a report on his own operations and the report on the operations controlled by his immediate subordinates.

Frequency of Reporting

The frequency of a report should be decided according to the information needs. It may be necessary for some information on critical factors to be reported more frequently. For instance, in a union an exceptional societies flash report in respect of societies showing abnormal figures for Fat %, SNF % and sour % should be reported at once to the manger-procurement. On the other hand, information on growth rate of membership, growth rate in number of societies, development in milch herd, availability of trained manpower, etc, may be reported on a quarterly basis. Similarly information on complaints from customers or market shares may also be reported only once in a quarter.

MIS FOR A VDC

At the VDC level a one page MIS report would be prepared on monthly basis. Most of the items shown in the report can be obtained from the daily milk register maintained by each VDC. The format for VDC report is shown in Exhibit IV for reference. It will be seen that apart from showing the quantity of milk procured and the quality of milk procured, the report also provides information on:

(*i*) Number of AIs

(*ii*) Number of minikits distributed

(*iii*) Number of animals diagnosed

An important piece of information required to be generated at the VDC is a progress cared for crossbred cows. The information provided by this card is of critical importance for monitoring the progress and effectiveness of crossbreeding programmes.

Performance Review and Follow-Up System

A Management planning and Information System is not likely to be effective unless it is backed up by a formal and systematic performance reviews follow-up system. It is necessary that performance reviews be conducted periodically (preferably, at least once a month). Such reviews would be based on the MIS reports.

The attitude of the reviewer should be that of a 'positivist and an activist. There•should be an effort, between him and his subordinates; to formulate remedial action plans jointly. The subordinates should be encouraged to come up with their own suggestions and the superior should spell out possible alternatives for remedial action (based on his experience and knowledge) and the resources support, which has, would be able to provide (or muster) to his subordinates for accomplishing remedial action plan. The focus of such review must invariably be on achievement of common tasks (as distinct from tasks assigned from one level of authority to the 'next below' level) on a collaborative basis. In the context of a union, the MIS Administrator would have the responsibility for administering the MIS. He would act as the professional support service group for the performance review meetings.

It is useful to record the decisions during performance review meetings along the following dimensions:

(*a*) Nature of shortfall highlighted by the reported or identified during the review;

(*b*) Remedial action decided upon;

(*c*) Benefits identified from remedial action;

(*d*) Executives responsible for taking remedial action;

(*e*) Superior level management support required for remedial action;

(*f*) Deadline for completing the remedial action

Systems Administration

It must be realized that a management information System, which is excellent in terms of design, might prove to be relatively less effective if not administered and implemented properly. It becomes necessary, therefore, to appoint an executive with the full responsibility for implementing and administering the system. This is all the more important in an organization where the quantum of tasks involved in MIS is relatively large. An MIS administrator could have any background such as accounting, Procurement, animal husbandry production or marketing. He need not necessarily be an accountant. He has essentially to play a role which is supportive to the line mangers. He will not exercise any line authority over the managers who have to take decisions based on the MIS reports, nor does he develop the budgets on behalf of a manger and give it to him for his comments and approval. On the contrary, he should help the managers in coming up with their own budgets.

His role and responsibilities would include the following:

(*a*) he would be responsible for preparing the various MIS reports and circulating them to the mangers concerned along with his analysis and comments for their action.

(*b*) He would provide assistance to the mangers in their tasks of formulation of budgets and setting up of targets.

(*c*) He would coordinate the performance review excise and ensure that appropriate follow-up takes place with regard to the remedial action plans decided upon.

(*d*) He would carry out economic analysis, cost analysis and other analysis which might be required by the mangers of the organization.

(*e*) He would guide and advise the VDC secretaries about the preparation of the MIS reports at the VDC.

(*f*) He would be responsible for preparing the reports required by NDDB/ IDC.

(*g*) He would also be responsible for sending information required by the Federation.

Role of Management levels in Administration of MPIS

Top management involvement at the design stage is critical if the system is to gain acceptance in an organization. It should not be restricted to more circulation of memos or presence in the various briefing meeting. The top management should closely monitor the implementation of the systems and ensure that the various formats are provided to the mangers concerned in time, the activities relating to target setting are carried out appropriately and in time, the managers in the organization understand what the system is all about.

During the stage of administration of the system, the top management has to ensure that the system is being used. The only way in which this can be manifested is far the to management itself to use the system. For example, if the managing director conducts a review of the operation with his immediate subordinates, he would be in a position to percolate the discipline of a performance review down the line and ensure that the MIS reports are being used at all levels. This again cannot be achieved by merely exhorting the immediate subordinates to review operations of their subordinates.

The top management has to be closely involved in the annual budgeting exercise and ensure that their assumptions about the budget are made know to the various mangers before they develop their budgets. The managing directors of the Unions and the federation have a particularly important role here because thy are informed about the thinking of the Federation and the apex institutions like NDDB and IDC in a much better manner being in regular touch with those organizations.

The other mangers like the Manger-procurement, Manager-animal Husbandry, manger – Production, in the unions or manger - Marketing, in the Federation also have a key role to play in the successful implementation and administration of MPIS. They would be closely involved in providing the inputs for form formulating the plans for the unions/federation. They would also be involved in reviewing the performance of their subordinates and in providing their guidance and support to them in formulating plans for overcoming the shortfalls in the performance.

MIS FOR SUGAR COOPERATIVES

The modern view of an organization is to consider it as an integration of several interlinked sub-systems. The sub-systems are make up an organization are (*i*) Organizational goal and values (*ii*) Technical sub-system (*iii*) Psycho-social subs-system (*iv*) Structural sub-system and (*v*) the sub-system which actually establishes and integrates all these systems in the Managerial system.

Though Managerial system encompasses all the other sub-system, Technical, psycho-social, goals and values and structural sub-system, it is not the scope of our study to discuss psychological and goals and values sub-systems. The management information system has to be essentially built around the organization structure; therefore we discuss the structural sub-system, the decision centers and information flow.

Identification, Specification and Problem in Selection of Data Processing Equipment (computer) in Sugar Cooperatives

A large variety of computers are available in the market starting from micro to mini frame to super computer. First one has to choose a proper computer system along with the essential software and hardware. Due to these variety of computers price also varies from few thousands to few cores. Moreover as these are electro-mechanical instrument associated problems also these like: temperature, dust, space, after sales support, up gradation, obsolence, continuous and stabilized power supply etc. However, suitable choice of the best combination of hardware and software for specific application in a given time is the most important. Technically a relational database management systems (RDBMS) under multi-use (UNIX) platform will be appropriate for developing the above systems to meet the requirement of large data transaction processing and frequent variations in report generation. This will not only require a relatively very higher level of professional expertise but will also be more expensive. N the basis of detailed analysis with regards to systems requirements, rural development, users limitations and cost effectiveness, it is proposed that the Foxpro data base management systems. The system integration concept can also be achieved while designing the systems using foxpro. In a typical sugar factory main items for consideration in small application are:

(*i*) Personal computers: PC-ATs and PC-super ATs,

(*ii*) Local Area Networks (LANs), and

(*iii*) Computers with multi-user and multi tasking facilities.

Due to advancement in technology in computer industries PC-ATs and SUPER ATs are available in very lower and affordable costs. In most of the computer based office automation work PC-AT or PC-Super At are adequate and appropriate. Local Area Network is the most suitable choice for office automation.

Most of the sugar factories in our country are located in rural areas skilled and knowledgeable manpower in computer field is not easily available at all the places. So one should start computerization activities in step by step. So the sugar factory employees could get trained in the process and could be acquainted in the computer environment. Moreover that could give a balance between investment and utilization of computers. In the first phase 2/3 PC-ATs along with OS (Operating system) DOS, data base packages like DBASE. Foxbase packages etc with dot matrix printers may be purchased and installed in one or two departments of sugar factory. Then small application systems like payroll. Inventory control, cane billing, financial accounting etc may be computerized one by one. Side by side local employees can be trained and build confidence in computerization work. After computerization of one or two department, plan for another system which can be networked with the first system. This could be considered as first stage. Having competed the first stage one can go for multi terminal system i.e. LAN consisting of one file server, based on the powerful central processing unit like 80486, working on Novel Network system along with a few diskless PCs and additional dot matrix printers and a suitable uninterrupted power supply. All the application systems developed in the first phase can run very smoothly on LAN environment without much modification in the soft wares. System based on MS DOS and Novel Netware Operating System are easy to handle and operate. Special maintenance is not required for this operating system. So whatever purchased in the first phase now become nodes of the new LAN system. Moreover complete failure of LAN SYSTEM cab be avoided, because if some terminal failed remaining terminal work and emergency job can run on other terminals. Further expansion in the LAN SYSTEM is always possible without discarding the earlier machinery

The above approach of system design and implementation can be followed in all those factories, where computerization is taking place so as to make the uniformity and standardization of system.

Strategy for Application Systems Design, Development and Implementation

In line with the modernization trends using computer system in the sugar industry all over the world computerization of the factory can be done in four stages putting priority to the main application (*a*) Cane Billing. (*b*) Cane accounting (*c*) Transportation (*d*) payroll, (*e*) Harvesting and (*f*) Financial accounting.

Stage I

In stage I the primary emphasis should be on analyzing the need of user and following the systems integration design concept. The system should be compatible with Novel LAN, due importance should be given to training and educational of the users. The users should be involved in the system analysis phase. The following sequences should be followed while communization:

- Formation of systems group as an independent unit of the organization.
- Formation of MIS group consisting of systems group and one key person from each department

- System analysis and design
- Installation of hard ware
- Implementation of systems
- Training of staff.

Stage II

On successful implementation of phase I, a suitable local area network (LAMN) should be installed using existing systems such as inventory, personal information etc should be implemented.

Stage III

In this phase, an effort towards implementing an integrated information system as identified in phase I should be made. This will provide flexibility in MIS report generation. A decision support system can also be easily designed. The computerization of production process control and chemical analysis may be done in order to automate it.

Stage IV

All those factories which have successfully implemented their systems can connected through wide area network(WAN) communication channel.

Management Information System for Planning and Control in Cooperative Sugar Factories

The activities of all the three levels of management may look to the same e.g. top management formulates the plan and also the lower management helps in formulating the plan but the emphasis given to the various activities at different levels of management would be different and this emphasis determines the decision areas of a particular level of management based on the following questions:

(*i*) Where is the sugar factory stand now ?

(*ii*) What are factories objective in future?

(*iii*) What does management want the coop. sugar factories to be like in about five years?

(*iv*) How will management get to this desired position?

There are broadly two areas in sugar factories where information technology based-tools, technologies and system can play a vital role in overall working environment. There are:

- Factory Automation, and
- Transaction.

Factory Automation

The management of sugar factories is planning in a big way to automate the manufacturing process of sugar by introducing microprocessor based control systems in view to quality sugar production and to increase recovery by continuous monitoring of production process. At present, three areas of production needs automation. These are:

- Juice Evaporation Process
- Sulphitation Process.
- Vacuum pan Boiling process.

The other areas of automated production process are the chemical analysis of the products and by-products at various stages of production processes and automation of weighing of cane and sugar by interfacing the weighing machines with the personal computers.

Transactions

The following functional areas have been identified for computerization to increase the overall performance of the sugar cooperative factories.

- Harvesting Schedule
- Cane growers' Information
- Cane Billing
- Financing Accounting
- Transportation
- Inventory management
- Distillery product Accounting
- Shares Accounting
- Personnel information systems
- Payroll

System Integration Concept and Design Strategy in Sugar Factory

The primary purpose of implementing computerized information system in the sugar factories is to provide a multi-level, cross-functional,. And timely flow to accurate, relevant information to all components of the organization and to make the report generation flexible. This can be achieved only by introducing the system integration concept while designing the system in the sugar factories.

It is basically to reduce the redundancy by providing common database and to enable the cross-migration of data among the different departments in the organization. The integration can either be implemented in the beginning or even after implementing different systems independently, if care is taken while designing the systems which special emphasis on the following points:

- A group consisting of persons from MIS and at least one key person of each department should be formed to coordinate the integrated system design.
- Elaborate security and access control should be enforced in the system and it should be checked for turning.
- The system should be preferable on-line so as to update the database instantaneously.

Information Sharing for Comparative Performance Analysis through Computerized Networking

The information technology network will enable the factories to share the relevant information with other factories. They may share information relating to sugarcane production and factory performance to begin with, but at a later stage they can also share information relating to inventory management and go for maintaining common inventory of some items. Information on some of the important performance parameters relating to sugar cane production, factory personnel management, finical management etc. can be shared for comparative analysis and competitive advantage. These parameters are mentioned below:

Crushing and Production Information

- area and other details of sugarcane cultivation of members,

- Yield of sugarcane production per acre.
- Recovery percentage of cane.

Factory Performance Data

- Average crushing rate (2500Mt/Day std)
- Time lag between harvesting and crushing.
- Fiber percent
- Juice per cent
- Loss in Molasses and Bagasse.
- Recovery loss and its reasons. Lime and other chemical consumption
- Factory loss and its reasons
- Lime and other chemical consumption

Personnel Management Data

- Number of permanent employee - Number of casual employee
- Number of technical employee - Number of head of department

Financial Data

- Sugar bags sold - levy (Qty)
- Cash/Credit amount - Average sugar price/kg
- Harvesting cost - Transport cost
- Total income - Total Expenses
- Expenses per ton - Deficit

Objective of Computerization of Sugar Factory

- Ensures availability of sugarcane during crushing season by helping in better planning procurement and control.
- Helps in achieving farmer's satisfaction with improved services.
- Helps in attaining higher recovery of sugar by introducing efficient sugarcane management programme.
- Contends to reduce cost of operation.
- Helps in maximization of overall profits

- Better management of men, machines materials and money.

Benefits of Computerization

- Increase in availability of sugarcane as a result of better sugarcane programme.
- Rise in sucrose content of the sugarcane due to enhanced monitoring capabilities of sugarcane development programme.
- Farmers are more satisfied lot especially due to prompt payments and overall improved services.
- Time-consuming and tedious manual jobs like basic-quotacalculation, bonding, scheduling of day-wise procurement of sugarcane and generation of sugarcane supply tickets are accomplished accurately in no time.
- Reduction in time between harvesting and crushing thus saving sugarcane from getting perished and losing vital sucrose content.
- Correct weighment of sugarcane at mill-gate through better weighbridge control. Also improve estimation of driage while sugarcane being transferred from center to mill.
- Comprehensive preventive maintenance programme for plant, along with complete facility for monitoring production status
- Complete handling of all types of payment to farmers ad transporters through bank or cash or both.
- Complete handling of fiscal related matters be it loans, sales or financial accounting issues.
- Handling of all subject related with materials management so that overstocking of materials can be checked.
- Facility to handle all human resources related matters and helps in providing overall improved management information services.

The points discussed in the paper may provide the basis framework of system design and strategy for computerization of sugar cooperative factories. It will also help them in selecting the appropriate application software and hard ware platform uniformly across the factories, which is desired in order to implement information Technology Network in sugar factories.

BUSINESS MANAGEMENT SUPPORT SYSTEMS IN COOPERATIVES

Cooperatives are economic as well as social enterprises. They are doing business with social objective and social obligation. Cooperatives are not an exception regarding business management support systems. They are in need of gathering, processing and disseminating information within and outside ie., internal and external environment of their business.

In cooperatives all types of business management support systems can be applied based on their requirement and nature of business that they are performing. As in the case other business enterprises cooperatives using all types of support systems not only for gathering, processing and disseminating information but also for making right business decisions for improving cooperative business so as to serve all the stakeholders. In this section, an attempt is made on the applications of support systems in cooperatives.

Operations Support Systems in Cooperatives

Transaction Processing Systems (TPS): TPS can be applied in almost all types of cooperatives since they have transactions in their business. They have to enter, maintain and process all transactions as records. In this regard, they have to use/apply TPS. Cooperatives like consumer cooperatives, multipurpose cooperatives, marketing cooperatives, housing cooperatives, and dairy cooperatives and similar other cooperatives can apply TPS to process their routine daily transactions.

For example, in a consumer cooperative, there are major transactions such as purchase, sales, inventory and accounting. Consumer cooperatives can apply TPS to process these major transactions.

Management Information Systems (MIS): Management Information Systems (MIS) is widely used by some types of cooperatives like cooperative banks, dairy cooperatives, sugar cooperatives, consumer cooperatives and the like. The application of MIS is dealt with elaborately in various types elsewhere in this chapter.

Enterprise Resource Planning (ERP): ERP can be applied in large-scale cooperatives or industrial cooperatives where transactions, business processes are more. Actually ERP is system, which integrates all business functions and processes of an enterprise. ERP can be applied in fertilizer manufacturing cooperatives, sugar cooperatives, mass level dairy processing cooperatives, cooperative spinning mills, etc. In such cooperatives we can have more processes and functions. Those functions and processes can be integrated by means of ERP.

For example, in a fertilizer manufacturing cooperative, the activities and functions like sales, production, etc is possible through ERP systems. There is integration of all activities such as shop floor control, production planning, production scheduling, procurement of inputs / raw material, inventory tracking with sales activity. The manufacturing resource planning is linked with sales activity through inventory system.

Management Support Systems

Decision Support Systems (DSS): DSS are designed in such a way that they support management to make proper decisions to improve effectiveness and thereby efficiency of the enterprise. Cooperatives are not exceptional cases to apply DSS to their decision making process. In cooperatives group decision making process is followed. All members are given equal chance to make decisions.

Group Decision Support Systems (GDSS) are used in cooperatives. GDSS offers an interactive environment for users and this permit manager to experiment with data and models to develop the optimal decision making strategy in a given situation. DSS are data oriented and model oriented. Cooperatives which are engaged in mass production and large scale cooperatives can go for GDSS applications to make both structured and unstructured decisions ie., during predictable and unpredictable situations they can make decisions by the application of decision support systems by building blocks of DSS.

For example, in a sugar factory, DSS can be applied in the areas of production and finance. In the area of production, DSS can be applied for procurement analysis (sugar cane), cost estimation in all respects, sugar production planning and scheduling, make or buy decisions, inventory planning and control, manpower loading, etc. Under finance – capital budgeting, financial planning, tax planning, budgeting, cash and working capital management, foreign exchange risk management, variance analysis, etc.

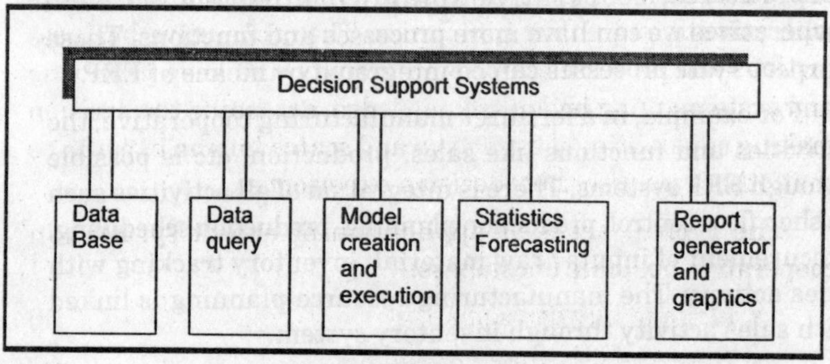

Fig. 16.5. Building Blocks of DSS

Executive Information System (EIS) or Executive Support System (ESS): Top executives need fast access to up-to-date, aggregated, concise information and exception reports with facilities to personalized information and analysis. The information systems designed to cater such needs of top executives are called executive information systems. In cooperatives, particularly large scale cooperatives and cooperatives which are engaged in international marketing, this type of support systems can be applied. Cooperative federations at national and regional levels can employ such systems in the following areas:

- *Executive Briefing* – The information is automatically downloaded periodically from databases in the form of finished reports.

- *Personalized Analysis* – It offers facilities for data analysis using the models of user's choice.
- *Exceptions Reporting* – It is a module of EIS. This is used for identifying variations, reasons thereof, and possible impact of proposed salvage operations.

Expert Systems: The increasing complexities and dynamism in the emerging business environment require greater interaction of functional managers with the experts so as to get timely advice. Cooperatives are not exception and they have to seek the advice of experts on a regular basis for their survival and sustainability. Cooperatives are in a position to compete with private and public companies. The cooperative business expert systems simulate human activity and keep capturing and systematizing business knowledge, extending the decision making capabilities of expensive and scarce human experts, so that others can use their decision experiences.

The typical areas of application of expert systems in cooperative business encompass:

- Make or buy decisions;
- New product launch decisions;
- Determining credit limits;
- Product design and development;
- Investment analysis;
- Project and Performance evaluation;
- Incentive systems;
- Customer query;
- Product scheduling; and
- Routing decisions, etc.

Holsapple identifies three basic components of business expert systems namely, user interface, inference engine, and knowledge system. These components can be applied for cooperative business experts systems also. The following figure (Fig. 16.5) presents the building blocks of cooperative business experts systems.

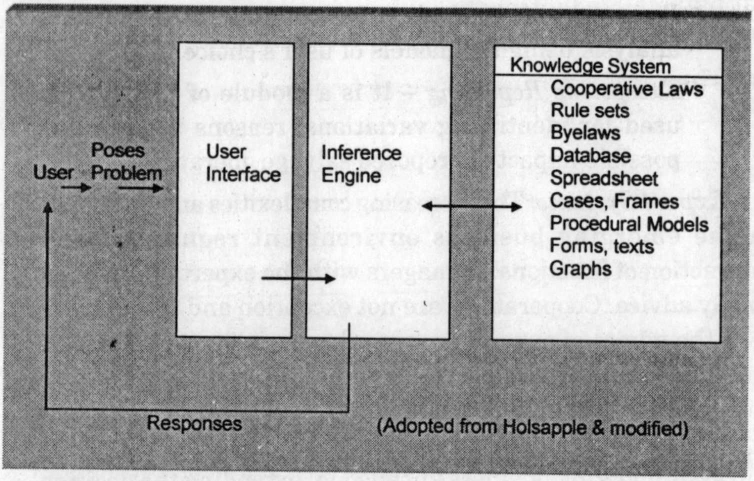

Fig. 16.5. Components of Cooperative Business Expert System

A user poses a problem before the cooperative business experts system using the user interface. The inference engine tries to understand the problem, structure it in such a way so that the knowledge system can be used to solve the problem. This is how the cooperative business experts system works. In the modern competitive business environment, cooperatives should apply experts systems for their survival and sustainability.

Office Automation Systems (OAS)

The productivity of knowledge workers in cooperatives can be improved by providing secretarial support and better communication facilities. This can be supported by the systems called office Automation Systems. Cooperatives are using all types of office automation systems in their regular business operations. The OAS types used in cooperatives can be presented as in the following figure. Cooperatives are using text processor and related systems for processing word and text, document management systems for keeping records and storing data / information, using message communication systems to communicate information. For this, they are using email, facsimile (fax), etc. Moreover, a few well-established cooperatives at national and international level are using teleconferencing and video conferencing systems.

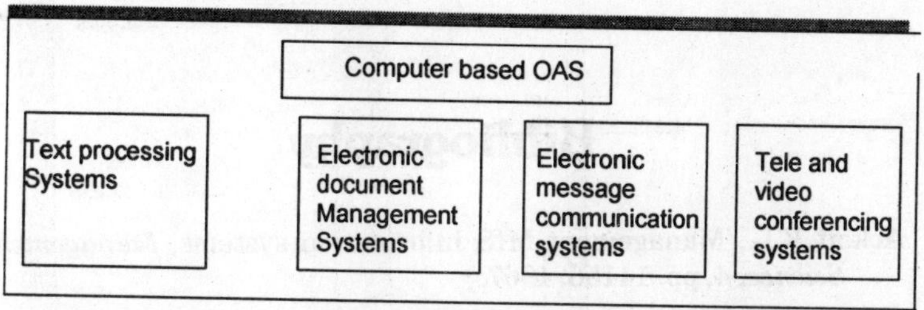

Fig. 16.6. Office Automation Systems used in Cooperatives

Most of the cooperatives cannot afford cost of installation and maintenance of such systems in their business operations. In future, cooperatives may use all types of business support systems widely. Cooperatives at secondary level and national level are using widely OAS, TPS, MIS and some DSS. Cooperatives are yet to go for using widely EIS, ES. No doubt, they will use properly the support systems for improving their performance and sustainability.

Bibliography

Ackoff R.L., Management MIS information systems, *Management Science*, 4, pp. 14156, 1967.

Ahituv, N., Neumann, S., & Riley, H. N. (1994). *Principles of information systems for management* (4th ed.). Dubuque, IA: Wm. C. Brown Communications.

Awad, E. M., and Gotterer, M. H. (1992). *Database Management.* Danvers, MA: Boyd & Fraser.

Balwan T.K and Dr. G.N. Acharya Computer application in sugar Factory in second workshop on Maharashtra cooperative sugar business

Banerjee, U.K., and Sachdeva, R.K. (1995). *Management information system: A new framework.* New Delhi: Vikas Publishing House.

Bartow Hodge, Robert A Fleck Jr. C. Brain Honess, *Management Information System* Reston publishing co. Inc., Reston Virginia 1984

Benbasat, I.B. and Taylor, R.N., The impact of cognitive styles on information system design, *MIS Quarterly*, 2, 2 June, 1978.

Boddy, D., McCaloman J. and Buchanan D.S. (Eds). *The New Management Challenge: IS for Improved Performance,* Croom Helm, London, 1988.

Bryant, J.W., *Financial Modelling in Corporate Management*, 2nd edition, Wiley, New York, 1987.

Carlson, John R., Dawn S. Carlson, and Lori L. Wadsworth. "On the Relationship Between DSS Design Characteristics and Ethical Decision Making." *Journal of Managerial Issues.* Summer 1999.

Chandra Mohan, R. 1999, "Cooperatives in Water Management", *Tamilnadu Journal of Cooperation*, TNCU: Chennai: 7-9.

Chaudhry, Sohail S., Linda Salchenberger, and Mahdi Beheshtian. "A Small Business Inventory DSS: Design, Development, and Implementation Issues." *Computers & Operations Research.* January 1996.

Chellappan, K, 1998, "Towards image building by Cooperatives in the changing environment", *Khadi Gramodyog*, 44(7), KVIC: Mumbai: 254-257.

Cherry, C., *On Human Communication*, MIT Press Cambridge, Massachusetts, 1957.

Clutterbuck, D., *Information 2000*, Pitman, London 1989.

Cretien, P.D., Ball, S.E. and Brigham E.F., *Financial Management with LOTUS 1-2-3,* Dryden Press, New York, 1987.

Datta, K, 1996, "Strategies for the fishery cooperatives of tomorrow", in *Rediscovering Cooperation* Vol.II (Ed) R.Rajagopalan, IRMA: Gujarat: 359-368.

Datta, K, 1996, "The Mudiali Society: A model for freshwater fishery cooperatives", in *Rediscovering Cooperation* Vol.II (Ed) R.Rajagopalan, IRMA: Gujarat: 413-421.

Davis, G.B. and Olsen M.H., *Management Information Systems*, McGraw-Hill, New York, 1984.

Davis, G.B., and Olson, M. H. (1985). *Management information systems: Conceptual foundations, structure, and development.* New York: McGraw-Hill.

Editorial, 1991, "Towards greener India: Save the Blue Mountains", *Tamilnadu Journal of Cooperation*, 83(1), TNCU: Chennai: 3-4.

Executive information systems (January 1994). Retrieved June 17, 2006, from http://www.cs.ui.ac.id/staf/sjarif/eis.htm

Feltham, G.A., The value of information, *The Accounting Review*, Oct, pp. 684-696, 1968.

Forester, T., *Computers in the Human Context*, Basil Blackwell, Oxford, 1989.

Forester, T., *High-Tech Society*, Basil Blackwell, Oxford, 1988.

Glimpses of Cooperatives, "Recent achievements in Cooperative Sector: Some highlights", *The Cooperator*, 37(2), NCUI: New Delhi: 60.

Government of Tamil Nadu, 2000, "Announcements of Food

Department", *Tamil Nadu Journal of Cooperation*, 92(3), TNCU: Chennai: 14.

Gupta, Jatinder N.D., and Thomas M. Harris. "Decision Support Systems for Small Business." *Journal of Systems Management.* February 1989.

Handy, C., *The Future of Work*, Basil Blackwell, Oxford, 1985.

Human, Development Report (10th), 1990, "Globalisation with a human face", in *The Cooperator*, 1999, 37(2), NCUI: New Delhi: 41-43.

Imboden, N. (1980). *Managing information for rural development projects.* Paris: Organization for Economic Co-operation and Development.

Jaiswal, M.P. and Mr. N.P. Singh, Information Technology Networking in sugar cooperative management in Second workshop on maharashtra cooperative sugar business.

Jerome, Kanter, *Management Information System*, Printice-Hall of India private Limited, New Delhi, 1984,

Jha, D and S.K. Jha, 1998, "The challenge of leadership for Cooperative Development in the forthcoming years", *The Cooperator*, 35(11), NCUI: New Delhi: 487.

Keen, P.G.W., and Morton, M.S.S. (1978). *Decision Support Systems.* Reading, MA: Addison-Wesley.

Khurana, M.L, 1999, "Cities for All", *The Cooperator*, 37(5), NCUI: New Delhi: 199-204.

Khushalani A.V, and K. Kavita, 1999, "Intellectual Property/ Royalty rights determination for empowering Bio-diversity conserving Cooperatives and Strategic G-77 and Indian Ocean RIM countries commonwealth", *The Cooperator*, 34(1), NCUI: New Delhi: 35-42.

Kimball, Ralph, and Kevin Strahlo. "Why Decision Support Fails and How to Fix It." *Datamation.* June 1, 1994.

Kumar, Ram L. "Understanding DSS Value." *Omega.* June 1999.

Laudon, Kenneth C., and Jane Price Laudon. *Management Information Systems: A Contemporary Perspective.* New York: Macmillan, 1991.

Lewis, C., *Management With Micros*, Basil Blackwell, Oxford, 1988.

Liskin, M., *dBase IV Made Easy*, Osborne/McGraw-Hill, Berkeley, California, 1989.

Long, R., *New Office Technology: Human and Management Implications*, Croom Helm, London, 1987.

Lucas, H. C., Jr. (1990). *Information systems concepts for management.* New York: McGraw-Hill.

Mallik, R.M, 1996, "A Micro-Analytical investigation into community Vs. private dugwells: findings from a study of two villages in Orissa", in *Rediscovering Cooperation* Vol.II (Ed) R. Rajagopalan, IRMA: Gujarat: 25-39.

Martin, J. (1990). *Telecommunications and the computer* (3rd ed.). Englewood Cliffs, NJ: Prentice-Hall.

Martin, J. and McClure C., Buying software off the rack, *Harvard Business Review*, Nov.-Dec., pp. 32-60, 1983.

Mason, R. D., and Swanson, B. E. (1981). *Measurements for management decision*. Reading, MA: Addison-Wesley.

McKenny, J.L. and Keen, P.G.W., How managers' minds work, Harvard Business Review, May/June, pp. 79-90, 1974.

McLeod, R., Jr. (1995). *Management information systems: A study of computer-based information systems* (6th ed.). New Delhi: Prentice Hall of India.

Mintzberg, H., *Impediments to the Use of Management Information, Society of Management Accountants of Canada* and NAA, Canada, 1975.

Muller-Boling, Detlef, and Susanne Kirchhoff. "Expert Systems for Decision Support in Business Start-Ups." *Journal of Small Business Management*. April 1991.

Nabar, Veera, 2000, "Cooperatives on the upsurge – some success stories", *Tamilnadu Journal of Cooperation*, 92(3), TNCU: Chennai: 29-36.

National Economic Development Office, IT Futures...IT Can Work, NEDO, Millbank, London, 1987.

Neb, D.P. 1997, "Environment Protection and Cooperatives", *The Cooperator*, 35(6), NCUI: New Delhi: 317.

Parkinson, Chris. "What If? Decision Shaping Systems." *CMA—The Management Accounting Magazine*. March 1995.

Pawar, Rajendra S. "planning for an organized change" computers Today, April, 1986, 2(4).

Raggad, Bel G. "Decision Support System: Use It or Skip It." *Industrial Management and Data Systems*. January 1997.

Raheja, S. K., and Jai Krishna (1991). *Manual for monitoring and evaluation of T & V agricultural extension system*. New Delhi: Centre for Agricultural and Rural Development Studies.

Ramanujam, K.N, 2000, "Concern for Community – New Principle of Cooperation", *Tamilnadu Journal of Cooperation*, 92(3), TNCU: Chennai: 20.

Ramesh Babu, A., and Singh, Y. P. (1987). Management information system in an agricultural extension organization. In *Proceedings of the national seminar on management of information system in management of agricultural extension* (p. 1-15). Hyderabad: NIRD.

Ramesh Babu, A., and Singh, Y. P. (1990). Agricultural administration at block level: A case study. *Indian Journal of Extension Education, 26* (1 & 2), 88-90.

Rao, C. S. S. (1985). Agricultural extension management system in India: Past, present and modalities in future. *Indian Journal of Extension Education, 21* (1 & 2), 32-35.

Raymond, Louis, and Francois Bergeron. "Personal DSS Success in Small Enterprises." *Information and Management.* May 1992.

Robert, G Murdick and Joel E. Ross, "Information System for Modern management" Prentice-hall of India private Limited New Delhi, 1982.

Rochester, Jack B. (1996). "Tools for Knowledge Workers." I *Using Computers in Information*. Indianapolis, In: Que Education and Training.

Rowe, C., People and Chips: The Human Implications of Information Technology, Paradigm, London, 1986.

Rowe, C., *People and Chips: The Human Implications of Information Technology,* Paradigm, London, 1986.

Russell, H. M. (1979). A review of management information systems for agriculture. In H. M. Russell (Ed.), *Information for agriculture: Proceedings of the national workshop on agricultural information* (pp. 41-51). Melbourne: Department of Agriculture, Victoria.

Sachdeva, R. K. (1990). *Management Handbook of Computer Usage.* Oxford: NCC Blackwell.

Salmeron, Jose L. and Herrero, Ines. An AHP-based methodology to rank critical success factors of executive information systems. *Computer Standards & Interfaces,* Volume 28, Issue 1, July 2005, Pages 1-12.

Sanders, D. H. (1988). *Computers today* (3rd ed.). New York: McGraw-Hill.

Shah, 1996, "Organisation for the Bhagiratha lift canal project for irrigation and domestic supply: outline of a design and its framework", in *Rediscovering Cooperation* Vol.II (Ed)

R. Rajagopalan, IRMA: Gujarat: 3-21.

Sharma.M.L, 1996, "Community is the main Concern" (Editorial), *The Cooperator*, 34(5), NCUI: New Delhi: 139.

Sharma.M.L, 1997, "IFFCO – One more feather in its Cap" (Editorial), *The Cooperator*, 34(12), NCUI: New Delhi: 327.

Sherman B., The New Revolution: The Impact of Computers on Society, Wiley, Chichester, 1985.

Simon, H. A. (1977). The new science of management decision. New Jersey: Prentice-Hall.

Singh, Y. P., & Ramesh Babu, A. (1985). Basic management issues in extension. *Indian Journal of Extension Education,* 27 (1 & 2), 20-31.

Smita Nair, 1994, "Community Health through Cooperatives – An Agenda", *Cooperative Perspective*, 29(1), VOMNICOM: Pune: 42-44.

Sprague R.H. and Carlson E., Building Effective Decision Support Systems, Prentice Hall, Englewood Chiffs, N.J., 1982.

Stair, Ralph M. (1996). *Principles of Information Systems and Managerial Approach*, 2nd ed. Cincinnati, OH: Boyd & Fraser.

Stonier, T., The Wealth of Information: A Profile of the Post-Industrial Society, Methuen, London, 1982.

Sugar, Mill Management system. - Technical Literature of UPTRON INDIA LTD.

Thierauf, Robert J. Executive Information System: A Guide for Senior Management and MIS Professionals. Quorum Books, 1991

Toffer, A., The Third Wave, Morrow, New York, 1980.

Turban, E., Decision Support and Expert Systems: Managerial Perspectives, Macmillan, New York, 1988.

Vishwanathan, B.S, 1998, "Challenges before Cooperative Sector", *The Cooperator*, 35(10), NCUI: New Delhi: 459.

Wentling, T. L., & Wentling, R. M. (1993). *Introduction to microcomputer technologies. Rome: FAO.*

Zorkoczy, P., Information Technology: An Introduction, Pitman, London, 1985.

Websites:

http://www.environment.tn.nic.in/ENVIS.htm#soe

http://www.envis.nic.in

http://envfro.nic.in

http://www.google.com

http://www.ica.coop

http://www.worldenvironment.com

http://www.wisc.edu/uwcc

http://www.epa.gov/eims/papers.html

www.answer.com